THE LEGISLATOR

The Legislator
German Parliament as a Centre of Political Decision-making

KLAUS VON BEYME

Ashgate
Aldershot • Brookfield USA • Singapore • Sydney

© Klaus von Beyme 1998

All rights reserved. No part of this publication may be reproduced, stored in a retrieval system, or transmitted in any form or by any means electronic, mechanical, photocopying, recording or otherwise without the prior permission of the publisher.

Published by
Ashgate Publishing Limited
Gower House
Croft Road
Aldershot
Hants GU11 3HR
England

Ashgate Publishing Company
Old Post Road
Brookfield
Vermont 05036
USA

British Library Cataloguing in Publication Data
Beyme, Klaus von
 The legislator: German parliament as a centre of political decision-making
 1. Legislative bodies – Germany 2. Germany – Politics and government
 I. Title
 328.4'3

Library of Congress Cataloging-in-Publication Data
Beyme, Klaus von.
　　　The legislator: German Parliament as a centre of political decision-making / Klaus von Beyme.
　　　　p.　cm.
　　　Includes bibliographical references and index.
　　　ISBN 1-84014-433-5 (hc.)
　　　　1. Legislative bodies—Germany. 2. Legislators—Germany.
　　3. Representative government and representation—Germany.
　　4. Germany—Politics and government—Decision making. I. Title.
　　JN3971.A71B44　　1998
　　328.43'074—dc21
　　　　　　　　　　　　　　　　　　　　　　　　　　　　　　　　98–18565
　　　　　　　　　　　　　　　　　　　　　　　　　　　　　　　　　CIP

ISBN 1 84014 433 5

Typeset by Bournemouth Colour Press, Parkstone, Poole, Dorset.
Printed and bound in Great Britain by MPG Books Ltd, Bodmin, Cornwall

Contents

List of Figures, Matrices and Tables — vii
Abbreviations — ix

1 Introduction — 1
The policy cycle — 2
Typology of decisions — 4
The network approach — 7
The decline of parliament and the growth of legislation — 10

2 Policy Formulation — 15
Agenda-setting and the media — 15
Agenda-setting and policy steering by the parties — 20
The preparation of bills by the administration — 22
Scientific policy advice — 23

3 Parliamentary Decision-making — 29
The introduction of bills in parliament — 29
Committees in parliamentary decision-making — 37
The hidden part of the decision-making network: the interest groups — 48
Parliamentary hearings — 63
Plenary sessions and public debates in the decision-making process — 69
Strategies of the oppositions — 76
Voting on bills — 81
The federal state and the decision-making process — 95

4 Control of Legislation — 105
Judicial review of legislation — 105
Control of the feasibility of legislation: Implementation by the bureaucracy — 114
Control of efficiency and efficacy: the stage of evaluation — 119
Amendment of laws — 133

5	Conclusion	137
	Appendix: The 150 key decisions of the German Bundestag	**149**
	Bibliography	**191**
	Index	**205**

List of Figures, Matrices and Tables

Figures

1.1 The policy cycle and the phases of the legislative process   2

Matrices

1.1 Structures of conflicts and types of legislative act   6
1.2 Typology of policy measures   6
1.3 Typology of policy networks   8
2.1 The prospects of issues getting on the political agenda   17
2.2 Mobilization and demobilization of the public for legislative bills   19
3.1 Typology of network structures in interest articulation   53
4.1 Actors and goals in the steering process of German Reunification   118
4.2 Types of symbolic legislation   125

Tables

1.1 Innovative laws and amendments   3
1.2 Top positions in the hierarchy of parliament and parliamentary groups   11
1.3 Laws passed and legislative initiatives in the Bundestag, 1949–94   12
2.1 The influence of media on the stages of decision-making   18
2.2 Attempts to influence the legislative process of the 150 key decisions   25
3.1 The initiator behind the formal initiator: impulses for bills in the policy fields, 1949–94   35
3.2 European impulses on German legislation   38

3.3	Work of the parliamentary committees	41
3.4	Number of deliberating committees and frequency of sessions in policy arenas and types of regulation	46
3.5	Intervention of offices and parties in the process of legislation	47
3.6	Interventions of interest groups according to types of parliamentary decision	61
3.7	Interventions of interest groups according to types of policy field	62
3.8	Hearings of parliamentary committees	67
3.9	Length of the mandate in the German Bundestag (in years)	72
3.10	Amendments during the legislative process	75
3.11	Amendments of the opposition parties (in percentage of all motions for amendments among the 150 key decisions)	75
3.12	Sanctions imposed in the German Bundestag	79
3.13	Instruments of control in the German Bundestag	81
3.14	Unanimous decisions	85
3.15	Roll calls in the Bundestag	86
3.16	Voting on bills according to types of regulation	89
3.17	Voting on bills in policy fields	89
3.18	Types of coalition in the *Länder* in the 1990s	97
3.19	Amending motions of the West German *Länder* (1st–12th Bundestags) 1949–94	98
3.20	Number of contributions to the parliamentary debate by members of the Federal Council	99
3.21	Appeals to the conference committees	103
4.1	Policy fields in which laws were declared null and void or not compatible with the Basic Law (1951–91)	107
4.2	Key decisions in front of the Constitutional Court	108
4.3	The efficacy of laws	123
4.4	The speed of legislation	128
4.5	Consequences of evaluation	134

Abbreviations

BR	Federal Council
BT	Federal Diet
BTcomm.	Committee of the Federal Diet
BVerfGE	Decision of the Federal Constitutional Court
FLO	Federal Labour Office
GOBT	Common Standing Order of the Bundestag

Quotations from the minutes of the parliamentary debates are marked by the number of the electoral period, the date and the page.

1 Introduction

'The legislator' is a standard formula among lawyers. Social scientists use it only in quotation marks because they know there is a 'legislature', but in a pluralist democracy there cannot be a 'legislator' but only 'legislators'. The juridical formula has, however, still some of its suggestive power: Moses, Solon and Lykurg are associated with it and promise emanations of God's and the people's will. Lawyers on the continent discovered the 'will of legislator' or even 'the will of the law' until legal positivism demystified it and 'the will of the law' was downgraded to a hypothetical construct of legal dogmatics.

With its demystification, political science lost its interest in the legislator, abandoning as in other fields, certain topics to the lawyers. The policy approach in political science declared legislation as old-fashioned – just as abstract painting abandoned the central perspective. Legislation as a subject was suspected of treating policy arenas as if the political actors met only with a passive environment, although legislative studies – especially in the United States – have never neglected the non-statal actors in the process of law-making.

Enthusiasm for the aspect of *implementation* led to a preference for the *meso-level* of politics and a neglect for the macro-level of legislatures. Legislation was handed over to the jurists who increasingly became interested in social science issues. As sociology – the torchbearer of modernization in the social sciences – has abandoned its general outlook and dissolved into fragmented fields, policy analysis did the same for political science. At worst, the result was a kind of *West Side Story*: research was restricted to 'school boards' or 'hospital administrations' in certain quarters of New York.

In parliamentary studies most research focused on deputies and their social background. The international influence structure of decision-making escaped into case-studies – a complaint also voiced by the best scholars in the field in other European countries (Esaiasson and Holmberg, 1996: 215).

2 *The Legislator*

The Policy Cycle

For heuristic and didactic purposes, this study of 150 key decisions in the first 12 Federal Diets (1949–94) is arranged along the policy cycle. Because the actors dealt with are not restricted to the respective phase of government and legislatures certain views back and forth have to be inserted. The *cosy triangles* discovered by American research have been recognized as a too narrow focus even in the United States. In Germany there are rather *uncosy pentagles*, including not only parliamentary elites, administration and interest groups but also party management and the actors of the federal *Länder*.

The policy cycle schema (see Figure 1.1) needs a caveat: it suggests a constant relationship in the strength of actors and institutions over a period of 12 legislatures, which does not exist. The centre of gravity in the networks of actors is shifting permanently. The *Länder*'s competences have diminished, but their influence on central decision-making via *intergovernmental decision-making* is increasing. Judicial review of the Constitutional Court has an increasing importance, given the legalism of German political culture. All the agencies of control have an impact and develop an 'anticipated' obedience among the majority of the legislators.

German parliamentary statistics are probably the most developed in the world – besides those of the US Congress. They already operate with the concept of 'crucial laws' (Schindler, IV, 1994: 846). 'Important' and

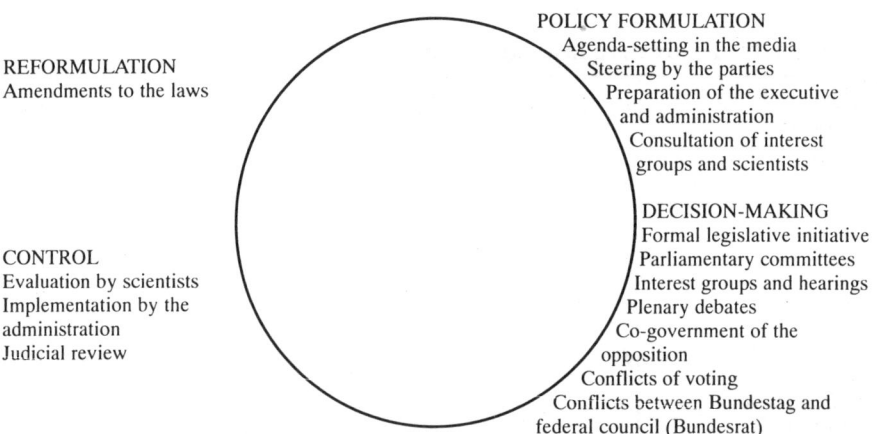

Figure 1.1   The policy cycle and the phases of the legislative process

'marginal laws' are the two other categories. My 'key decisions' do not completely correspond to these 'crucial laws', because my criterion is not simply that a law is completely *new*. Many *amending* laws, such as the fourth or fifth reform of the penal law were much more important than most of the 'new laws'.

Among the 150 key decisions one-sixth (24) were formally amendments and almost one-third (46) an amendment *de facto*. Very occasionally – contrary to American custom – laws in Germany were abolished (2). The importance of laws is tested by constitutional lawyers according to the dichotomy:

- codification laws which are *innovative* and *new* regulations (77), and
- *limited interventions* in favour of certain interests (73).

Both types are distributed in the sample of 150 key decisions (see Table 1.1).

The 150 key decisions are not equally distributed over this period of almost four decades. Some legislatures (the first two and the twelfth after Reunification) have been necessarily more active and more innovative than the others. The fifth legislature under the Grand Coalition (1966–69) did not tackle new social and economic regulations, but nevertheless dealt with important leftovers from the last two decades, including some 'crucial' laws. Every choice is disputable. Although I consulted policy specialists in selecting the key decisions, I am sure that some people will disagree with my choice. Nevertheless the bunch of decisions offers a fair overview over

Table 1.1 Innovative laws and amendments

Legislative Period	I	II	III	IV	V	VI	VII	VIII	IX	X	XI	XII	Total
Formal amendment	0	1	1	2	1	2	2	3	1	3	4	4	24
De facto amendment	4	4	3	5	4	4	5	5	3	2	3	4	46
Revocation of a law	–	1	–	1	–	–	–	–	–	–	–	–	2
Key decisions	16	19	10	10	10	15	16	11	5	8	12	18	150
Laws regulating important questions in a coherent way	10	13	5	5	7	7	13	2	1	2	5	7	77
Ad hoc laws	6	6	5	5	3	8	3	9	4	6	7	11	73

various policy arenas and types of regulation or distribution (cf. Matrix 1.2).

In addition to the 150 key decisions, ten *non-decisions* have been included in order to constitute a control over the outcome of many legislative efforts. Even key decisions are frequently only the final compromise after a couple of non-decisions.

Typology of Decisions

Decision-making studies normally start with classifications of decisions. One of the most general typologies is that of *opinions* and *interests* (Zintl, 1992: 107). Conflicts of opinions are organized by public interest groups and promotional groups in a kind of 'collective ombudsman politics'. Opinions are launched for the benefit of third parties and non-actors. The defence of other interests is less organized.

The arena of interest conflicts can be subdivided into two principal categories:

- *class conflicts* of relatively symmetrically organized large groups
- *status conflicts* in which the dominant interest often has no organized counter-interest but has to fight loose coalitions of resistant state and social actors.

Each type of conflict has a different organizational basis, pressure potentials and ethos of actions.

Various indicators have been applied in the selection of the 150 key decisions in the German Federal Diet in 12 legislatures:

- the innovative character of laws
- the public attention to the issue received in the media and in society
- the conflicts which a measure has generated.

'Routine legislation' has been excluded.

The statistical office of the German Bundestag (Federal Diet) listed 2 per cent of all the laws as 'crucial laws'. Not all of them were highly controversial: 26.5 per cent of these were decided on unanimously (Schindler, IV, 1994: 846).

Parliamentary conflict can be measured by various indicators:

- the amendments proposed in the committees and in the plenary sessions
- the length of debates in parliament and the importance of party leaders involved

- the use of roll call voting
- the margin of the majority
- the echo in the media (and sometimes in the streets by rallies of organized interests)
- the use of the conference committee to settle disputes between the Bundestag and the Federal Council and/or the opposition's attempt to stop a decision via a trial in the Constitutional Court.

I have resisted the temptation to select only 'interesting' decisions which were highly controversial because such a procedure would not reflect 'business as usual', even in the sphere of innovative decisions.

Another criterion for the selection of cases was a certain *balance of the decisions in various policy arenas:* to this end, foreign policy and security policy decisions are represented (23). The biggest field proved to be legal policy (36), followed by economic policy (33), social policy (29), environmental protection (11), construction and housing policies (13) and education (5). It proved to be easier to place a measure in a policy field than to have an uncontradictory placement in the typology of policies.

Different types of conflicts (see Matrix 1.1) give rise to different types of legislative response and measures. 'Policy determines politics' was a famous slogan (Lowi, 1964) and it has been tested time and again. Lowi's typology initially showed the normal trinitarian design (regulative, distributive, redistributive). Later a fourth type was added – constituent policy. Lowi's three elements of a typology are not on the same logical level. It seems to me that it has to be completed. If we differentiate between regulative and distributive levels of decision we end up with a sixfold typology (see Matrix 1.2). Each of the three columns in this matrix centres in one of the main ideological camps: conservatism, liberalism and socialism. This does not mean that conservatism is exclusively restrictive or protective and that socialists can afford to govern only via redistribution. Conflicts in the legislative process are most intense in the right and left. Protective measures are normally highly consensual.

Distributive politics – frequently referred to in the United States as 'pork barrel' decisions – are normally 'no zero-sum' games. Some groups benefit and most have no serious losses – or at least the losses are not felt directly and are hidden in taxes. Social benefits financed by means of taxation have often been denounced as 'creeping redistribution', but, since all these measures normally do not disturb the balance between privileged and underprivileged groups, these benefits are accepted.

Redistributive politics normally create winners and losers. The losses are, however, exaggerated in the legislative battles (1. BT 7.5.1952: 9055D). The German 'equalisation of burdens law' (1952) for the refugees was meant to

Matrix 1.1 Structures of conflicts and types of legislative act

Opinions		Interests	
		Class politics	Status politics
Those who benefit	Virtually everybody	Large groups	Limited groups
Types of games Organizational basis	Recognition games Opinion groups, advocacy groups, new social movements	Distributive games Large groups with approximately equal potential and weapons (strike/lock-out) Conflicts limited by labour regulations	Status groups with high membership density Large degree of autonomy, no organized counter-interest, but only ad hoc adversarial coalitions
Pressure power	Unconventional behaviour	Refusal of certain services	Refusal of certain services (in the case of civil servants limited by law)
Ethos of political action	Common good orientation Utilitarian *Kaldor criterion* for virtually all groups	Special interest orientation according to the *Pareto criterion:* benefits for at least one important actor; no losses for the rest of the actors	
Predominant type of legislative acts	Restrictive extensive, protective, occasionally regulative	Distributive, redistributive	Distributive, protective

Matrix 1.2 Typology of policy measures

Regulative level (low input of financial means)	Restrictive limitation of existing rights (24)	Regulative regulations neutral to the question of gain and loss (33)	Extensive extension of rights (17)
Level of distribution	Protective protection via norms with limited inputs of finances (35)	Distributive distribution without a great coalition of losers (32)	Redistributive redistribution with winners and losers (9)

Note: Figures in brackets = number of cases.

impose serious losses on the investors. Only later was it discovered that the state and the refugees themselves – via taxes – paid most of the funds needed for redistribution (cf. Chapter 4, pp. 105–36).

The legislators are not always in agreement as to which type of measure they have in mind. *Protective* laws create a high degree of consensus. If this is not the case it is mostly because the idea of protection has been superseded by others goals. In the discussion of a law on gene technology (1990) the SPD opposition suspected that it was more a law to support certain industries than a protective law (11. BT 29.3.1990: 15981B). Implementators at a post-legislative stage quite frequently shift the balance of various goals in a law.

Restrictive measures were initially suspected as a first step towards an authoritarian regime (emergency laws 1968). Later the problem of fighting terrorism or regulating immigration and the influx of asylum-seekers have extended this type of measure. With hindsight, Adenauer – frequently suspected as a semi-authoritarian politician – was in charge during an era when much more *extensive measures* granted new rights to the citizens. Thus the 'Adenauer era', in some respects, has been glorified as the 'freest time in German history'.

Even if my typology is accepted, the rubrification of individual key decisions can nevertheless be controversial. Decisions are controversial, and parties tend to advocate quite different measures when a governmental bill is proposed. Abortion is a typical case: conservatives will call a restrictive measure 'protective'; the left wing will argue that they have a protective measure in mind as well, but that it protects the rights of the mother rather than those of the unborn child. In cases of doubt such a rubrification should not be set according to the personal preferences of the author, but according to the intentions of the parliamentary majority which decides. If the usefulness of the typology of policy measures is doubted, my quantitative results in the sphere of policy arenas will probably be accepted.

The Network Approach

The network approach has been elevated from a method to a theory. There is much loose talk about networks, which pretends to explain everything when they drop the catch–all notion of network in cases former generations of scholars talked about 'influence' or communication.

The network approach has the virtue of helping falsify approaches which start from the assumption of compact *power elites*. It recognizes that there is no unified 'will of the legislator'. Even the coalition parties in power may not agree and, moreover, in each decision many actors such as interest groups, oppositional parties, citizens' movements or federal *Länder* – take part who do not share the intentions of the government initiating the bill concerned (Pappi *et al.*, 1995: 36). This network analysis seems to be appropriate for the fragmented reality of post-modern societies. Even corporatism, with its search for a unified actor – albeit a kind of 'holy trinity' of actors (state, investors, trade unions) – was still an approach of classical modernity. Network theory has paid back in terms of severe criticism the corporatists just as they did to the older pluralists who suddenly experienced a revival.

All the while corporatism remained a growth sector in the scientific debate, many attempts were made to identify whole countries, such as Sweden or Austria, as corporatist. Germany never completely fitted the model but had important corporatist arenas. Corporatists and pluralists chose their favourite arenas and thus were able to demonstrate their preferred model of interest mediation – although only for a limited time and a restricted field of decision. When network analysis moved from being a methodological instrument to a theoretical hypothesis the nationwide dominance of certain patterns of decision-making were demystified. New typologies discovered the coexistence of several models of interest representation between the extreme poles of 'dominance of state' or 'dominance of society' (see Matrix 1.3).

European systems showed a certain tendency to implement one or the other model: France (I), Italy in the time of the Democrazia Cristiana dominance II and III, Germany IV and V. But no country ever exclusively used one or two models.

I never did participate in the intellectual civil wars between corporatists and pluralists. The analysis of decision-making in detail shows that there are

Matrix 1.3 Typology of policy networks

	Dominance of the state			Dominance of the society		
Actors	I State agencies	II Cartels of parties	III One great interest group	IV Two conflicting large interest groups	V Moderate pluralism of groups	VI Unlimited pluralism of groups
Dominant model of intermediation	Pantouflage, state corporation	Parentela relations	Clientela relations	Liberal corporatism	Sponsored pluralism sub-government	Pressure pluralism

Sources: Variation of Jordan and Schubert, 1992: 25; van Waarden 1992: 50.

applications for both of them. The proliferation of groups participating in decision-making has reduced the power of monopolizing groups and therefore, in some countries, also the number of laws (Gray and Lowery, 1995: 533, 547). The classical iron triangles accepted only a restricted number of actors: the permanent players had a minimal consensus on the procedure. Recent networks encompass greater number of actors which do not participate on a permanent basis. Each arena is characterized by 'exit and voice' (Jordan and Schubert, 1992: 13). The fundamental consensus is rather minimal.

The typology of networks shown in Matrix 1.3 does not symmetrically represent types of network acting in Germany. The French type of *pantouflage* is rare in central decision-making but happens at local level. *Parentela relations*, such as investigated by LaPalombara for Italy, are also more of a regional phenomenon. *Clientelistic networks* are diminishing with the withering away of the power of certain status groups, such as the refugees or farmers. The variations in German policy arenas concentrate on types IV and V.

The picture is complicated by mixed types. Networks in health policy are characterized by a juxtaposition of self-regulating and corporatist forms of interest mediation (Döhler, 1990: 178). Compared to the United States, German policy arenas are still dominated by fewer relevant groups and more stable coalitions of interests.

Network analysis was the result of deficits of the old institutional approaches (Benz, 1993: 185). Networks diminish the costs of decision but they do not render valueless the formal constitutional and parliamentary rules of the political game. Uncontrolled networking has its limits in a parliamentary democracy. Networks are no general remedy against the shortcomings of institutions. There is a fruitful tension between the more egalitarian structures of networks and the hierarchical structures of parliamentary and governmental institutions. *The nerves of governance* are not identical to the *nerves of government* but are more efficient in creating the information and communication necessary for political decision.

Highly fragmented systems develop a minimum of *core beliefs* among the actors (Mayntz and Neidhardt, 1989: 384). They proved to be weak in Germany according to one survey, but this does not mean that they do not exist. In countries where corporatism prevails, networks unify the actors by strong beliefs in science and rational solutions. 'Policy determines politics' is partly reversed: 'network determines policy.'

Reputational studies have shown that all the actors rank parties and ministerial elites very highly in terms of their influence on the legislative process (Pappi *et al.*, 1995: 181): Indeed, some studies have ranked party in the first place (Schönbauer, 1983). 'Legislative leviathans' have been discovered in the United States and this has revived interest in the parties as coordinators of decisions. In non-American field situations the parties have never been neglected. There is much speculation on the 'decline of parties' in terms of membership density and party identification, but certainly not in terms of decision-making in central institutions (Table 1.2).

The formal hierarchy of parliamentary and party elites is increasing. The larger circle within the network has grown from 127 (10th Bundestag) to 158 (12th Bundestag). Parliament seems to verify the autopoietic system theory: it is steering itself rather more than society. Even the Green Party, originally reluctant to be steered from behind, has given up its bias in favour of plenary open debates and increasingly applies 'planning by the parliamentary group'. Oddly enough, the managers of the parliamentary group were the stable element, as long as the deputies were forced to rotate all the time. Michels' (1989: 340) prediction that even libertarian movements cannot escape the 'iron law of oligarchy' seems to be correct.

The Decline of Parliament and the Growth of Legislation

Wagner's law of growing state activities has been applied to legislatures (cf. von Beyme, 1985a) and the 'legislative flood' has been discussed time and again. Is there a such a thing? *Prima facie* the figures in Germany deny it. The first German legislature passed 545 bills, the twelfth 507. These two peaks of legislative activity were caused by a regime consolidation after 1949 and German Reunification in 1990. Between those two figures the rates were much lower, averaging out at just over 100 laws per year. The figures show that the initiatives from within parliament have increased (see Table 1.3).

How big is 'big'? If we follow the literature we must assume that there is a flood of legislation. In international comparison Germany falls way below the principal Western democracies in terms of legislative activity. In the 1980s Germany passed about 111 laws per year compared to 452 in the USA, 588 in Italy, 148 in the UK and 93 in France (Rose, 1984: 69). However, the higher proportion of *leggine* and 'private member bills' comprising part of these figures in Italy and the United States have their origins in special circumstances which are not comparable to Germany.

The argument concerning the 'legislative flood' has to be reversed. Since in most consolidated democracies most important issues have been regulated, the number of laws should decrease. This is actually not the case. As in other countries there is not a single, but rather several reasons responsible for this trend:

Table 1.2 Top positions in the hierarchy of parliament and parliamentary groups

	10th Bundestag 1983–87					11th Bundestag 1987–90						12th Bundestag 1990–94				
	Offices	CDU/CSU	SPD	FDP	Green Party	Offices	CDU/CSU	SPD	FDP	Green Party	Offices	CDU/CSU	SPD	FDP	not represented Green Party
Speaker, deputy speakers	5	2	2	1	0	5	2	2	1	0	5	2	2	2	–
Leaders of parliamentary groups or working committees	60	29	14	11	6	60	30	13	11	6	78	35	15	13	–
Chairmen of parliamentary committees	20	10	8	1	1	21	9	8	2	2	23	11	9	3	–
Members of government	17	14	0	3	0	19	15	0	4	0	19	14	0	5	–
Parliamentary secretaries of state	25	22	0	3	0	27	23	0	4	0	33	26	0	7	–
Total	127	77	24	19	7	132	79	23	22	8	158	88	26	39	–

Table 1.3 Laws passed and legislative initiatives in the Bundestag, 1949–94

Legislative	1	2	3	4	5	6	7	8	9	10	11	12
Bills proposed by:												
government,	472	431	394	368	415	351	461	322	155	280	321	419
parliamentary groups,	301	414	207	245	225	171	136	111	58	183	227	297
Federal Council	32	16	5	8	14	24	73	52	38	59	47	179
Total	805	861	606	621	654	546	670	485	251	522	595	895
Laws passed and proposed by:												
government,	392	371	348	326	372	259	427	288	104	237	267	345
parliament,	141	132	74	97	80	58	62	39	16	42	68	99
Federal Council,	12	8	2	3	9	13	17	15	8	32	15	28
government/ parliamentary groups	–	–	–	–	–	5	10	12	11	9	19	50
Total	545	511	424	426	461	335	516	354	139	320	369	522

Sources: Schindler, 1983, 1987, 1994; Stand der Gesetzgebung 11. und 12. Bundestag.

- *Citizens' expectations* are met by a populist style of government which urges 'action', even if only a symbolic law is passed. There is a democratic paradox: the steering capacity of the state becomes weaker because the autonomous self-regulation of subsystems is growing. Nevertheless the state is pushed towards regulating even those problems which can hardly be regulated. The democratic state interferes in problems where no absolutist ruler would have dared to regulate, as, for instance, in an issue actually discussed as a bill – 'marital rape' (1997).
- Competition is becoming tougher, the *majorities are decreasing* and make coherent regulations more difficult. The problems are therefore chopped into smaller pieces and regulated in different laws.
- The influence of the *European Community* has an impact on legislation. In Germany one-fifth of all the laws are caused by the European level.
- A special German reason for the increasing pressure for regulations was the *Constitutional Court* and the German tradition of emphasizing the legal state rather than democratic participation.

According to constitutional rules the Bundestag is the 'institutional centre of the people's sovereignty'. Parliament *de facto* declined in importance because rivalling institutions – such as the Constitutional Court, the administration, the parties and the media – grew stronger.

The Constitutional Court contributed most in shifting the balance between legislative and jurisdictional power by the doctrine that all important matters are a domain of parliament and cannot be regulated by other institutions, such as the executive or the administration (by decrees and administrative regulations). The German concept is that of *der allgemeine Gesetzesvorbehalt* (BVerfGE 7: 301; 40: 249) which has caused numerous trials in the courts and forced parliament to envisage new regulations. This doctrine contributed to the growth of legislation as much as the growing tasks of the state in general. The Constitutional Court was not able to develop all the issues which are a domain of parliament. Instead of writing a textbook outlining all the imaginable cases it postulated a rather cloudy 'doctrine of essentials' (*Wesentlichkeitslehre*). The principle of the legal state (Rechtsstaat, Art. 20.3 GG) and the principle of democracy (Art. 20.2.1 GG) oblige the legislator to regulate all 'essential' (*wesentliche*) questions and not to leave them to the administration (BVerfGE 47: 55, 33: 158; 40: 237). The Court ruled that the *negative liberal principle* which reserved laws for cases of interference with freedom and property of the citizens was obsolete and demanded the 'positive intervention of the state' in order to grant benefits and opportunities to the citizens (BVerfGE 40: 249). Classical liberalism favoured 'regulative measures' and was strictly against redistribution. The new concept extended the responsibility of parliament to the bulk of protective and distributive measures.

The doctrines of the Constitutional Court have not only increased but also the amount of work combined with legislation. The legislator is obliged:

- to investigate the consequences of a law (BVerfGE 50: 334; 65: 55)
- to respect scientific knowledge at any given time, which is problematic in the case of new technologies (BVerfGE 49: 90)
- to offer prognoses about future developments (Karpen, 1986: 22)
- to accept the duty to amend a law after unintended consequences have been recognized (BVerfGE 49: 50).

These principles seemed to strengthen parliament, but in reality increased the influence of the administration and of certain 'think-tanks' advising policy-makers.

The doctrine of the 'legislative domain' was meant to strengthen parliament, but it strengthened the ministerial administration as well. Increasing legislation entailed an increasing number of decrees. In the 1st Bundestag there were 50 per cent more decrees than laws; in the 3rd Bundestag decrees were more than twice as frequent as acts of parliament (Loewenberg, 1967). Apparently the citizen cannot really select between transparent and less transparent forms of juridification because there is no trade-off between the two sources of regulation.

2 Policy Formulation

Agenda-setting and the Media

Idealized views on the political discourse suggested that parliament in an open egalitarian discussion sets its own agenda. Parliaments have a high degree of autonomy – financially and, to a certain degree, even in front of the courts – because representatives cannot be accused without parliamentary consent to lift the protection of immunity. Nor are parliamentary deputies bound by an index-linked pay agreement – taking the salaries of civil servants as a yardstick – parliament has the autonomy to decide.

The autonomy of agenda-setting exists only insofar as nobody can impose a topic on parliament. But it is a negative defensive autonomy. The positive autonomy in agenda-setting is lost – if it ever existed. Democratic systems have a high capacity to create themes for the agenda which exceeds the capacity of parliaments to regulate the pending issues. Early parliamentary theory still accepted parliament's teaching function. This was taken over by the parties and later by the media.

The decline of ideology-based politics has led to a migration of topics from party to party. There are hardly any restrictions in the agenda of parliamentary party groups. Even the Green Party discovered that it is not enough to specialize on topics such as environmental policy, disarmament and gender policy.

Parliamentary agendas react most quickly in case of riots and mass demonstrations. The first response is a commission of inquiry, but its recommendations usually come too late to have a major influence, except in the case of repressive and restrictive measures, such as fighting terrorists and strengthening internal security (Willems *et al.*, 1993: 245).

The opposition has an important function in agenda-setting because it can influence the decision-making process. In the first years of opposition to the Adenauer regime, the SPD neglected the fact that efficiency in agenda-setting has to respect a rational strategy of theme-finding, avoiding launching too many questions at the same time particularly when the topics do not attract media attention (Sebaldt, 1992: 71, 334).

The opposition has to respect certain rules in order to guarantee media coverage:

- Issues have to stimulate a *clear profile of dissent*.
- Issues should be capable of *attracting media attention*. The SPD, and, later, the Green Party frequently fought for tiny little groups (such as artists or special groups of women) which had little 'news value'.
- Issues should *not be restricted to the class interests* of a single party.
- Issues should be *safeguarded against the 'theft of themes'*, as happened to the 'Green' issues of environmental protection. But all parties, and especially the unorthodox new ones, have to take account of the fact, in their strategy, that the 'new politics' is spreading quickly in 'old parties' (Schmitt, 1987) and that the innovative themes have to be offered carefully in well calculated doses.

In a survey, about one-third of the German deputies confessed that they feel influenced by the media (Puhe and Würzberg, 1989: 12) and see this as a one-way communication because they have no influence on the media, except occasionally on the local newspaper. However, party politicians in particular do not believe that the media creates the issues, but that it offers only reinforcement for certain trends and topics. New social movements have been much more successful in creating new agendas. The media reacted to their initiatives. The media has, however, an important function in emphasizing already existing topics on the agenda: when smoking lost its virile, positive 'Marlborough-country' image and fear of cancer dominated the public debate, the old issue was viewed differently by the politicians because of the anti-smoking campaigns in the media (Baumgartner and Jones, 1993: 114). But, on the whole, the media is more reactive than interest groups and social movements which do not wait until an issue is on the agenda. Surveys among German media journalists have discovered that only 13 per cent perceive their role as active influence on the political system and only a minority accepted a 'teaching function' for the media (Schönbach *et al.*, 1994: 145).

The data on the 150 key decisions show that the media rarely directly appears as a pressure group in the decision-making process and during hearings. In the early days of the system, German politicians had to learn to communicate with the media and to tolerate criticism. Under Adenauer newspaper articles sometimes became an item on the agenda of cabinet meetings (Die Kabinettsprotokolle, vol. 3, 1986: 47, 59). The responsible minister would be asked to take action and Adenauer would use this incident to fix the agenda and to confront the opposition and the media with his new

Matrix 2.1 The prospects of issues getting on the political agenda

	Dimension of direct experience of citizens and of the degree of concern of citizens	
Dimension of actors mobilizing citizens via the media	Obtrusive issues (high concern)	Unobtrusive issues (creation of concern only with help of media campaigns)
	Entrepreneurs organizing an agenda	No entrepreneurs organizing an agenda
Examples of issues in the German parliament	Popular census Protection of data Deployment of new rockets Abortion	Protection of embryos Experiments with European rockets Euro-currency

guideline (Nowka, 1973: 140). Many German politicians had little talent in using the media. Committee members of the Bundestag in the early days of the system considered the media not so much as an opportunity but as a disturbing intervening factor (Schatz, 1970: 131). Only more recently German politicians recognized that communication with the media is more than a one-way declaration of the so-called *Verlautbarungsjournalismus* which demonstrated a paternalistic attitude towards the media.

The prospects to put issues on the agenda are dependent on two factors: the concern which issues raise and the existence of political entrepreneurs who push an issue (see Matrix 2.1).

The influence of the media in decision-making is not equally strong at all stages (see Table 2.1). As a rule, committees in Germany work secretly, but even if they do not – and during the hearings – the media is not very interested in details of the parliamentary work. It prefers plenary debates where the cleavages are clear and compromises do not make the clutter and obscure the proceedings (Sarcinelli, 1994: 148f). On the other hand, the media complains that it is excluded from the meetings of the steering committees of the coalition parties and from mediation sessions at the chancellor's or a minister's office.

The democratic creed demands complete openness of all political processes. The politicians, however, insist on the necessity of bodies where compromises can be found without the presence of the media which looks for statements which appeal to the public rather than to the partners in negotiations. The more important a meeting, the less it is open to the media. If coalition steering committees or chancellor's mediation sessions were open to the public, the real discussion would move from the 'chamber' to the 'anti-chamber'.

18 *The Legislator*

Table 2.1 The influence of media on the stages of decision-making

Decision-making style	Degree of media influence
1 Formation of policies	
Pressure from the street	++
Opposition counterproposals	+
Interest groups' proposals in the ministries	−
Party proposals in the Bundestag	+
2 Decision-making	
Conflicts in the committees	−
Public hearings	+
Demonstrations in front of parliament	++
Plenary debates	+
Conflicts within the coalition	++
Mediation at the chancellor's office	−−
Committees of the coalition parties	−
Roll calls	++
Veto of the Federal Council	+
3 Implementation	
Manipulation of laws by the implementing administration	−
Unintended consequences of laws being denounced by the administration	+
4 Evaluation	
The parliamentary minority turning to the Constitutional Court	++
Scientific evaluation of councils and agencies	+

The Media and Mobilization of Support and Opposition for a Bill

Most of the 150 key decisions did not stimulate a media campaign. Extensive measures (codetermination, representation of civil servants in administrative agencies), restrictive measures (limitations of basic rights) or redistributive measures (burden-sharing for the benefit of refugees) are susceptible to public mobilization campaigns, but the bulk of regulative, distributive and protective legislation does not lead to a mobilization of the citizens outside parliament. Political actors frequently talk about 'the public' as an 'outside' force, neglecting the fact that they themselves sometimes mobilize the public in support for their views in parliamentary debates or, alternatively, deliberately try to demobilize them (see Matrix 2.2).

In the consolidation phase of the 1949–57 regime, protests mobilized by a parliamentary group – at that time still the Communists (KPD) – could cause

Matrix 2.2 Mobilization and demobilization of the public for legislative bills

	Mobilization	Demobilization
From within parliament and parliamentary groups	burden-sharing (1952) codetermination (1951, 1952, 1955, 1971, 1976, 1986) Rearmament (1955, 1956) Emergency Laws (1968)	Law on refugees (1953) Representation of civil servants (1955) Saar statute (1955) Biotechnology (1990, 1993) Treaties with socialist countries (1972, 1973)
From outside parliament and the established parties	Regulation of conscientious objection (1977, 1982) anti-terrorism laws (1977ff) Regulation of asylum-seekers (1978ff) Census laws (1981, 1985) Abortion laws (1992, 1994)	Law on the capital 'Berlin' (1991) Constitutional reform (1994)

so much trouble that the emergency powers of the Allied occupation forces were discussed in the cabinet (Die Kabinettsprotokolle, vol. 4, 1988: 403). The resistance against rearmament encompassed even parts of the coalition parties. Minister of Domestic Affairs Heinemann (CDU) – later the first SPD federal president – resigned and founded a small pacifist group. The refugees were another major group to organize resistance from within parliament by summoning tens of thousands to march into the capital, Bonn (Kather, 1964: 158ff.). The trade unions were moderate in their mobilization efforts from the outset. They organized rallies but took care that the more radical workers did not proclaim a 'general strike'. The emergency laws (1968) attracted the peak of protest mobilized from within. Even some Social Democrats participated in the counter-rally in the Paulskirche in Frankfurt – although the SPD majority carried the laws in a Grand Coalition. The granting of the 'right to resistance' according to the Basic Law was a kind of recompensation for the trade unions for their moderation in organizing the public against the emergency laws (Oberreuter, 1978: 243).

There was a popular widespread view that the media are 'leftist' and in favour of all the reforms. This has not always been true. In the debates on a reorganization of the retirement allowances in the mid-1950s, the media took the conservative side (Hockerts, 1980: 394). When, however, a status group defended its status quo in a reckless way, as the medical doctors sometimes did (Naschold, 1967: 222), most of the media felt obliged to advocate the 'public good'. Sometimes the resistance in the media was not motivated politically, but directed against badly prepared initiatives – from the bill on 'recompensation for losses because of inflationary tendencies' (1952) down to a bill for the 'protection of the honour of soldiers' (1996).

Despite exaggerations of media power, the legislative processes show that the media on the whole is reactive rather than active – in agenda-setting as well as in the pressuring for the carrying of a bill.

Agenda-setting and Policy Steering by the Parties

Comparative research on party manifestos came to the conclusion that programmes matter for the policy of parties in power (Klingemann et al., 1994: 240ff.). Majoritarian political cultures emphasize the idea of a 'mandate'. Fragmented systems on the European continent, characterized by the persistence of traditional cleavages, cannot emphasize the 'programme of the winner' but take cognizance of the need for coalition.

The programmatic steering of the agenda in Germany has several aspects as exemplified by the subjects of the following documents:

1 party platforms
2 coalition agreements
3 governmental declarations.

The second and the third documents under Kohl became increasingly congruent because of the publication of the coalition agreement. In the early CDU governments, the coalition agreement was kept secret. Over time, governmental declarations have been the most important source of programmes. Among the 150 key decisions only about one-quarter have been announced and carried through in one legislative period of usually four years. Another third of issues was introduced ad hoc without major prior announcement and another third was announced in a governmental declaration but carried through much later. In some cases, the issue had to be announced several times. On the whole, governmental declarations – varying according to the style of the chancellors – avoid offering a concrete list of projects for governmental bills which could be used by the opposition as a checklist to denounce the failures of governmental policies (cf. von Beyme, 1979).

All the governments in the Federal Republic have been coalition governments, even when Adenauer won the absolute majority for his Christian Democrats. He used a satellite party (Deutsche Partei, DP – a regional conservative group) as a 'savings bank' of votes which, in the event, he did not need at his second re-election in 1957).

Parties and their parliamentary groups have a steering function on several levels:

- *The party tries to influence the parliamentary group and its activities.* In Germany the old Duverger wisdom of extra-parliamentary and intra-parliamentary parties was no longer valid after 1949. Four types of relationship between party and parliamentary group have been discovered (Thaysen, 1976: 74f).
  – The parliamentary group is dependent on the party (for example, the SPD under Schumacher 1949–52).
  – The parliamentary group is the centre of decision-making (for example, the SPD 1958–66).
  – The parliamentary group is but an appendix to the government (for example, the CDU under Adenauer 1953–61).
  – The government is subservient to the parliamentary group (for example, the CDU and SPD under the Grand Coalition 1966–69).
  None of the four types proved to be pure over time. Under Schmidt after 1974 the government also tended to dominate the parliamentary group, but the Adenauer syndrome was limited by the account that Schmidt had to take of his liberal coalition partner. In the Grand Coalition, as the leader of the SPD parliamentary group, Schmidt still fought for the autonomy of the party in parliament and told the party convention: 'It would not be helpful if you fetter us completely' (SPD-Parteitag, 1968: 185).
- *Coalition parties develop a coalition committee to control the agenda.* In the Kohl era such committees were called 'coalition round tables' and became an important steering instrument (Schreckenberger, 1992a: 141; 1994: 330).
- *A coalition working group is created.* Some issues on the agenda exceed the working capacity of coalition round tables, such as the reform of retirement allowances (RRG 1992). In this instance, a coalition working group for the 'structural reform of the pensions' was formed.

The impact of these coalition steering bodies cannot be quantified, but they have increasing importance. The media complains about a lack of transparency and, from time to time, the coalition steering committees have been suspected of serving as a kind of 'co-government'. The chancellor's guidelines and the cabinet's competences are occasionally weakened by the machinery of coalition consensus-finding. This trend was considered as detrimental for parliamentary autonomy because the leading figures of the party hierarchy in parliament usually need representatives from the administration in order to steer the agenda in a responsible and action-oriented way (Diskussionsveranstaltung, 1994: 415).

The Preparation of Bills by the Administration

The German cabinet is more a 'board of managers' than a cabinet in the British sense. Textbooks envisage a balance between the chancellor, the cabinet and the individual ministers, but cabinet is the weakest of the three elements, serving mainly to mediate conflicts between the ministers. The weakness of the cabinet has been analysed as a consequence of the strength of the chancellor. But the opposite is the case: weak chancellors, such as Erhard or Kiesinger, have usually caused a cabinet to work inefficiently (Müller-Rommel and Pieper, 1991: 3). The government in Germany has no formal hierarchy as in the UK, but there is an informal hierarchy of the chancellor and the vice-chancellor, the old ministers and the newcomers (Vogel, 1996: 1973). Moreover, there is a hierarchy of ministers according to the importance of the ministry. The ministers of labour and social affairs frequently had such a degree of autonomy in their arena that no 'chancellor's democracy' worked in that field (Hockerts, 1980: 123). The minister of finance even has certain formal veto powers.

Before the cabinet works on the coordination of bills, the administration has to prepare them. Quite often, bills are presented to the minister who is urged to push an issue. The minister does not always have the effective leadership in the preparation of bills. The 'cosy triangles' have their equivalents at this stage of the legislation: political leaders, administrators and interest group representatives form a restricted network.

Interest groups have several ways of influencing the administration:

- Of the personnel in the ministries 70 per cent has certain links with interest groups – mainly with economic groups (43.9 per cent), (Benzner, 1989: 157).
- In many arenas interest groups have certain rights to be heard at this stage of the legislative procedure (common standing orders of the federal ministries (GGO II, §25)). But even unsolicited influences are not regarded as 'illegal' (Schröder, 1976: 73) or different (Ammermüller, 1971: 86f). The only criticism is of a lack of transparency. A formal presentation of the statements of the groups, as in the Swiss procedure of consultation (*Vernehmlassung*), has been discussed but not yet introduced in Germany.

Scientific Policy Advice

Science as an actor at the stage of policy formulation has four organizational forms:

- permanent scientific advising councils (almost 300)
- scientific institutes under the auspices of ministries (54)
- ad hoc advice by hearings or invited memoranda
- advice by autonomous parastatal institutes such as those of the Max Planck Society, Science Center Berlin, Fraunhofer Society, common institutes of the Federation and the *Länder* (82) (Bundesbericht Forschung, 1993; Hohn and Schimank, 1990: 297ff; Murswieck, 1994: 110).

In rare cases among the 150 key decisions, new forms of ad hoc advice have been developed, such as:

- *An experimental game.* This is used with fictitious actors at a round table to search for optimal solutions in preparation of a bill (for example, Federal construction law, 1986).
- *A test of a legislative draft* after the end of the preparatory work of the ministry. This form of policy advice is used to anticipate the difficulties of implementation for a given law (Böhret and Hugger, 1980: 21ff). A protective and distributive measure which not only regulates but also distributes funds, such as the Youth Protection Act (1980), is a typical case for applying the test.

New forms of experimental politics were restricted to certain policy fields, such as construction and education; and later also traffic policy (Hellstern and Wollmann, 1983: 50ff). Since legislators are under time pressure, the instruments have so far been rarely used. Another form of experimentation – a bill limited for a certain timespan ('sunset legislation') – has been discussed but not yet introduced.

Scientific policy advice is used at both the policy formulation and policy implementation and evaluation stages.

The administration usually has better access to scientific advice. But parliament tries to compensate for the advantages of the administrators by organizing its own forms of policy advice:

- through commissions of inquiry
- hearings (see Chapter 3 'Parliamentary hearings', pp. 63–69)
- reports of commissions and scientific offices

- special institutions evaluating the consequences of technologies.

Commissions of inquiry are not a voluntary exercise in gathering knowledge. They are explicitly (GOBT §56,1) meant to prepare decisions. According to the legislative statistics, which try to mention the source for each bill, commissions of inquiry are much more rarely the source of a new regulation than the Constitutional Court of the European Community. Some of the key decisions in this sample have been prepared by a commission such as that on the 'regulation of gene technology' (1990) and were carried by all relevant groups. In other cases, such as the 'structural reform of health insurance', the SPD opposition has imposed the commission of inquiry against the will of the majority (11. BT, 4.6.1987: 1041ff).

Commissions of inquiry are increasingly important because laws have to regulate technologies which involve high risks. They are, however, under constant danger of serving an alibi function and politicians respond to pressure by reporting without acting. Commissions of inquiry are not the solutions (Gill, 1991: 109). They are less influential than they could be because the ministries have a highly segmented outlook, and the commissions have no competence to force private actors to deliver the necessary information, as in the case of the 'commission of inquiry into the protection of the atmosphere'. In some arenas, parliament has renounced the idea of establishing a commission because of this dilemma of information (Rehfeld, 1981: 255; Ismayr, 1992: 505).

Governmental reports (Schindler, vol. III, 1988: 330ff, IV: 488ff) are increasingly used as a source of information for legislation, especially in cases of amending laws. Since the Law of Agriculture (1955) and the Anti-monopoly Law (1957) many key decisions have been accompanied by a duty to report regularly. Moreover, there are many ad hoc resolutions to work on a report about the consequences of legislation – because either the government or a parliamentary majority has required it. Some of these reports are:

- *Reports on a whole policy field.* Again, the reports on agriculture, required by law since 1955, became a model. From economics and finances to health, education and environment, this model has been copied. Nowadays each ministry has such a report and regards it no longer as a burden imposed by parliament but rather as an opportunity for reporting on successes and work in progress.
- *Reports on special issues.* These range from vocational training and the protection of animals to cancer and rheumatic diseases and are proliferating. They can be used as a check on the need for further legislation.

To date, 114 duties to report have been registered. The government is not obliged to follow them, but it cannot usually ignore them. Although the reports were meant to reduce the informational advantage of the administration, the administration also benefits from these parliamentary activities, and sometimes there is information kept by the ministerial bureaucracy which never enters the parliamentary report.

Since 1989 the 'society of risks' (Beck) has created a *permanent task to evaluate the consequences of technology.* The committee on research and technology added 'evaluation of consequences of technologies' to its name. In 1990–91, an 'office for the evaluation of consequences of technologies' (TAB) was created. It had some difficulties being accepted by the deputies, but in the meantime communication between scientific experts and parliamentarians has improved (12. BT 4.3.1993: 12334ff; Petermann, 1994: 81). The new instruments had a considerable influence on the amendments to the law on gene technology. Experts, however, (Vitzthum, 1993: 237) were not yet satisfied with the results of the amendments and considered the first amendment to the law on gene technology (1993) a hardly convincing compromise.

Besides the institutionalized forms of policy advice, there are not only unsolicited attempts to influence the legislative process but also invited influences, mostly by inviting individual experts to hearings of the parliamentary committees. Scholars are most frequently engaged in legal policy (42.3 per cent of all the interventions, followed by construction policy (15.2 per cent) and environmental policy (14.6 per cent – see Table 2.2).

An increasing problem of scientific advice to legislators is the formula imposed by the Constitutional Court (BVerfGE 49: 90) that legislation has to consider the 'contemporary level of scientific knowledge' and the 'contemporary level of technological knowledge'. The Constitutional Court itself has sometimes not known the actual level. When it had to evaluate the census law (BVerfGE 65: 55), it ruled that a universal census surveying the whole population was still indispensable but that, in the future, a

Table 2.2 **Attempts to influence the legislative process of the 150 key decisions (%)**

	Foreign and Security	Legal	Economic	Social	Construction	Education	Environment	Total
Individual scholars	8.5	42.3	11.9	5.9	15.2	1.6	14.6	100 N=184
Advisory Councils	7.6	11.5	3.8	7.6	27.3	3.8	38.4	N=26

micro-census' might be more appropriate to represent the contemporary level of scientific knowledge.

Scholars may disagree about the appropriate level of knowledge. But the actors in the network disagreed still more about the actual level of technology because economic interests were involved. The evaluation of the 'federal law of immissions' (1974) showed the disagreements of the experts: economists tended to measure its appropriateness within the enterprise, whereas other scholars judged it more by the consequences for the environment outside the factory. Formulas such as 'the most progressive procedure' proved to be empty when experts were unable to agree. The administrators usually defined the standards according to their standards of efficacy and the parliamentarians could only afterwards state that they had other intentions when passing the law.

In the case of routine legislation, a minimal consensus may be found. But great innovations were frequently imposed by the political leadership against the huge majority of experts. When Erhard began his liberalization of the German post-war economy, most experts considered him as a 'utopian professor', Hayek Haberler and Sohmen being the few exceptions (Ferdinand, 1985: 118). After 1989, in many East European countries Erhard became a demi-god and his devices were accepted – sometimes too early – without taking account of the fact that Germany after 1945 was integrated into the Western economy which was not the case with Eastern Europe at that time.

In conflict situations, the experts of the parliamentary groups used to criticize their adversaries for starting from an 'outdated level of scientific knowledge' (Law on pensions 2. BT 18.1.1957: 10424, 10426) and sometimes, when the experts were equally divided in opinion, each party accepted only the advice of 'its' experts, as in the case of the codetermination law (7. BT 18.3.1976: 16003A).

'Expert packing' of advisory committees is a usual practice or was at least imputed by the opposition (11. BT 29.3.1990: 15974D). Rarely was a non-organized minority of experts able to obtain influence against the official experts, as in the case of the reform of the penal law (5. BT 7.5.1969: 12717A). The higher the risks the more even the parliamentarians felt guilty that they had to vote on the basis of insufficient knowledge – as in the case of gene technology (11. BT 29.3.1990: 15964B). German deputies who approved a complicated law resorted to alleged 'American experiences' without legitimation by science. Those who disapproved used all the possibilities of science fiction. In one case even Goethe and his creation of a 'homunculus' in Faust, Part II, was used to prove that the great poet would not have accepted this law (11. BT 24.10.1990: 18218A).

The parties usually agree on the necessity of rigid scientific standards. But trust in science has not always been equally distributed, being weakest among the Bavarian branch of the Christian Democrats, the CSU, and strongest among the liberals (Müller, 1977: 295). The more conservative Christian Democrats most frequently cited 'moral responsibility' rather than trust in scientific research. In the case of the penal law they argued that 'Law has not the task to be torchbearer of the sexual revolution' (5. BT 9.5.1969: 12832D).

In the debates on the key decisions there were five reasons why parliamentarians failed to follow the advice of the majority of scientists in their final decision:

1 consensus on values and the so-called 'sound sentiments of the people'. Acceptance was also a consideration for technocrats
2 moral reasons which had to be clarified by 'ethical commissions'
3 difficulties in implementing a law
4 lack of financial resources
5 the risk of unintended consequences.

The key decisions showed again that 'games of recognition' could not be smoothed by scientific expertise, whereas conflicts of interests usually found some minimal consensus with the help of experts. In many cases, parliamentarians also use science for 'trial balloon' to scapegoat functions (Beneviste, 1977: 228; von Beyme, 1988: 355f). Scientific policy advice proved to be the least dangerous form of engagement of scholars in politics – but frequently it was also the least influential means of intervention.

3 Parliamentary Decision-making

The Introduction of Bills in Parliament

Germany has a parliamentary system with a strong executive. The main actor is the chancellor and his parliamentary majority. It is not by chance that, in such a system, the majority of bills is introduced not by parliamentary initiative but by the executive (about 60 per cent – see Table 1.3, p. 12). In the 12th Bundestag (1990–94) the share of governmental proposals diminished to 50.9 per cent (Schindler, 1995: 561), not because the government was less active but because German Reunification had created such an enormous need for new regulations that the government chose the parliamentary initiatives of their parliamentary groups to save time. There are several reasons why a government might cede the initiative to its parliamentary group:

- In cases of parliamentary bills the first consideration of the bill by the Federal Council can legally be avoided. Quite frequently, the government and the Christian Democratic parliamentary group have submitted identical proposals. Moreover, there were a certain number of key decisions in which the party leadership could not impose party discipline, such as with a new abortion regulation (1992, 1994), towards which the GDR took a rather liberal line which the East German people were not ready to accept, or the decision about the capital which was a controversial issue in all parties.
- When elections approach, the handing over of a proposal to the parliamentary group of the leading party in the coalition has propagandistic effects because it raises the party's profile and does not leave an issue to a 'coalition'.
- In cases of dissent within the cabinet, ministerial bills are in greater danger of being substantially amended than parliamentary initiatives. Sometimes an opposition parliamentary initiative has attracted

support from ministerial staff and the governmental party has tried to steal part of the show from the opposition. This happened in the case of a bill on 'allowances for children' (1953).

In all these cases there are no 'authentic' parliamentary initiatives. Not only was the idea born in the executive but also the whole draft – which, however, is increasingly the case with all the bills introduced by a governmental party and, in rare cases, even with those of an opposition party.

The proportion of parliamentary initiatives passed by the majority reveals the imbalance. Whereas 9.7 per cent of the initiatives in the 10th Bundestag and 14.4 per cent of the initiatives in the 11th Bundestag were successful, oppositional SPD bills were passed only in 0.3 per cent of the cases and the Green Party had no success in a single of its numerous proposed bills. Government was the most busy actor in the collective right to propose a bill. The ministries contribute unequally to these bills, with the ministry of justice usually having the greatest share. Research and technology initially ranked lowest in 1980 and 1991 but this is changing with the development of a 'society of risks' (Schindler, IV, 1994: 832f).

Contrary to the conventional wisdom of many comparative studies, the Federal Council is not a part of parliament, nor a true second chamber. Nevertheless it has the right to propose a bill. It has a share of only 6.6 per cent of the initiatives and, in this sample of 150 key decisions, only of 2.6 per cent. A total of 3.3 per cent of all the bills that become law have their origin in the Federal Council. We do not include them into the parliamentary bills, because Bundesrat proposals are usually initiatives of the *Länder* executives.

Occasionally the opposition tries to initiate a bill via the Federal Council, as in the case of the 'law against organized crime' (1992). When the opposition has a majority in the Federal Council – which happened under Schmidt (SPD) as well as under Kohl (CDU) – Federal Council initiatives can be called quasi-parliamentarian. The opposition initiates these initiatives via the Federal Council because it has more leverage in this body and calculates that this approach gives its proposals a better chance of success against the *Länder* which sometimes develop common interests, irrespective of the party in power. Even if there is only a remote chance of winning over *Länder* governments ruled by the national majority party, the launching of bills is used as an instrument of propaganda (Ismayr, 1992: 281f).

Among the 150 key decisions of this sample, one-third (33.3 per cent) was proposed by the parliamentary groups of the coalition in power and in more than one-quarter (26 per cent) the opposition launched an initiative at the same time. In 11.3 per cent of the cases, the government and parliamentary group acted simultaneously, a procedure which became popular under Kohl's governments (see Tables 3.1 and 3.2, pp. 35 and 38). This is above the statistical average which oscillates between 2.8 per cent (10th Bundestag) and 7.9 per cent (11th Bundestag) and can be taken as a proof that key decisions are more frequently protected against parliamentary failure than routine bills.

If we compare the parliamentary bills they concentrate on legal and construction policies which are the subject of more than half of the initiatives. Oppositional bills are centred in social and legal policies. The types of measure show that bills proposed by the parliamentary groups focus on restrictive, distributive and protective legislation. The opposition focuses on protective laws – understandably, since they usually involve low costs and appeal even to the majority in power. Among the restrictive measures, predominant are those which do not influence the rights of the average citizens but are nevertheless highly controversial in the media, such as 'limitation of basic rights for soldiers' (1956) and laws against terrorism (1977, 1990). In the first case the coalition parties even succeeded in including the SPD opposition in a common initiative of the main parliamentary groups. Some decisions in restricting the right of asylum-seekers (1982, 1992) show a similar consensus of the three established parties (CDU–CSU, SPD, FDP).

The opposition has various strategies at its disposal. For example, it uses the introduction of a bill to influence the governmental bill (Sebaldt, 1992: 331f). The amending power of the opposition seems to be greater when it can show a coherent counterproposal as a point of orientation for dozens of amendments which it can propose in the committee meetings. Sometimes the opposition is so strong that it runs the risk, in a deadlock, of producing a non-decision, as in the case of the 'health insurance law' (1960) where the government was forced to select the less controversial points of its bill and offer it as a partial regulation to its voter in an election year under a new popular label 'Security of workers in case of sickness' (1961).

Occasionally the opposition has been quicker off the mark with its proposal than the minister in charge. In such a case, all means of irony are used to demonstrate the greater efficiency of the opposition, as in the case of a question by the responsible minister Blüm (CDU) in the discussion on a 'Law on widows' and orphans' pensions' (1985). The expert of the opposition turned it down:

> The deputy Blüm can talk later in his capacity as a minister. In the meantime he should take care that the governmental bill is punctually forwarded to parliament. Otherwise his behaviour is a contempt of the legislative. (10th BT, 21.6.1985: 10915C)

Since the rise of the Green Party, which entered the Bundestag in 1983, a healthy competition between the Social Democrats and the Green Party has mobilized the opposition. Previously, the SPD had proposed 4.1 per cent of the bills (9th Bundestag); however, after this new competitor had emerged, it launched 11.4 per cent of the bills. In the eleventh legislature (1987–90) the Green Party even overtook the SPD in terms of the number of bills proposed, but this parliamentary activism remained 'symbolic politics' because not one became law. Unfortunately the two opposition parties rarely combined their efforts.

In the history of the German parliament there have been cyclical fluctuations of the activities of the opposition. Young oppositions, such as the SPD in the first two legislatures and the Christian Democrats in the sixth legislature (1969–72), tend to be more active in submitting complete bills. Later they economize their efforts in amendment politics. Occasionally, a coherent oppositional bill could cause a non-decision, as in the case of the 'health insurance bill' (1960) because a legislative deadlock caused neither of the two bills to get a majority. In other cases the oppositional proposal was amended by the government parties to such an extent that the initiating SPD was no longer able to accept it (for example, the 'Reduction of the planned economy in housing', amending law, 1963). The opposition has been most successful when it has found a popular issue which the governmental parties could hardly turn down, such as 'minimal labour conditions' (1951), 'protection of mothers' (1951) or the 'law for a more coherent insurance for workers' pensions' (1951). All three of these oppositional bills were passed with huge majorities or even unanimously. The CDU opposition had a similar success with the bill on 'improvement of social services' (1972).

Germany has an old tradition of *consociational democracy*, interrupted by the Weimar and the Nazi period. Cogovernment of the opposition has been denounced. In cases of emergency the opposition has been willing to cooperate on a bill of all the major parliamentary groups as in the issues of fighting terrorism (1977), the procedure for asylum-seekers (1982) or even the 'reform of retirement allowances' (1992). In cases of restrictive measures, the governmental parties try to win over the opposition in order to 'share the blame'. This happened when the parliamentary groups had to pass a law which gave the parties certain benefits, such as the 'party law' (1967, 1983), or in questions of *Weltanschauung* where party discipline could not be imposed, as in the decision on the capital (1991) or the 'constitutional reform' (1994).

Consociationalism had its peak under the Grand Coalition (1966–69). The parliamentary initiatives of that period show interesting deviant behaviour of the parliamentary parties. There were, of course, many common bills by the two principal parties in power (CDU–CSU and SPD) instead of proposals by the government. The most spectacular case which almost tore the SPD to pieces was the common initiative for the 'emergency laws' (1968). In other cases during the fifth legislature, the CDU and the SPD had a common idea but could not agree on a common bill, as in the case of 'payment of wages in case of sickness' (1969).

From the outset, the Grand Coalition was a transitory emergency solution. This was documented by the fact that both governmental parties occasionally cooperated with the mini-opposition of the liberals (FDP): the SPD in the case of 'the right to resistance' as an amendment to the Basic Law (1969), and the CDU in the case of the 'law on vocational training' (BBiG, 1969). Major initiatives of the liberals, as in the first two reforms of the penal law (especially the issue to depenalize homosexuality), legally remained one-party proposals. Nevertheless, many Social Democrats sympathized with the 'homosexuality' bill from the outset, but the party as a whole did not dare to antagonize the conservative wing of their Christian Democratic coalition partner.

The formal initiator of a bill frequently is not the real actor who first launched the idea of a law. There are two types of initiators behind the formal initiators:

- the actors of the parliamentary decision-making network
- the actors outside parliament.

Among the actors behind the formal actors, *unobtrusive parts of the decision-making network* can push an issue; these might include the ministerial bureaucracy, the parliamentary group and the rapporteur of a parliamentary committee who usually has close contacts with the administration – even if he happens to be a member of the opposition party.

The hidden initiator can use his influence secretly. Parliamentary groups, especially those of the oppositional parties, use the instrument of a motion which tries to pressurize the government to act. In 1986 one-quarter of all the motions contained a request to regulate a matter by law (Ismayr 1992: 492). During the 11th Bundestag (1987–90) the number of such motions rose from four to 20, seven which were launched by the parliamentary groups and 13 by the parliamentary committees. In six cases the government reacted with a bill; four of them were passed as a law (Schindler, 1995: 562). Some scholars took this as a proof for increasing parliamentary activity, but it could also be interpreted as the reverse: parliament sees the necessity for regulation but feels too weak in its working capacity to prepare a bill and leaves the initiative to the government.

The *external initiators of a bill* are often listed in the parliamentary statistics under the rubric 'reference': 33 such references are differentiated

(Schindler, IV, 1994: 834) which, for our purposes, are reduced to four. One-third of all the key decisions can be reduced to an impulse from outside parliament if we include the interventions of the Allied occupational powers in the first two legislatures under international politics. These initiatives behind the formal initiative for a bill do not include the interest groups whose influence is difficult to assess. Only in the early legislatures, in policy fields dominated by one powerful status group and the related ministry considered almost as a 'domain' of this interest group (the so-called 'interest group duchies'), could a pressure group almost dictate a bill to the ministerial administration as happened in an arena following the clientelistic model – namely, the case of the refugees' and the farmers' associations. This model is restricted to *status politics*. In the model of *class politics* the investors were rarely able to impose their views, except in cases where the labour unions chose not to be involved because mere interests of investments were discussed. The unions sometimes requested a kind of initiating right in the sphere of codetermination (Borgmann, 1986: 43) but admitted, that in a case of conflict their organizations had no special legal rights to formulate a policy for the parliament.

More frequent than the formulation of a whole bill by a single association is the veto against a bill proposed by the executive. In many cases the industrial associations of the capital owners preferred to avoid a regulation, as in the case of the 'federal law on immissions' (1974) or the 'insurance for nursing of sick elderly people' (1993) (Götting and Hinrichs, 1993: 63). Where investors were interested in social regulations they frequently tested the solutions by including them into the wage agreements with the unions. No such step was taken in the case of the nursing issue. The investors' associations were most frequently active as initiators in issues such as privatization (privatization of Volkswagen, 1960) or the 'law to overcome the restrictions for investments' (1991) in the former GDR. On the other hand, when deregulation of social policy is discussed, the high status organizations are rather reluctant to push the state towards abandoning its responsibilities in the field (Wellenstein, 1992: 461). The influence of interest groups is hard to isolate. It can be described, but to count it would lead to rather arbitrary results.

As shown in Table 3.1, impulses for bills (33.9 per cent of the key decisions) can be quantified for four actors outside parliament: impulses from international politics; from the European Community; from the Constitutional Court; and from committees of policy advice and recommendations in their final reports.

1 **International politics**. Germany was not a sovereign state until 1955. Later it became a 'penetrated system' suffering more external

Table 3.1 The initiator behind the formal initiator: impulses for bills in the policy fields, 1949–94

Actors	Foreign and external Security	Legal	Economic	Policy areas Social	Construction	Education	Environment	Total
International politics	23 34.7%	36 2.7%	33 6.0%	29 –	13 –	5 –	11 –	150 7.3%
EU	13.0%	8.3%	3.0%	–	–	–	18.1%	6.0%
Constitutional Court	4.3%	25.0%	12.1%	10.3	7.6%	20.0%	–	12.6%
Policy advisory committees	–	8.3%	9.0%	13.7%	7.6%	–	9.0%	8.0%
Total	52.0%	44.3%	30.1%	24.0%	15.2%	20.0%	27.4%	33.9%

interventions than other national states. The Allied powers had many reserved rights which, after 1955, were reduced to emergency cases which never happened. At the beginning of the 1950s, parts of the legislation stood under the saving clause of the Allied powers. The high commissioners issued guidelines and had a 21-day veto in many fields such as de-armament, decartelization, the control of the Ruhr industry and respect for the constitution. Among the key decisions, only in the case of a provisional 'law on the civil service' did the Allies use their rights but, as the parliamentary documents of the committees show, there were memoranda and warnings *ex ante* without a formal veto *ex post facto*. The veto has been used more frequently against the laws of the *Länder* before the foundation of the Federal Republic in 1949. But former vetos had some impact on the anticipated obedience of the legislators, as in the case of the 'Law on the company constitution' (1952).

Later, the reintegration of Germany into the international community was the most important motive for legislative impulses from abroad. It is not by chance that more than half the foreign policy and external security laws had such an impulse from outside the system (see Table 3.1). The first agreements with the GDR are also listed under this heading.

2 **The European Union**. The European Community is responsible for 6 per cent of all the external reasons for drafting a bill. This figure is low compared to previous legislatures. The eleventh and twelfth legislatures show that about one-fifth of all the laws were actually initiated in Brussels (see Table 3.2); in communication and service during the twelfth legislature already 100%, in environmental policy 75% in the 12th legislature. Agriculture, which used to be the EU's classic sphere of national legislative influence, is not listed separately from economics in our sample (Töller, 1995: 47). The trend towards Europeanization is growing. If the twelfth legislature (1990–94) showed a slightly declining tendency this was only a statistical artefact, due to the fact that, after Reunification, the number of purely national regulations rose for a limited period. There is much complaint about the erosion of national legislation, which is felt still more painfully because many impulses from Brussels are based on a statutory order and not on a European law.

3 **The Constitutional Court**. The impact of the Constitutional Court has been studied as an important contribution to the anticipated obedience of the legislator (Landfried, 1996) but hardly ever in terms of its importance on the initiation of bills. In this sample, 12.6 per cent of all the key decisions owe their existence to a judgment of the Constitutional Court. Sometimes a bill is proposed by the legislators in 'anticipated obedience' to the Court in an attempt to clarify certain norms in advance in order to

avoid its interference (Görlitz and Voigt, 1985: 136). The legislators are mobilized in certain periods when the Constitutional Court exercises 'judicial activism' and judgments (such as the 'soldiers are murderers' judgment or the question whether in Bavarian schools 'crucifixes should be mandatory in class') and the conservative majority in power disapproves the liberal and laicist connotations of the sentences.

4 **Advisory committees.** A fourth impulse for introducing a bill comes from advisory committees, enquête commissions and other bodies. They constitute about 8 per cent of the cases. The causal link between the advice and the bill is certainly the weakest, because most of these bodies have hardly any pressure power to urge the legislators to act.

All these initiators behind the initiators limit the scope of activities for the deputies. Some studies of individual legislators came to rather pessimistic conclusions. The Federal Diet is active principally as an institution of control or of ratification of the work of the ministerial bureaucracy (Schulze-Fielitz, 1986: 82). The analysis of all the laws identified only the abrogation of two paragraphs in the penal law and a new definition of the office of the military ombudsman as a true purely parliamentary initiative and, even for these, parliamentarians used help from the administration – a devastating result for the autonomy of the Bundestag. The German parliamentary barely steers the initiation of bills but parties in parliament – the parliamentary groups – are an important link which explains why government, with the help of the ministerial bureaucracy, successfully steers a large part of the legislative process.

Committees in Parliamentary Decision-making

Surveys among German deputies show that they perceive themselves primarily as 'legislators' (Johnson, 1979: 129). This is strengthened by the growing importance of the committees which, legally, prepare the decision. *De facto* the committees' recommendations are often almost identical to the final decision of the majority after the debates in the plenary sessions. The Constitutional Court has endorsed this trend by ruling that the committees 'anticipate a part of the decision-making in order to unburden it' (BVerfGE 80: 188, 13.6.1989).

There are only few parliamentary committees, such as Foreign affairs, defence and petition, required by the Basic Law (Art. 45a, 45c GG). Recently, the committee on European affairs was added (Art. 45). Additional committees were created on the basis of standing orders or by means of a law. In the first legislature there were still 50 committees with 200

Table 3.2 European impulses on German legislation (%)

Policy areas	10th BT (1983–87)	11th BT (1987–90)	12th BT (1990–94)
Domestic affairs	6.7	2.3	13.0
Justice	9.8	37.5	14.8
Finance	22.9	25.6	20.0
Economics	16.7	14.3	15.8
Agriculture	64.7	33.3	42.5
Labour and social security	3.0	5.7	7.7
Youth, family, wealth	26.2	30.4	31.4
Traffic	30.0	33.3	22.2
Communication	33.3	0.0	100.0
Housing and construction	0.0	10.0	10.0
Education, science	0.0	0.0	25.0
Environment	20.0	66.7	75.0
Average	16.0	20.9	20.6

Source: Töller, 1995: 48.

subcommittees (Schneider and Zeh, 1989: 1089); only in the 1960s was a rationalizing concentration process begun.

Unusual for majoritarian systems is the proportional representation of parliamentary party groups which is required by the statutes (GOBT §57, 1 §12). The Constitutional Court promoted the image of the ideal committee as a 'small model of the plenary assembly'. The parliamentary groups nominate the committee members. In a ruling on the representation of dissenters who left their parliamentary group, the Constitutional Court held a mandate theory: when a deputy leaves his parliamentary group, the group can withdraw the mandate in a parliamentary committee. The dissenter got only the right to continue to work on the committee, but was denied the right to vote because such a right would disturb the balance between government and opposition parties (BVerfGE 80: 188, 13.6.1989). This ruling strengthened the party state without depriving the individual parliamentarian of all his or her participatory rights. Constitutional lawyers (Demmler, 1994: 503) have nevertheless denounced this compromise in the name of free individual representation.

The German committee system has shifted the balance from a debating parliament (following the British model) to a 'working parliament' following the US model. This system has, moreover, contributed to the fragmentation of deliberation and to the creation of a number of specialized parliaments within parliament (Zeh, 1989: 100). In the early days of the Bundestag the committee system was an ad hoc system. In the era of the

Grand Coalition (1966–69) and under the dominance of the coalition of SPD and Liberals (1969–82) committee and ministry were closely related. The Social Democrats demanded rational steering of legislative work. Rapporteurs proliferated and the committee members were forced towards increasing specialization and professionalization. In post-modern times, with the significant impact of the Green Party, new types of committee have been created. A new holism is applied to overcome excessive fragmentation and to coordinate legislation in overarching committees with broad vistas into the future. The rising importance of the commissions of inquiry and the committee on the assessment of the consequences of new technologies has also strengthened the holistic movement in parliament.

The committee system is now less differentiated than originally (22 instead of 50 committees) but nevertheless became more complex due to the proliferation of subcommittees. Most of the committees work without public access to the meetings. Although, in a survey, 51 per cent of deputies claimed to favour public meetings (Patzelt, 1996), experts on parliamentary procedure are rather sceptical about opening the meetings to the public, fearing that the committee work would be outer-directed and rendered less efficient by members delivering showcase speeches rather than finding a compromise between the parties. In a highly hierarchical parliament secret committee meetings afford the individual parliamentarian better protection against party pressures and also facilitate cooperation between governmental and oppositional parties. Open meetings would probably lead to an increasing number of sessions, because important and controversial matters would still be dealt with in secret preparatory meetings. Nevertheless the relationship of public and non-public meetings has become more democratic: in the 9th Bundestag (1980–83) the relationship was 1:8.3; in the 11th Bundestag (1987–90) it was 1:4.9 (Schindler, 1995: 560).

Since 1969 work in the committees has become polarized (Veen, 1976: 85f). Deputies of the governmental parties more frequently advocate governmental policies. On the other hand, the opposition still cooperates to some extent despite the discouraging fact that compromises reached in committee are usually perceived as successes of the governmental coalition. The governmental coalition will, however, try to find a true compromise when it expects a Federal Council veto – that is, situations where the opposition is stronger in the Federal Chamber than the governmental parties. In certain matters, such as social policy, the experts dominate. The most permanent network is established by the 'retirement allowance men'. They usually are men, and there are hardly any women, and they develop 'antagonistic friendships' between government and opposition experts, as in the case of Stingl (CSU) and Schellenberg (SPD) or later between Blüm (CDU) and Dreßler (SPD). 'Antagonistic party friendships' are, however, sometimes disrupted by oppositional networks of certain interest groups which form a 'social security opposition', including the minority of the expert committee 'social council', the employers' associations (BDA), the Federal Bank and the Council of Economic Advisers plus certain Liberals (Nullmeier and Rüb, 1993: 69, 119). The experts develop a certain autonomy vis-à-vis the parliamentary group. Occasionally certain wings of the parties are overrepresented in the committees, such as the workers' representation among the Christian Democrats in matters of social security (Hereth, 1971: 37f). This independence is, however, compensated by an increasing dependence on certain pressure groups. Interest group dominance is not always negative. Sometimes it smoothes down the party ideologies and turns to more unideological debates. Still more important than the interest group representatives are the civil servants who outnumber the deputies in many meetings. They do not keep to a subservient role of providing the parliamentarians with information but are fully engaged in the political debate (Schäfer, 1982: 123): there is a formal 'co-legislation' by civil servants (Lohmar, 1975: 75ff, Vetter, 1986: 227).

The number of committees cooperating in the work on a bill is increasing. The responsible committee in all the 150 key decisions on average needed 12.5 sessions, but the Grand Coalition was so heterogenous that it needed 28 sessions for important decisions. However, certain reforms, such as the reform of the penal law, have distorted the statistics because the committee needed as many as 150 sessions. If we exclude these mega-committees from the calculation, the average number of sessions is rather modest (8.4 from 1966–69). There is no correlation between the frequency of committee meetings and the number of deliberating committees. On the contrary, the fewer committees cooperating the longer sessions of the responsible committee tend to be (see Table 3.3). The most controversial decisions extending rights to the citizens support the hypothesis: the number of committees involved was small (2.7 per bill), but the responsible committee needed more frequent and longer sessions. One explanation for the number of sessions could be the number of hearings scheduled. There is, however, no correlation here either. Construction policy (approximately 22 sessions) and legal policy (approximately 14 sessions) are above average, although the number of hearings, especially in housing and construction policy, was far below average (23 per cent against 63 per cent hearings in the average key decision). The reverse test can be carried out when we investigate the committees which schedule hearings most frequently in their key decisions (economic policy 71 per cent, social policy 60 per cent). Neither committee exceeds the average number of sessions (12.5 per bill).

Table 3.3 Work of the parliamentary committees

	8th BT (1976–80)	9th BT (1980–83)	Bundestag 10th BT (1983–87)	11th BT (1987–90)	12th BT (1990–94)	1st–12th BT (1949–94)
Number of committees (end of legislature)	19	20	21	21	25	–
Sessions	1586	916	1724	1780	2085	25509
Special committees	0	0	0	1	2	15
Sessions of subcommittees	262	168	379	517	499	4684
Enquête commissions	2	3	2	5	4	21
Public hearings	70	51	165	235	361	–
Proportion of public and secret sessions	1:7.8	1:8.3	1:4.7	1:4.9	nd	–

Source: Schindler, 1995: 560.

Committee Elites

The chairpersons of important committees belong to the parliamentary elite even when they use in their memoirs such terms as 'water lackey' (Hauck, 1990; Vogel, 1996: 183ff). The opposition usually has more top politicians among the chairpersons of committees because their parliamentary group does not lose top personnel to the executive. Candidates for the office are sometimes elevated to the rank of a 'potential minister'. Originally, between 1969 and 1972 the parliamentary secretaries of state were often at least deputy members of committees but their profile subsequently shifted towards the executive and nowadays they no longer sit on parliamentary committees. Former ministers do not usually join the committee of their former responsibility in order to avoid conflicts of loyalty with their former collaborators in the ministry. It is an unwritten rule that the budget committee should be led by a parliamentarian from the opposition. Parties have further domains – for example, the committee for labour and social policy (SPD) and economics (FDP).

When the governmental composition changes committee leadership is reviewed. In 1982, when the Christian Democrats came back to power a constructive vote of no confidence against Schmidt (SPD)), 12 out of 20 committees were handed over to a new chairperson in 1983. The committee chair opens privileges of information which are attractive, especially for oppositional politicians. The chairperson has, moreover, not only the privilege of presiding but – contrary to the rules for the parliamentary speaker – he or she can at any time also intervene in the substance of the debate. Chairpersons have opportunities for a higher profile in the media and have privileged access to auxiliary manpower for their work. They do, however, have to put in a lot of time – with 26 hours per week, they spend twice as long in meetings as the ordinary deputy (Kevenhörster and Schönbohm, 1973: 28).

The rapporteurs of the committees in the plenary sessions also belong to the parliamentary elite because they frequently dominate the whole debate in parliament. They are often the experts of their parliamentary group in a given policy field and are key links in the decision-making network because they are the favourite target of interest group contacts. Rapporteurs from the oppositional parties have a certain influence in representing the problems and in the strategy of finding compromises (Schneider and Zeh, 1989: 1122). Sometimes they have important coordinating functions, as in the case of the 'drug law' in which the rapporteur confessed that he had written several thousand letters to inform about the state of the legislative process (Sayn Wittgenstein, 7th BT, 6.5.1976: 16682C).

The chairpersons, rapporteurs and coordinators of the parliamentary groups (*Fraktionsobleute*) are the only deputies who get a deeper insight into the substance of a pending bill. Oral presentation of the results of committee work is becoming rare, being replaced largely by submissions of short additions to the written reports. Frequently the parliamentary speaker has to criticize the tendency to speak about the substance, rather than the detail of the procedure. In cases of complex legislation, such as constitutional reform (1994), a special steering body is necessary: meetings between the rapporteurs and the responsible civil servants gave certain privileges to parts of the decision-making network (Batt, 1996: 78).

Steering of Committee Work by the Parliamentary Groups

Working groups of the parliamentary groups are constantly involved in the work of related committees. A 'trustee' (*Obmann*) of the parliamentary group has coordinating functions and tries to keep the committee work in tune with the resolutions of the parliamentary group (Vetter, 1986: 226). The chairpersons of the working groups also have coordinating functions. They are usually members of the steering body of the parliamentary group. The committee elite and the steering bodies of the parliamentary group are linked by the secretaries of the committees, most of whom have party affiliations but try to cooperate loyally with a chairperson from another party (Hauck, 1990: 46f). The collaborators of the parliamentary groups have a certain note

(GOBT §57.4), but these 'unelected representatives' have neither the weight of their equivalent in the US Congress nor the importance of the secretaries of the committees.

In the American context, confessional wars have been fought over whether the representatives decide according to their 'policy goals' or rather to rational choice considerations concerning their re-election (Fiorina, 1977). After years of rational choice dogmatism new actors have been rediscovered – the parties behind the 'legislative leviathan'. American scholars have found that not every issue can be carried by mere rational coalition-building (Baron, 1994: 269). The individualistic approach tended to neglect collective entities such as party groups behind the parliamentarians. Institutions were also rediscovered, such as the customs and traditions of autonomous committees (Cox and McCubbins, 1994: 227). But, in comparative perspective, American committees have probably more autonomy than German committees: *ex ante* they function as a goalkeeper who does not admit all the proposals and *ex post* they try to streamline the amendments. Some schools perceive the committees as 'interest group islands' (Ray, Weingast and Marshall); others (Krehbiel, 1991) emphasize instead the autonomous decision of deputies after cross-cutting information from various sides. The debate ended in a differentiating view: some committees are independent on the plenary composition of the House and closely related to influences from outside networks; other committees more faithfully reflect the majority will of the House (Londregan and Snyder, 1994: 233, 262). The same is true of German committees, but on the whole the influence of the parties is as significant as that of interest groups.

Opposition parties try to compensate the deficit of their access to the ministerial bureaucracy by a closer cooperation with the party apparatus. But the policy expertise of the parties is limited, despite the work of party foundations (subsidized by the state budget) and their scientific staff and the party working groups in parliament. The steering of the coalition parties officially emphasizes the common guidelines of the coalition agreement, but internally they try to stress their party domain in the ministry. This is one of the reasons why German governments tried to delegate a parliamentary secretary of state into the ministry held by another coalition party. But even this little control could not prevent ministers attributing their ministry's successes to their respective party as well.

The problem of party discipline is more tricky than in the plenary sessions because the smaller number of deputies in the committees melts away the smaller margins of a governmental majority more quickly. Therefore party steering is essential: on Tuesday the executive board of the parliamentary group precedes the committee sessions on Wednesday and the plenary sessions of parliament on Thursday and Friday. Another form of party steering is the attempt of some ministers to be frequently present in the committee meetings. When they send their parliamentary secretaries of state this is usually denounced as a 'contempt of parliament' by the opposition (12th BT, 4.6.1992: 7832D). In one controversial case, the Minister of Youth, Women and Health Ursula Lehr (CDU), was sufficiently imprudent to hint at the voting relationship in the committee, inviting the counterattack: 'You don't know anything about that. You don't even know where the committee holds its sessions' (11th BT, 29.3.1990: 15985A).

The work of the committees is characterized by a good deal of opposition. Cooperation in the committee is later relativized for the sake of the opposition's image in the media, as in the case of the bill on gene technology. The co-rapporteur of the SPD reported:

> The opposition has declared its readiness to cooperate and we have pushed you [the government] for years to act. But this does not mean whatever the result of the bill – the main concern is that we get the law. (11th BT, 29.3.1990: 15955A)

In many cases, opposition co-government is suspected to undermine the autonomy of parliament and to work for a party state which finds its agreements with the opposition outside the House (Kewenig, 1970).

The networks of the decision-makers have not been constant over time. In the United States the devolution of the old subgovernments has been noted, with power dispersed in various subcommittees (Fiorina, 1977: 36). This process has its equivalent in Germany. The oligopolistic dominance of many status groups has diminished. New groups enter the arena and new actors, such as the new social movements, bid for participation. The German Bundestag has, however, resisted meeting this challenge by concessions in the proliferation of subcommittees. Sometimes the establishment of a subcommittee is more due to the search of a co-governing opposition party for an opportunity to boast of having carried through its motion for a subcommittee (11th BT, 29.3.1990: 15954A). Occasionally special committees have been created for complex issues causing ideological disputes throughout the country, as in the reforms of the penal law in the 1970s or in the regulation of abortion in the early 1990s.

Networking and Committee Work

The increasing number of actors in decision-making led to an increasing number of influence-seekers on the part of interest groups. In this sample the first legislature saw 4.5 deliberating committees per key decision; in the 12th Bundestag (1990–94) there were 8.5 committees involved in the average key decision. Some committees only send a memorandum. Only the budget committee is obliged to participate in the decisions. *Redistributive measures* are the most controversial, and it is not by chance that eight committees participate in this type of decision. *Regulative decisions* have an average of six committees. *Extensive measures* – though also controversial – are mainly concentrated in labour policy that fewer influence-seekers seek to participate. The number of committees involved is therefore the lowest (2.7 per key decision).

According to the types of regulation, environmental policy solicits the most frequent aspirations of other committees (6.8 per key decision). Legal policy (3.7) and education (4 committees) are so highly specialized that they attract fewer demands for codetermination (see Table 3.4).

These superficial indicators hint at the size of the networks, but offer little information about the dominant influence. How can influence be measured in this respect? Party managers will prefer the indicators of a tight timetable: success is quick when passing a law with little amendments by the committees, interest groups, administrators and experts involved. The best indicator is parliament-centred – the number of amendments. Hardly any bill is passed without amendments. But most of the amendments counted by the Statistical Office of the Bundestag are concerned with formal changes, sometimes only corrections of orthography (Schulze-Fielitz, 1986: 367).

The number of amendments is quite unevenly distributed among the 150 key decisions. Some bills, such as the bill on gene technology, have given rise to 254 amendments from the Federal Council alone. Sometimes the opposition triumphs: 'You have liquidated the bill under the disguise of amendments and you practically move a new bill' (11th BT, 29.3.1990: 15953C). Only occasionally has this triumph also included that of parliamentarians who have acted against the control of their parliamentary group hierarchy (ibid., 15967B).

The *uncosy pentangles* are of various sizes and compositions in different arenas. In some arenas, old-fashioned 'interest group duchies' have survived. Loose cooperation, neopluralistic and corporatist arenas have been differentiated (Liebert, 1995: 320). Neocorporatist networks dominate in the economic sphere (Hirner, 1993: 175), with the exception of agriculture which is still dominated by one status organization.

Classical interest group theories tend to identify institutions with groups. This may be more appropriate in non-American field situations where administrative actors are among the most important influence-seekers in the decision-making process. It we exclude in this chapter the interest groups (cf. Chapter 4) there are four other important actors who try to intervene in the decision-making process: ministries; executives and parliaments of the federal *Länder*; offices; and parties or their working groups.

The balance between the actors shows important variations. The ministries

Table 3.4 Number of deliberating committees and frequency of sessions in policy arenas and types of regulation

	Policy fields						
	Foreign	Legal	Economic	Social	Housing	Education	Environment
Number of deliberating committees	5.7	3.7	5.6	4.0	4.3	4.0	6.8
Number of sessions of the responsible committee	9	14	12	11.5	22	9	11

	Types of regulation					
	Restrictive	Regulative	Extensive	Protective	Distributive	Redistributive
Number of committees	4	6	2.7	4,5	4	8
Number of sessions of the responsible committee	10	14	13.7	11	13	17

*Reform of the penal law excluded.

were more active in the first Diets than later. The Grand Coalition (1966–69) witnessed the paternalistic presence of many civil servants in the committees again. Many interventions constitute guidance in terms of background material rather than a direct influence. More important is the impact of legal help in finding the appropriate formulations in a bill. Civil servants intervened most frequently in legal policy (53.7 per cent) and in distributive regulations (29.3 per cent).

The federal component of ministries of the *Länder* is also important. It was dominant in the first legislature when the Federal Republic had no experience with statehood, since between 1946 and 1949 the *Länder* were the only existing German part of government. The influence of the *Länder* executive increases when the opposition dominates in the *Länder* and in the Federal Council. In the eighth legislature (1976–80) the CDU opposition was so powerful that motions of the *Länder* – in concert with motions from the Federal Council – were used as an opposition strategy. The *Länder* intervened most frequently in restrictive regulations (31.6 per cent) and in the arena of legal policy (51.1 per cent) because they knew that they had to implement many decisions of the Federal Diet as the federation

Table 3.5 Intervention of offices and parties in the process of legislation

	Policy fields							
	Foreign (%)	Legal (%)	Economic (%)	Social (%)	Housing (%)	Education (%)	Environment (%)	Total No.
Federal ministries	6.6	53.7	5.3	3.8	18.8	3.3	8.5	601
Länder executives and Diets	11.6	51.1	7.4	11.9	7.4	3.7	6.9	215
Offices	1.8	42.4	8.4	18.6	13.8	2.4	12.6	166
Parties and their working groups	4.4	32.5	5.5	25.5	21.1	4.4	6.6	90

	Types of measure						
	Restrictive (%)	Regulative (%)	Extensive (%)	Protective (%)	Distributive (%)	Redistributive (%)	Total No. (%)
Federal ministries	10.6	6.8	19.4	10.3	29.3	23.6	601
Länder ministries and Diets	31.6	17.2	8.3	11.8	21.8	9.3	215
Offices	21.6	19.2	5.4	26.5	18.6	8.7	166
Parties and their working groups	7.7	38.8	2.2	11.1	26.6	13.6	90

had only a restricted number of administrative substructures at its disposition. Offices, mostly municipal offices, intervened most frequently in the sphere of protective measures (26.5 per cent) and in legal policy (42.4 per cent).

Foreign authorities rarely intervened directly. Mostly they sent their memoranda to the ministry of foreign affairs which forwarded it to the responsible committee. In the first legislature the Allied powers sent their views to the committee. Later they also chose the proper channel via the foreign office. Parties, and particularly the management of the parliamentary party groups, have tried to intervene occasionally. Parties intervened most frequently in *regulative measures* (38.8 per cent) and in distributive decisions (26.6 per cent). Among the policy areas, social policy (25.5 per cent) was their favourite target for influence-seeking. Among these interventions it is less the central party organization which is noteworthy – because they have other channels – but more the regional and functional groups of parties which try to develop an initiative of their own.

The Hidden Part of the Decision-making Network: The Interest Groups

The data in this section are based on interventions of interest groups in the decision-making process. The larger organizations intervene already in the preparatory stage when ministerial bureaucracies work out a bill. Mostly they intervene twice in the parliamentary arena – in the stage of parliamentary committee work and in the hearings. Innovative decisions – except in the field of foreign policy and politics of foreign and internal security – are frequently accompanied by public hearings. Since the fifth legislature, when they were introduced according to the American model, almost two-thirds (64 per cent) of the 96 key decisions in that period were based on a hearing.

The 150 key decisions between 1949 and 1994 reduced to 110, because certain areas invited scarcely any interest group interventions or were not completely documented. Some decisions had to be excluded because the sheer quantity of the case would have distorted the sample, such as the reform of penal law (1969, 1973, 1974). The constitutional reform of 1994 caused 800 000 interventions, 170 000 of these alone in the sphere of protection of animals. The tail would have wagged the dog in a sample in which almost 3000 interest group interventions have been counted – on average about 30 attempts per pending bill to influence parliamentary decision-making.

The interest groups were classified according to four groups:

1 *class politics* in a dualistic situation of great corporatist organizations of workers, employees and civil servants, on the one hand, and organizations of the capital owners and employers' associations on the other (969 interventions)
2 *status groups*, subdivided into nine fields (1394 interventions)
3 *territorial political associations* which, in a state-dominated society such as Germany, play a special role (125 interventions)
4 the old *promotional groups, public interest groups* and *new social movements*, which are basically interested in non-material issues, (422 interventions).

The analysis of interest group interventions in various legislatures is unrewarding. The number of cases is small (about 12–13) and more important: the dominance of certain policies varies over time: construction policies after the Second World War; economic policy in the period of consolidation and under the Grand Coalition (1953–69); and educational and environmental policies under the first Social Democratic–Liberal coalition (1969–82). Constantly strong over time was the intervention of interest groups in legal and social policies. Promotional groups and new social movements have increased their efforts since the rise of the Green movement in 1983. Certain groups of underprivileged people and groups (such as refugees and the handicapped) claiming compensation for losses during the war were naturally most active in the Adenauer era. They renewed their efforts after Reunification in the twelfth legislature (1990–94) when the legal norms of the Federal Republic were transferred to the former GDR territory.

This imbalance of the representation of interest groups over time is one of the reasons why the data have to be compiled by a typology of policy measures. In the policy areas, economic interest dominates in more than one-third of the interventions (35 per cent). The trade unions are not symmetrically represented (19 per cent), not even in some favourite domains such as housing policy (20.2 per cent) or social policy (16.7 per cent). Trade union interventions are above average only in foreign and security policies (23.3 per cent, chiefly because the unions intervened on behalf of the social needs of soldiers), economic policy (18.8 per cent, neglecting mostly decisions where investment policy was shaped) and legal policy (13.7 per cent) although, in the latter, most interventions did not come from the unions in a narrow sense, but from organizations representing employees and civil servants. The number of actors is large in policy areas where a corporatist dualism is typical. Previous studies (for example, König, 1992: 237ff) have come to a similar conclusion.

Status-oriented interest groups – with their nine various subgroups – represent almost half of all attempts to influence the parliamentary decision-making process (47.9 per cent). Since most of the organizations – with the exception of some professions – operate in a narrow policy field, it is not surprising that the interventions concentrate in certain policy areas rather than others. Above-average interventions outside their domain status groups, such as legal professions, show up in the field of external and internal security policy. In the latter field these associations act 'on behalf of other interests' as a kind of 'public interest group' – favouring, for example, asylum-seekers, foreign immigrants, terrorist sympathizers. The associations of farmers also demonstrate wider interests than others, intervening frequently in construction policy. Consumer associations were more active than others in foreign policy. In some policy fields the specialized interest groups in the field dominated, such as associations of educational and cultural interests in educational policy (80 per cent of all interventions) and groups of investors and customers in housing and construction (40 per cent).

A model of a *symmetrical corporatist cooperation* of employers and trade unions was developed most often in the fields of economic and housing policy. Many areas, such as education, legal policy and social policy, experienced an asymmetrical corporatism. Trade unions were more frequently involved in these arenas than the investors' interest groups. The territorial–political associations of the cities and regional institutions intervened most frequently in economic policy.

Individual citizens most frequently engaged in legal policy. When restrictive measures were envisaged to limit certain citizens' rights individuals sometimes flocked together in actions of mass petition. This type of 'shotgun pressure' – as opposed to a more specialized 'rifle-type' influence – was rare, however, except in the great reforms of penal law and in the case of major constitutional amendments. Social policy was another field in which individual citizens intervened in an attempt to strengthen protective measures in favour of limited groups.

The policy measures of legislation show a strong veto position for interest groups in the domain of health protection (30.3 per cent), when restrictions are envisaged. Social organizations, lawyers and associations of underprivileged groups were active in their capacity as 'public interest groups'. In the field of regulation the dualistic cooperation of economic interests and trade unions dominated (41.4 per cent). The status groups (40.1 per cent) were also strong, but less dominant than usual. The territorial and regional organizations reached their highest degree of activity in this field (11.8 per cent of all interventions).

Extensive measures for greater rights are dominated by the groups in the field of labour relations (41.4 per cent), especially when the extension of codetermination was discussed. In subfields where equalization of work conditions for men and women or rights within educational institutions were concerned, the status organizations dominated again.

Protective measures showed a certain balance between class and status politics (31.2: 30.5 per cent). Social organizations and interest groups of the underprivileged and handicapped were unexpectedly underrepresented.

Distributive measures were accompanied by two-thirds of the interventions on the part of status organizations. Even in battles over the distribution of funds from the state budget the trade unions were underrepresented (8.4 per cent). The promotional groups were also weak in this field, as would be expected (4.8 per cent).

Redistributive measures are expected to polarize society more than distributive measures since sacrifices are imposed on privileged groups in favour of underprivileged groups. The model of symmetric corporatism in economic and construction policies is most frequently found in this type of decision. The underprivileged interests in these fields are above averagely represented by social associations and organizations of the handicapped and underprivileged rather than by trade unions.

The territorial interest groups of cities and regions are strong in economic and foreign policy (in the latter field as far as questions of foreign trade are involved). The strength of these associations is, however, the relative absence of other organized interests.

Promotional groups and new social movements engage in interest representation in a wide variety of fields (foreign policy and security policy 40 per cent, legal policy 39.1 per cent, environmental policy 24.3 per cent). In all the other fields their influence-seeking activities are below average, especially in all areas and measures where interest articulation is more important than the *politics of recognition* (for example, economic policy).

The Structure of Interest Conflicts in the German Political System

The figures on attempts to intervene in the legislative process cannot be taken as a proof of influence. But, since part of these interventions is 'invited interest representation by the committees' and these committees, their leaders and those who report in the plenary sessions have a clear perception of the importance of groups in a respective field, the invitations to hearings are an indicator of influence. However, even influence via unsolicited proposals to the committees and comments on the draft of a bill often hint at influence. The Statistical Office of the Bundestag does not record whether a committee leader has called an interest group or whether it sent its opinion against the will of the committee managers. This can only be evaluated by reading the text. If it starts 'We protest...' it is unlikely that the intervention is made on the basis of positive cooperation.

In comparative perspective the German parliament is rather open to broad access of interest groups (Sturm, 1989: 326), especially in decisions on the state budget. The final degree of influence resulting from these interventions can be evaluated only by case studies. But even the most detailed ones (Stammer *et al.*, 1965) dared this only in a very vague and wholesale manner. Only occasionally did one of the key decisions show striking similarities between the presentation of an interest group and the final text of the law. The chemical industry, in this respect, was more influential than many other important organizations.

Influence does not depend only on an interest group's level of activity. Equally important is the counteractivity of other groups. In the field of status politics, strong organizations have a better position, because farmers or physicians have no permanent counterorganization. Only when physicians annoy the clients of other interest groups – by high costs for treatment, for example – can a negative countercoalition be organized. There are arenas of monopolistic or oligopolistic organizational structures. The typology of networks in Germany has shown (Matrix 3.1), that the Federal Republic has avoided the extreme poles of dominance by state or society. Most policy areas are therefore located between corporatism and moderate pluralism. In the light of the figures on 110 key decisions (out of a total of 150) in which interest groups played a significant role the intellectual wars between corporatists and pluralists proved to be superfluous because both concepts will find evidence for their hypotheses in certain arenas.

Deviating from the above model, developed in international comparisons, I processed another typology of six network structures in interest articulation which is closer to the political reality of the country. This dualistic *corporatist model* can be found in several variations:

1 **Symmetrical corporatism**. This involves a zero-sum game between employers' and workers' associations. Only in 10 per cent of the key decisions was this model dominant, most frequently in economic policy (60 per cent of the cases). This model sometimes developed into a model of *double corporatism*, especially in the field of housing and constructions policies (20 per cent). A dualistic antagonism of property and customer interest completes the usual corporatism of investors and trade unions. Occasionally decisions in social policy also create a second corporatism of status groups which behave like groups in a class conflict: status groups of privileged and underprivileged groups.

   This textbook type of corporatism, so dear to the corporatists in the 1970s and early 1980s, is rare. When it happens, the frequency of

Matrix 3.1 Typology of network structures in interest articulation

	CORPORATIVE DUALISM		CORPORATISM PLUS PLURALISM OF STATUS GROUPS	STATUS–GROUP PLURALISM		DOMINANCE OF PROMOTIONAL GROUPS
	Symmetrical dualism	Asymmetrical dualism		Oligopoly of status groups (limited pluralism)	Variety of status groups	
Criteria of demarcation	Dominance of class Political dualism of economy and trade unions	Dominance of one pole in the dualism of corporatism	Cumulation of class Political corporatism and status political pluralisms	Restricted pluralism of status groups ruling a policy field	Extended access for many groups	Pluralism of many groups Promotional groups give the key Status groups work as advocats in favour of third groups
Focus in policy fields	Economic policy 60% Housing policy 20%	Economic policy 69% Environmental policy 16%	Social policy 34% Environmental policy 23%	Social policy 28% Legal policy 24%	Legal policy 35% Housing policy 35%	Legal policy 76% Environmental policy 11%
Cases 110 (= 100%)	9.1%	16.4%	23.6%	22.7%	12.7%	15.5%
Attemps of interventions per law	37.9	16.0	60.9	6.6	36.7	21.2
Focus in types of parliamentary decisions	Protective 30% Distributive 30%	Distributive 27% Protective 22%	Distributive 38% Protective 30%	Distributive 48% Regulative 19%	Regulative 35% Distributive 35%	Protective 52% Restrictive 29%

interventions is high (37.9 interventions per parliamentary bill). Key decisions in Germany, involving, in two-thirds of the cases, public hearings, tend to strengthen the trend towards corporatism because German legal-mindedness is excessively preoccupied with a concern to invite the principal interests in the field symmetrically.

In times of crises in certain policy arenas when deadlocks in parliament threaten a solution – especially when the opposition parties have a majority in the Federal Council and block the decision by means of their power in the *Länder* – symmetric invitations to the chancellor's office can strengthen the dualism, as in June 1987 during the steel industry crisis and in December 1987 during the coal industry crisis. This type of 'auxiliary ad hoc corporatism' was most successful when the opposition was invited. In Central Europe corporatism was only successful when parties supported the model. The predominance of attention paid to the parties in decisions should not lead to exaggerated claims for the opposite when some corporatist scholars tend to neglect the parties altogether.

When, in February 1996, the class organizations were seeking a compromise in the question of retirement pensions a corporatist ad hoc solution was initiated by Chancellor Kohl. This is regularly cited as an instance of the 'final downgrading of parliament' (Fromme 1996: 1). But in most cases the compromise did not last and parliament soon re-entered its rightful position as a legal framework for decision.

When class politics is organized in a strictly dualistic and exclusive way it makes little sense to speak of 'networks' since these tend to develop in cases of asymmetrical types of corporatism and in mixed systems where status group pluralism is strongly involved.

2 **Asymmetrical corporatism**. In 16.4 per cent of the key decisions from 1949–94 a model of asymmetrical corporatism prevailed in the type of networking for interest groups. Economic decisions mainly affecting problems of investments regularly followed this model. They were frequent after German Reunification (for example, the Privatization and Investment Act 1991, the GDR Investment Act 1990 and amendments to the Law of Foreign Trade 1990). In other cases (for example, the Promotion of Employment Act 1985) the trade unions were more strongly engaged. The more aspects of social and employment policies involved, the more status groups competed as influence-seekers in the asymmetrical corporatist arrangement. This type of network is dominant in the economic arena (61 per cent of all cases) and environmental policy (16 per cent of all the decisions in that field).

When the corporatist wave had broken and even labour relations no longer functioned in the corporatist way, the corporatists emigrated to other arenas, especially health policy (Wiesenthal, 1981). But even in this field – after the change of the paradigm and the revival of neopluralist approaches – a combination of corporatist concertation and status group pluralism has been shown (Döhler, 1990: 178). Cooperation proved to be successful only when a grand coalition for the legislation could be formed, as in the case of the Pension Reform Act 1992 (1989) and the Health Sector Structural Reform Act (1992). In the first instance the implied interest groups consented with the major parties. In the second, a grand coalition of the parties (including the largest opposition party, the Social Democrats) had to overrule the opinions of the most powerful interest group associations. This was possible only by deparliamentarizing the decision (Nullmeier and Rüb, 1993: 222). In such a case an initially asymmetrical corporatist arrangement can be made more symmetrical by excluding certain powerful status groups.

3 **Corporative dualism plus pluralism of status organizations.** At the borderline between corporatism and pluralism a mixed type has been developed which I call 'corporative dualism plus pluralism of status organizations'. It is more typical of the German decision-making process than the two other more corporatist types of organization of the policy arena and encompasses almost one-quarter of all the key decisions (23.6 per cent). Because of this combination of two principles it is not by chance that the number of interventions is the highest (60.9 per cent per bill) of all the six types. In this type of model the class organizations (employers and trade unions) usually multiply their efforts by sending the subassociations into the battle of parliamentary decision-making. A kind of double corporatism (see above) is watered down by many promotional groups. This type of organization of the arena dominates in social (34 per cent) and housing policies (25 per cent). The non-solicited interventions tend to resemble the pluralistic model. The invited statements in hearings, on the other hand, show a more dualistically streamlined image which leans towards corporatism.

4 **Limited pluralism.** Germany is often counted among the countries which experience a 'limited pluralism' with strong groups holding an oligopolistic position. This type can be found in 22.7 per cent of the key decision-making processes. The number of interventions is the lowest of all of the six types (6.6 per bill). This type of organization of interest group representation dominated in the field of social (35 per cent) and legal policies (35 per cent). Some decisions – for example, the Armament Regulation Act (1972), hold little interest for the great associations of class and status politics. Nevertheless a lively debate is launched by associations of weapon enthusiasts which the average citizen has never heard of.

In almost one-quarter of the decisions some great and more important status groups dominate the scene of interest representation ahead of the parliamentary decision-makers. This model is close to the clientela type of Matrix 1.1 (p. 6). It is not by chance that laws on agriculture and measures in favour of the underprivileged, the handicapped and the refugees after the war showed this type of arena. In some restrictive measures (the crown witness law 1989 and the law against organized crime 1992) status organizations of lawyers achieve this prominence because nobody else is interested, but they intervene not for themselves but as a kind of public interest group on behalf of the 'legally underprivileged' groups, such as asylum-seekers, criminals or terrorist sympathizers.

5 **Enlarged pluralism**. This type shows little barriers of access for interests of non-insiders in the arena. It is closest to the model of pressure group pluralism which was introduced from the United States into the continental European debate which rarely reflected the conditions of European decision-making – in Germany only in 12.7 per cent of the decisions. Only true symmetrical corporatism is rarer. The number of interventions is naturally high (36.7 attempts per law) which is equivalent to symmetrical corporatism (37.9 interventions per bill). This type dominates in the fields of legal policy (35 per cent) and housing and construction (35 per cent). More local and small groups show up in this model than in other types of interest representation.

6 **Extreme pluralism**. The final type, extreme pluralism is characterized by the dominance of promotional groups and new social movements. Issues of *Weltanschauung* and protection of non-material interests are strongly represented. The model produces decisions closer to the Kaldor principle (potential benefits for the aggregate interests of all groups) than to the Pareto principle (benefit for one interest with no losses for the others). This type was represented in 15.5 per cent of the German key decisions. The frequency of group intervention is in the middle field (21.2 per bill). This type of interest representation occurs most frequently in legal policy (76 per cent of the interventions of promotional groups), and in environmental protection (11 per cent).

Extreme pluralism is often accompanied by mass petitions. There is a great degree of polarization although there are no organized counterinterests. Active groups confront the veto of silent majorities. Non-regulation is generally preferred to regulation, although a number of protective decisions – where influence promoted far-reaching regulations – belonged to this type (for example youth protection, 1951; protection of mothers, 1951; equal opportunities for men and women, 1957; Conscientious Objectors Act 1982). This type of interest representation is often accompanied by noise in the media and in the streets. The dominant groups in the field have no sanctions like corporatist class and dominant status organizations (for example, strike, lock-out, work-to-rule and so on) but resort to deviant behaviour. The prevailing types of class and status politics mitigate conflicts via log-rolling. In conflicts of *Weltanschauung* and religion no concerted action at the chancellor's office helps to soothe the conflict. No round table and extensive goodwill can force the Catholic Church to change its mind on abortion or divorce. In these cases instruments of moral discrimination are frequently used by the interests and their respective supporters in the parliamentary parties. In the abortion debate of 1992 (twelfth legislative, 25.6.1992: 8250C), a Liberal politician belonging to the government coalition had to defend his views against the campaign. He resorted to survey statistics: when 67 per cent of members of the Christian Democrats, according to a survey, endorse the Liberal position on abortion, 'you cannot blame a group of citizens, allegedly without responsibility and ethical conviction'. Despite the broad pluralism the ethical controversies in this type of discourse can be more difficult than in issues of tough class conflict.

The German parliamentary process is chiefly organized as a limited pluralism – limited by means of building cartels and oligopolistic arenas. This result is implemented by large class and status organizations with a monopoly of representation in certain policy fields rather than by a deliberate illiberal policy of the state. State agencies and parliamentary decision-makers try to equalize the opportunities of access to decision-making, at least compared to the bureaucracy which favours big and powerful organizations. Half the key decisions are pluralistic (51.8 per cent). Policy does not always determine politics in a clear way, as Lowi (1964) has suggested. Economic decisions are dominated by corporatist models; legal policy is the domain of promotional groups. In all the other fields the situation has to be differentiated according to various issues. The affinities of policy arenas to certain interest group regimes do not exceed one-third in some of the policy arenas.

The policy measures show only two strong determinations: oligopolistic status politics prevail in almost half the distributive and redistributive decisions (48 per cent), whereas protective measures seem to invite the dominance of promotional groups (52 per cent).

The frequency of interventions is not tantamount to influence in all the arenas. In some arenas oligopolistic status – influence and intervention are closely connected – prevails, and corporatist intervention *ipso facto* limits influence because each intervention from one side provokes a counterreaction from the other side. Corporatism may be subdivided when suborganizations of the major associations (employers, investors and trade unions) intervene. The more status organizations are present at the same time, the more divergent the statements of the suborganizations tend to be. In decisions on social policy with a high degree of polarization the investors' organizations are frequently more divided than the trade unions because only the strongest organizations have an all-round interest in the issue (cf. Pappi *et al.*, 1995: 208).

Influence differs – especially in public hearings. German rites of *Ausgewogenheit* – that is, symmetrical invitation of interest organizations – leads to a representation in which not all the invited are equally involved. Some interests 'testify' but do not fight to the last ditch for the interests of their parent organization. In other fields, the symmetry of influence is disturbed by an *asymmetry of know-how*, as can be shown by the 'law on chemical elements', 1980. Moreover, certain goals are advocated for ideological reasons, such as ecological credos. In a case of conflict, however, in the regulations of pharmaceutic and chemical production trade unions tend to share efficiency criteria with the employers' side in order to protect workplaces. The groups working for environmental protection with their uncorruptible integrity, fighting for one goal only, tended to be so rigid that they marginalized themselves against a corporatist coalition of the two class organizations (Damaschke, 1986: 2).

In the United States a transformation of a *system of policy communities* has been discovered. The number and variety of views of the groups increased and former policy subsystems disintegrated (Baumgartner and Jones, 1993: 179). This development is certainly paralleled in Europe as well. Nevertheless the policy networks differed in Germany from the Anglo-Saxon prototypes in the 1990s. The networks were more decentralized in Germany, but vertical and horizontal interpenetrations were comparatively high. Sectoralization did not exclude the integration of interests. The number of relevant associations remained more limited than in the United States, although the fight for invitation to a public hearing is less difficult in Germany because there are fewer prospective testifiers than in the United States. Pluralist self-regulation and corporatist concertation were combined in arenas where, in the United States, a *pluralist lobbying model* continued to dominate (Döhler, 1990: 184). European systems were deeply influenced by American neoliberalist ideas. But despite the hailing of the market in Europe Thatcherism never prevailed on the continent and was not even able to delapidate completely the British National Health Service.

Interest group research in the United States has rediscovered the 'legislative leviathan' and the parties behind the calculation of parliamentarians' individual decisions and their links with interest groups. In Germany the discovery that parties matter would be a truism. The *cosy triangles* in the US Congress (legislators, bureaucrats and interest group representatives) have always been an *uncosy pentangle*, involving parties and the state agencies of the *Länder* in a system of vertical intergovernmental decision-making alien to the American federal system. The influence of interest groups in such a system ultimately depends much more on their capacity to penetrate the party organizations and the establishment of parliamentary groups than on influencing the legislators in the committees via interventions. These are rather an indicator of influence than the cause of direct causality between intervention and decision.

Pressure and Counterpressure in Conflicts of Interests

The term 'pressure group' has no equivalent in German, but certainly there is pressure. Pressure in a literal sense is, however, no proof of powerful influence because the most powerful groups, such as economic groups, hardly ever use it. On the other hand, the left-wing idea that industrial interest groups are so rich that they do not need pressure and simply 'buy' the compliance of state authorities has proved too simplistic (Mann, 1994: 153).

Pressure in a literal sense has been more used by trade unions and powerful status groups which are able to withhold important services to the society. The German tradition of the labour movement has never favoured the mystique of a general strike – although there were some during the Weimar Republic, which had no revival in the Federal Republic. Only the communists in the 1st Bundestag were sufficiently dogmatic to threaten a general strike against the Western occupation forces, even in parliament (Harig, KPD, 1st BT, 10.4.1951: 5071B). The more the communists used the vocabulary of the general strike the more cautious the Social Democratic majority in the trade unions treated it. Even when the Basic Law, the constitution, was created strikes for political reasons found no majority. The lack of agreement between the parties on this (and the right to lock out) was one of the reasons why the right to strike did not enter the constitution. Nevertheless also in parliamentary debates on key decisions an undue pressure of the trade unions was imputed by Conservative speakers in the house (1st BT, 19.7.1952: 10241B). There were even deliberations in the cabinet in January 1951 when the minister of domestic affairs asked for special powers in the event of a general strike (Kabinettsprotokolle, vol. 4, 1988: 111). By the time of the debate on codetermination in 1976 the social climate had changed. Trade union pressure was still mentioned but illegal actions were no longer imputed. Norbert Blüm, a CDU politician close to the trade unions, complained that the trade unions put most of their pressure on politicians who fought in parliament for the realization of certain of their demands (7th BT, 18.3.1976: 16014B).

In other conflicts both sides imputed undue pressure, as in the debate on a bill on vocational training in which the employers' associations were accused of having distributed a 'blackmailing letter' (FR 17.1.1975). The Left criticized the Social Democrats for failing to use counterpressure by mobilizing their votes and the trade unions (Offe, 1975: 300). However, threatening strike action in order to pass a law would probably have changed the majority, but would certainly not have been in the interest of the trade unions. Trade union threats had long been reduced to humorous gestures of symbolic politics when the DAG trade union sent Chancellor Adenauer a symbolic declaration of war, together with a tomahawk. Adenauer ignored the provocation and thanked the union for the gift, mentioning that it was the duty of the responsible committee in parliament to deal with 'your justified demands' (quoted in Hockerts, 1980: 371) The industrial associations were sometimes alleged to have used the threat of a transfer of their industries to foreign countries, as in the debate on the 'law on chemicals' (8th BT, 25.6.1980: 18176B), but research on this issue was unable to trace any blackmailing strategies used by the Association of the Chemical Industry (Zimmermann, 1982: 131).

In Germany interventions follow the type termed 'rifle type' in the United States – namely a carefully calculated intervention in the responsible bodies. Mass petitions of the American type of 'shotgun pressure' are rare. The media do not play such a privileged role in the process of legislation as in the United States (cf. Chapter 2, pp. 15–18). With the rise of the new social movements the mass repetition became, however, more prominent in the German decision-making process. Nevertheless when, in April 1970, the environmental organizations, BBU and BUND managed to solicit 2000 letters of protest against the 'law on chemicals' this was a rather modest result, compared to shotgun pressure in America (Damaschke, 1986: 135). In all the issues which involved mass mobilization, as in the case of rearmament, NATO and states of emergency, mass petitions also took place. The same was true in a limited sense for restrictive laws on fighting terrorism (1978), 'insurance for the case of sickness of retired people' (1993), in the 'compensation law' (1994) and the 'constitutional reform' (1994). Individual interventions constituted about one-third of the interest group interventions and were most frequently organized by promotional groups and new social organisations. Legal policy was the arena in which most of the individual interventions occurred, followed by economic and social policy. Unexpectedly environmental policy stimulated a rather average rate of individual influence-seeking (see Tables 3.6 and 3.7).

Table 3.6 Interventions of interest groups according to types of parliamentary decision (in %)

	Restrictive (13)	Regulative (18)	Extensive (10)	Protective (26)	Distributive (26)	Redistributive (7)	Total %	No. (2 909)
Class politics	**24.3**	**41.4**	**41.4**	**31.2**	**26.8**	**36.3**	**33.3**	**969**
Economic associations of employers and investors	12.7	29.0	16.7	23.5	18.4	27.2	21.9	636
Trade unions of workers, employees and civil servants	11.6	12.4	24.7	7.7	8.4	9.1	11.4	333
Status politics	**60.9**	**40.1**	**50.3**	**30.5**	**66.5**	**56.7**	**47.9**	**1 393**
Lawyers	7.6	1.6	2.2	2.6	2.2	0.8	2.7	80
Organizations of health protection	30.3	4.1	1.9	7.7	2.4	5.9	8.3	241
Self-employed	2.1	5.3	4.4	2.9	6.1	4.6	4.1	120
Agriculture	0.3	4.3	0.6	2.9	4.1	4.0	2.9	83
Education	5.3	6.9	35.8	3.6	16.2	1.9	10.2	296
Housing and construction	0.3	8.6	2.2	1.9	14.3	7.3	5.5	160
Consumers	0.3	2.9	–	0.5	–	1.3	0.8	24
Groups of underprivileged (refugees, handicapped etc.)	6.6	4.3	1.1	3.4	11.3	20.4	7.1	207
Social organizations	8.2	2.0	1.9	4.9	10.0	10.5	6.3	182
Territorial organizations (regional and municipal)	**3.7**	**11.8**	**–**	**5.4**	**1.9**	**3.0**	**4.3**	**125**
Promotional groups an new social organizations	**11.1**	**6.7**	**8.3**	**32.9**	**4.8**	**4.0**	**14.5**	**422**
Individual interventions	135	97	84	547	32	180		1075

Table 3.7 Interventions of interest groups according to types of policy field (in %)

	Foreign and security (5)	Legal (23)	Economic (25)	Social (21)	Education (5)	Housing (12)	Environment (9)	Total %	No. (2909)
Class politics	**23.3**	**31.0**	**53.7**	**26.1**	**8.2**	**26.5**	**42.0**	**33.3**	**969**
Economic associations of employers and investors	–	17.3	34.9	16.7	4.5	20.2	37.6	21.9	636
Trade unions of workers, employees and civil servants	23.3	13.7	18.8	9.4	3.7	6.3	4.4	11.4	333
Status politics	**26.7**	**27.2**	**36.5**	**61.4**	**88.9**	**59.2**	**29.6**	**47.9**	**1393**
Lawyers	3.3	8.3	1.5	0.7	–	4.4	2.2	2.8	80
Organizations of health protection	6.7	2.7	3.8	20.7	2.9	–	4.9	8.3	241
Self-employed	3.3	2.2	5.4	5.3	4.1	2.9	2.2	4.1	120
Agriculture	3.3	0.8	3.2	3.4	–	5.5	4.9	2.9	83
Education	–	5.1	5.9	1.9	79.8	1.5	6.6	10.2	296
Housing and construction	–	0.2	2.6	3.1	0.4	40.1	1.8	5.5	160
Consumers	3.3	–	1.3	1.0	–	–	–	0.8	24
Groups of under privileged (refugees, handicapped etc.)	6.7	3.9	7.8	13.6	1.2	1.5	1.8	7.1	207
Social organizations	–	4.1	5.0	11.7	6.4	3.3	5.3	6.3	182
Territorial organizations (regional and municipal)	**10.0**	**2.7**	**7.5**	**3.5**	**0.4**	**5.5**	**4.0**	**4.3**	**125**
Promotional groups and new social organizations	**40.0**	**39.1**	**2.3**	**9.0**	**2.5**	**8.8**	**24.3**	**14.5**	**422**
Individual interventions	10	474	252	148	48	32	111	–	1075

Parliamentary Hearings

Even at the time of Adenauer's government a former minister (H.-J. von Merkatz in Hübner *et al.*, 1969: 204) remembered that all important proposals for bills were sent to the interest group concerned. The procedure was considered useful. But most scholars criticized the secret procedure. In many cases, other interest groups than the dominant status group did not know about the bill, the members of cabinet were insufficiently informed about the background of a project and the members of parliament were uninformed altogether (Schröder, 1976: 189). These complaints led to the introduction of public hearings in the fifth legislature. Unsolicited groups can now ask to participate, which happens quite frequently. During the hearings the arguments forwarded by interest groups to the ministerial bureaucracy in the bill's preparation stage are repeated – this time in public. The introduction of the hearings has not satisfied all the wishes of interest groups. In particular, the demand for the right of associations to sue (*Verbandsklage*) in order to stabilize the group influence has never been introduced in Germany.

Parliamentary hearings usually serve legislation. But interest groups have also participated in long-term planning hearings (Wessels, 1987: 291). Hearings serve to improve the quality and quantity of information for the representatives and have an important function for the citizens who are alerted by the media reports on hearings. In some hearings the dominant status group dominates. If the influence becomes too strong, it is reversed. The hearing on the 'bill on chemicals' (1980) turned into a trial against the association of the chemical industry. The rapporteur in this case – usually inclined to limit group pressure – had to fight against the 'discrimination of the chemical industry' (8th BT, 25.6.1980: 18178C). This type of development is very likely when important groups, such as the trade unions, feel unrepresented, which they compensate by countermobilization in the media.

The share of public hearings increased from about 40–50 per cent (in the 8th and 9th Bundestags) to more than three-quarters of the important bills in the 12th Federal Diet. Hearings are used for various purposes, such as:

- an instrument of pressure by the opposition
- an articulation of party factions
- a means of overcoming the informational gap in competition with the bureaucracy
- disclosure of the interest group position, so far only known to some civil servants who have prepared the bill
- a means of resolving the divergence of views in a governmental coalition.

Interest groups compete with scholarly experts in the hearing. Whereas important groups can hardly be excluded, the nomination of the experts is highly controversial and each party tries to select experts close to its political views (Ismayr, 1992: 481). Scientific experts are, however, less predictable in their statements than interest groups. In the case of anti-terrorism laws when the 'key witness' problem was discussed, the parties were unexpectedly confronted with a unanimous negative attitude of the experts (BT, 14.11.1986). With some issues so many interest groups are invited that the deputies become confused and prefer to trust the expert's opinion. A third group present in the hearings are the administrative experts. In the early days of the Federal Republic there were discussions between bureaucrats and interest group representatives with hardly any participation of the deputies. This has changed. Unlike in the plenary sessions long lectures are hardly possible. Short dialogues prevail.

In the hearings associations which have had an initial opportunity to develop their views by means of consultations with the ministry testify. But the hearings are also attended by many other groups which do not have that initial opportunity. The quantification of the Bundestag sources is, however, incomplete: telephone calls and personal contacts are not listed. But, again, they usually strengthen those groups which have privileged access to the decision-makers. According to some studies (Schmölders et al., 1965: 142), true controversial deliberation prevailed only when the jurists were not a dominant group. This rarely happens because they prevail in all three angles of the 'cosy triangle'. Moreover the view that lawyers dogmatically think in terms of 'legal or illegal' is no longer justified. Administrators and constitutional lawyers increasingly think – like social scientists – in terms of problem solutions.

The hearings are well organized. Concrete questions are set out in the invitation letters. Before the 5th Bundestag there were occasional hearings, but too few in the perception of the opposition which sometimes scheduled a hearing of its own when its proposition did not find a majority in the responsible committee (for example, the second law for wealth formation, 4th BT, 5.5.1965: 5005B). In this case the results were biased because the symmetry of views was neglected and the expert-packing of specialists close to one's party was not avoided.

Access to the hearings has been regulated in the parliamentary statutes (Standing Orders, §73). In 1980 a compromise was reached on the persons eligible for invitation. The formula 'other experts' opened the door to increasing number of influence-seekers. In 1975 the always precarious symmetry between the groups was disturbed by granting the major associations representing municipal interests a privileged right to be heard (Standing Orders, §73).

As in other countries there are two types of interest groups – those which are invited and those which ask to be invited (Leyden, 1995: 434). The social partners of class politics and oligopolistic status groups do not have to ask for an invitation. Organized interests do not compete in the same composition in various areas: in some arenas of economic policy the economic associations dominate. In the Committee of Labour and Social Policy the trade unions are strong. Experts have also a different weight in different committees: the closer the arena is to one dominant organized interest, the less experts are defined in terms of their independent judgement, but rather in their capacity to streamline the arguments for certain interests (Wessels, 1987: 293).

Invitations to the hearings are more available in Germany than in the US Congress because fewer groups compete. Since 1972 Germany has registered interest groups. In 1991 the Bundestag Statistical Office counted 1578 groups (Schindler, IV, 1994: 892). Yet despite the corporatist ceremonies of social symmetry in Germany in some arenas important groups only obtained access to be heard after some pressure, as in the case of the trade unions in the procedure of the 'bill on chemicals' (1980). In many plenary debates complaints that symmetry in the committee stage has been neglected because the responsible minister has tried to save his project are discussed (2nd BT, 18.1.1957: 10438C; 'law on the reorganization of retirement allowances'). Such complaints occasionally lead to a second hearing. Only in rare cases of secular amendments (as in the case of the constitutional reform, 1994) have a whole series of (9) hearings been scheduled from the outset. Repeated hearings are not always beneficial for a dominant status group. In health policy the medical associations came under pressure from a broad coalition of parties and interests several times (for example, 1960, 1992).

Among the key decisions 64 per cent since the 5th Bundestag were accompanied by hearings. This is above average (about 20 per cent). In the 4th Bundestag only one bill out of 200 was discussed in a hearing. In the 10th Bundestag it was already one-quarter of all the bills (Schindler, IV, 1994: 720). Increasingly, the impact of hearings on legislation is only rather indirect. The commission of inquiry into 'Dangers of Aids' in the eleventh legislature conducted 21 hearings which had no immediate result in a law. Committees, such as Labour and Social Policy, Finances, Legal Policy or Domestic Affairs offer most of the hearings. The correlation between number of hearings and bills is, however, not always given. The Labour and Social Policy Committee, has most hearings but ranks in the middle in terms of the quantity of laws passed (Schindler, IV, 1994: 718f; Schüttemeyer, 1989: 1151). It is not so much the number of bills, but rather the conflicts in an arena that determines the number of hearings. Class politics usually needs more consultation than arenas dominated by a powerful status group (cf. Table 3.7, p. 62).

There is not only a flood of laws, there are also complaints about the proliferation of hearings. Critics question whether the parliamentary timetable allows for so many hearings which have only minor importance for legislation. There is, however, no correlation between the number of hearings and the strain of the timetable of committees: the committees with the longest and most frequent sessions are by far not those which schedule more hearings than others.

As can be seen from Table 3.8, among the 150 key decisions in this sample 58 per cent of all the laws were preceded by a hearing (1949–94). If we restrict the sample to the timespan of the 5th to the 12th Bundestags, when hearings became a normal practice, almost two-thirds of the laws (64 per cent) were passed after at least one hearing. Education which has 100 per cent is not typical because the number of decisions is small and the federation has few competences in this area. Moreover, educational policy was pushed by the Liberals and the Social Democrats during their first coalition (1969–72). As a consequence of the students' rebellion and Brandt's announcement that the government would dare to practise more democracy, public hearings in educational policy were almost mandatory. Social policy (72 per cent) and economic policy (69 per cent) are the areas with most of the hearings. In the twelfth legislature (1990–94) the proportion decreased because Reunification demanded so many new regulations that government and parliament agreed that the urgent need for decision did not allow for 'wasting' time in hearings. If we compare the types of regulation, hearings are most frequent in regulatory (66 per cent) and protective measures (62 per cent). With the proliferation of hearings the differences between various policy types diminished. Restrictive policies cause few hearings because many of the decisions are 'accelerated laws' which are speeded up, because certain populistic moods have to be appeased quickly. Foreign policy is not very suited for public hearings. Certain types of regulation, which are 'codification laws' and represent only a systematization of existing regulations, are not accompanied by public hearings.

The importance of hearings can be quantified, but their impact of hearings on the final decision is difficult to assess. Plenary sessions show that, in many cases, the arguments of the experts during the hearings are discussed and re-evaluated ('Conscientious objection reorganization law' 1982, 9th BT, 16.12.1982: 8892B). The opposition usually claims that the hearings serve only ceremonial functions. Politicians sometimes claim that hearings in the early days of post-war German parliamentarianism were more significant and deteriorated later to symbolic politics (Hauck, 1990: 51), but this is only true of the mainly secret hearings before the introduction of the

Table 3.8 Hearings of parliamentary committees (%)

Bundestag	Foreign	Legal	Economic	Policies Social	Housing	Education	Environment	Total
1st–12th	26	58	69	72	38	80	63	58 (88 out of 150)
5th–12th	17	50	48	37	15	100	63	64 (62 out of 96)

Bundestag	Restrictive	Regulative	Types of measure Extensive	Protective	Distributive	Redistributive	Total
1st–12th	58	66	52	62	56	55	58 (88 out of 150)
5th–12th	50	39	35	51	34	22	64 (62 out of 96)

public hearings in the fifth legislature. There are still secret hearings, but nobody has investigated whether interest groups and experts have been more successful in launching their views when the hearing is not public. If we use the findings of the few thorough early case studies on the influence of interest groups on legislation, as in the case of the 'representation of personnel law' (1955) (Stammer *et al.*, 1965: 213) the answer to this question is ambiguous: the early process of legislation in the Federal Republic was less affected by scientific policy advice.

Interest groups in the early legislatures were more directly successful in influencing the decision because there was less competition among groups and movements. The influence of experts in the hearings, on the other hand, was comparatively lower. Later, there was also a certain divergence in the assessment of success: scholars and experts were more interested in long-term regulations than interest group representatives and thus they were more readily disappointed by the meagre results of the consultation process (cf. Damaschke, 1986: 130). The expectations of the actors in hearings vary as one can see from the kinds of question they ask. A good example was the amendment of the 'law on gene technology' (1993, printed document 12/3658 Rabenstein, 1995: 19):

- The SPD opposition asked critical questions.
- The coalition parliamentarians asked rhetoric questions concerning the wishes of research and industry.
- Bureaucrats were apparently not interested in further deregulation as the representatives of the industrial sector hoped for.
- Science and industry were basically at one on further deregulation and weakening strict rules of bureaucratic supervision.

One criterion of success might be the number of amendments to the bill proposed after a hearing. But this indicator neglects the power structure: in certain cases where industrial interests dominated, as in the case of the 'law on chemicals' (1980) the hearing offered excellent counterarguments, but the lobby was so well organized that its views remained unshaken. Surveys among economic associations (Schmölders, 1965: 144) demonstrated that industrial lobbyists played down their impact on the decision: almost two-thirds of the interest group managers were unable to think of one instance where they were able to change a decision during a hearing. Nevertheless the interest groups do not consider hearings a waste of time, because they also serve a function in representing an issue in the media. This is particularly true of the weaker interests, such as the trade unions (Pappi, 1995: 181).

The parties value hearings more highly for decision-making, although the opposition only rarely boasted of having completely changed a governmental bill because of the hearing (11th BT, 29.3.1990: 15954, 'Law on gene technology'). For parliamentarians the hearings serve various useful functions:

- The lobby is 'outed' and the deputies get a clearer picture of who is pressuring behind the scenes.
- Hearings strengthen parliament's role in the public debate of the media – although not all the hearings get the media attendance of a hearing held on, say, 'pornographic literature'.
- The hearings strengthen, however, only one part of parliament against another: with rare exceptions, plenary sessions lose what committee elites gain in influence and media coverage.

Plenary Sessions and Public Debates in the Decision-making Process

Committees serve as a filter of governmental bills. But almost two-thirds of the less important bills are passed unamended to the plenary debate (see Table 3.9). The amendments after the committee deliberation are still less important (10.9 per cent in the seventh legislature, 3.0 per cent in the 11th Bundestag) (Schindler, 1995: 561). This does not mean, however, that the House has no importance in the decision-making process. Its activities can be measured by various indicators:

- the number of amendments
- the number of questions concerning pending bills
- the structure and intensity of the plenary debate
- how long parliamentarians stay in important positions
- the specialization and multifunctionality of parliamentary elites
- the importance of voting on the bills.

Most parliamentarians confess that committee work is more rewarding than participation in the plenary debate of the House (Hereth 1969: 58). A recent survey showed that 95 per cent of the deputies think that committee work is important and that 92 per cent consider sessions of the parliamentary groups to be important, but only 50 per cent rated plenary debates very highly (Patzelt, 1996).

The individual deputy felt colonized by influences outside parliament. This led to a number of decisions of the Constitutional Court (BVerfGE 10: 4ff, 70: 324ff, 80: 188f, 84: 304ff). Professors of political science who spent time in parliament were particularly frustrated about the individual deputy's lack of room for manoeuvre (Hereth, 1969; Schweitzer, 1979: 133). Many good speeches were never given and were buried in the minutes. But even those who got a chance to speak felt alienated by the stress of a hardly listening and newspaper-reading House which is almost empty (Lattmann, 1981: 21; Vogel, 1996: 448).

The debate is dominated by the committee speakers and the rapporteurs. Other deputies felt alienated by the secret linguistic code of the specialists in one arena. A professor of economics who complained was interrupted by a colleague and told that he, as a scholar, should be familiar with the jargon of the issue (2nd BT, 3.7.1957: 13142A). When a bill on the 'insurance of artists' (1981) was discussed the rapporteur had some difficulties making himself heard against the noise of uninterested colleagues. His mocking remark when thanking the Speaker who created silence for his report was typical: 'Usually we social policy experts are alone in the room and we listen carefully to each other' (9th BT, 26.5.1981: 2057A). The non-experts were perceived only as a nuisance potential.

Conflicts arise occasionally because representatives feel offended when the minister responsible for a bill discussed does not show up. The deputies have the instrument of 'calling in the responsible ministers' which has been used 54 times in 12 legislatures – 16 times successfully (Schindler, 1995: 565). Sometimes the instrument is only used for propaganda purposes. When, in a debate on the 'law on the national census' (1986) the Green Party called for the minister one deputy remarked that it was a waste of time: 'The majority is guaranteed anyway.' A Green deputy interrupted, 'We are 17 – the rest is only 13' (10th BT: 26.9.1985: 11916C). The Commission for Constitutional Reform under the SPD government (Beratungen und Empfehlungen, 1976: 174f) has made a number of proposals to streamline the debate and make it more efficient. Among these proposals was the reduction in the number of readings of a bill from three to two. Legislation by committees – as it exists in Italy – has not even been considered.

The visibility of politicians in the debate on bills can be assessed by the data which the Statistical Office of the Bundestag has collected since the eighth legislature (1976–80). The drawback of these data is that the computer does not weigh the interventions. It is no accident that a former Green obstructionist who left the parliamentary group was the most frequent speaker because the data include all his minor interruptions and motions concerning procedure (Schindler, IV, 1994: 559ff).

My own list of politicians' contributions during the debates on the 150 key decisions show some regular features of the process of debating bills:

- Representatives of small parties, such as the Liberals and the Green Party, are forced to be more present in the debate because the parliamentary group has few experts on various matters.

- The strategical generalists, especially the chancellors, are not always among the key speakers in the legislative process. Adenauer was more often present than his contempt for public debates would suggest. Kohl, who saw himself as Adenauer's heir, became rather lazy about influencing the debate during his later legislatures. The division of labour between strategic generalists and legislative specialists is growing. Many leading politicians are also among the most frequent speakers, but not necessarily in legislative debates.
- During the first two legislatures the Federal Republic had to consolidate. A peak of key decisions in foreign policy and external security led to a disproportionately *high presence of the chancellor* and the most important ministers in parliamentary debates. After the consolidation of the regime the division of labour returned to nearer the average.
- Some key speakers, such as Schmidt, Genscher or Strauss, were multifunctional *generalists* in many fields. Others were *single issue fighters*, such as Herbert Gruhl (CDU), who discovered a popular issue, such as environmental policy and was able to monopolize the debate in one field for quite a while. Fluctuations of fashionable topics increase or weaken the visibility of top politicians, especially of federal ministers. The number of bills passed per ministry is easy to count, but not very telling because the agenda changes from legislature to legislature.
- The visibility of key speakers depends on the fluctuations of the *length of an average mandate*. It went down from 8.17 years (11th Bundestag 1986–90) to 6.19 years (12th Bundestag 1990–94), but this was an artificial fall due to the influx of the new East German deputies. There is, however, no correlation between the length of mandate and engagement in the legislative debate. The top politicians are very active for two legislatures and later withdraw to more general aspects of the parliamentary debate – although they stay in parliament three or four or more legislatures (see Table 3.9).

There is an old debate on the professionalization of political elites: when social background data have been compared, it has shown a dominance of lawyers and teachers and this has been cited as evidence against growing professionalism (Armingeon, 1986). A better criterion is the kind of speeches and books which the elites produce. General titles such as *We Need an Unhurt World* (Gerhard Schröder, CDU, 1963) or *Views of a German* (Rainer Barzel, CDU, 1968) have been substituted by more substantial analyses of the political arena – even if ghost writers are often involved.

In some respects, little has changed. The proportion of women speaking

Table 3.9 Length of the mandate in the German Bundestag (in years)

	Length of mandate				
	8th BT 1976–80	9th BT 1980–83	10th BT 1983–87	11th BT 1987–90	12th BT 1990–94
At the beginning of the legislature	6.7	6.7	7.1	8.1	6.1
At the end of the legislature	9.9	8.7	10.5	9.0	nd

on women's issues remained almost constant from 'protection of mothers' (1952) to 'abortion' (1992, 1994). In some areas a professional group dominated in the debates on key issues, such as 'structural reform of the health system' (1992) in which out of 18 speakers five were medical doctors and eight social policy specialists. In the debate on 'insurance of health care for elderly people' (1994) among 13 speakers there were eight social policy specialists and one physician. In the debate on restrictive bills, such as anti-terrorism or asylum-seekers, the dominance of jurists is still more overwhelming.

Smaller parties cannot afford to develop monofunctional debaters in parliament. The most common combination of fields or specialization was legal and social policies. Only the top leaders of the parties combined two other issues: foreign policy and social security. Populistic criticism that modern politicians develop only one skill – to fight their adversaries (Hofmann and Perger, 1992: 150) – is correct only for one small group of generalists who try to keep out of the dull everyday work of legislation. The 'organization men' at the top have other skills besides special knowledge in one field, which is also essential to develop the steering capacity of the parties in parliament.

The 150 key decisions were not always accompanied by interesting parliamentary debates. In the sphere of protective and distributive policies – especially in the case of amendment laws – many debates on the bills were organized with a minimum of input from the parliamentary elite. Sometimes only the responsible parliamentary secretary of state was present in the debate. This study of 150 decisions is based on the analysis of 1707 contributions in the plenary sessions. The input was most intense in the twelfth legislature after Reunification. The parliamentary elite accounted for only one-third of the speeches on bills. The Grand Coalition had such a tight schedule that the proportions were reversed: the two giants in the governmental coalition (CDU–CSU and SPD) streamlined the debate and handed over two-thirds of all substantial contributions to the party elites.

This meant that, under the Grand Coalition, the newly created parliamentary secretaries of state achieved a certain prominence. Later they were substituted by ministers from the *Länder* cabinets who increasingly asked for the right to speak in the Bundestag.

The strategy of elite input into the legislative debates has also changed over time. The input was most noteworthy in the times of consolidation (first, second and twelfth legislatures). In other legislatures when the governmental coalition was on the defensive, as in the 8th Bundestag (at the end of the 1980s) the input of ministers was low.

The rapporteurs of the committees are part of the lower echelons of the parliamentary hierarchy. Their engagement in the plenary debate depended on the degree of conflict a bill aroused. After the first change of government composition (sixth–eighth legislatures) the rapporteurs took an increasingly dominant position in the debates on bills. Committee conflicts were carried over into the House. In some cases the Speaker offered the floor but hardly any deputy wanted it because the rapporteur experts had left nothing important to say. In 12 legislatures the rapporteurs have contributed one-eighth of all the interventions. In some key decisions the debate was short and apparently streamlined by the parliamentary group – for example, the bill on 'volunteers for military service' (1955), 'social services' and 'protection of animals' (sixth legislature), 'protection of nature' and 'protection of data' (seventh legislature), 'insurance of artists' (9th Bundestag), 'party law' amendment and 'national census law' (10th Bundestag) – were highly dominated by the rapporteurs with comparatively little contributions from the ordinary deputies. However, this did not mean that conflicts did not exist. The voting behaviour of the parliamentary groups show that the issue was far from being based on a broad party consensus.

The federal chancellors developed very different patterns of parliamentary visibility. Adenauer fought quite frequently for his bills in the Bundestag, mostly in foreign and security policy, but also in important social policy decisions. In social policy, however, the chancellor's interventions were tactical and restricted to critical moments, whereas in foreign policy his speeches were fundamental and systematic. Erhard, when minister of economic affairs had his hobby horses, such as the anti-monopoly law (1957). As the second chancellor he acted still more selectively in legislative debates, preferring fundamental appeals for consensus but avoiding the details of legislation. Not even in foreign policy which fascinated all the other German chancellors was he particularly active in the parliamentary debate. Brandt as the first chancellor of the SPD concentrated on foreign policy, but was also active in matters close to the Social Democratic credo, such as education or the codetermination of workers. Schmidt carefully prepared the legislation of his chancellorship but restricted his interventions to setting the chancellor's guidelines. With the exception of Kiesinger, who led the Grand Coalition (1966–69), Kohl was probably the chancellor who most avoided the details of legislative work.

The strategy of governmental presence in legislative debates usually gave rise to an intervention on the part of the minister responsible for the bill. In a case of emergency the chancellor would come to his support. Adenauer, in international matters, frequently called on Secretary of State Hallstein. In the second legislature (1953–57) the custom was established of showing up with several ministers in the legislative debate of key decisions such as 'law on volunteers' (1955), 'Nato treaty' (1955) and 'reconstruction of pensions' insurance' (1957) which was considered as a major event and was accompanied by interventions of one-third of the cabinet. Not even the 'state of emergency laws' (1968) caused such a mobilization of top politicians. The penal law reform (1973, 1974) led to a parliamentary debate of all the principal lawyers in the top elite. The 'basic treaty with the GDR' (1973 – one of the most controversial key decisions of the Federal Republic – mobilized almost half of the cabinet (eight ministers). The 'unification treaty' (1990) as a non-controversial key decision, needed only half the ministerial input (four ministers).

Generally the strategy of the debate includes three phases: in the opening debate the responsible minister and, eventually, the chancellor or top leaders intervene. In a second phase the floor is open to the middle field of elites and backbenchers. In a final phase the supporting ministers and leaders of the parliamentary group try to influence the arguments of the 'finale'.

The importance of plenary debates can be assessed by the number of amendments proposed at this stage of the procedure. The idea that parliamentarians consider the governmental bill as 'not obliging working material' (Hereth 1969: 71ff) is an exaggeration, but there are more amendments than one would imagine after the preparatory work of the committees, the government and the parliamentary groups. Amendment policy is a collective action. All the motions are usually coordinated in the parliamentary group. In June 1981 the SPD parliamentary group decided that non-coordinated motions from its members was to be considered as a breach of party solidarity (text in Hellstern and Wollmann, 1984: 78). In the parliamentary statutes of four federal *Länder* (Hamburg, Hesse, Lower Saxony, Saxony-Anhalt) individual motions for amendments are not even legally admitted, which is considered as non-constitutional by some public law experts (Demmler, 1994: 504).

As can be seen from Table 3.10, the committees already change about two-thirds of the bills, although most amendments are not very substantial. The amending power of the House – compared to that of the committees – has decreased. The second legislature (1953–57) was the heyday of

Parliamentary Decision-making 75

Table 3.10 Amendments during the legislative process (%)

Institutional origin	7th BT 1972–76	Bundestag 8th BT 1976–80	9th BT 1980–83	10th BT 1983–87	11th BT 1987–90
Committees	62.5	59.3	54.4	65.9	64.2
Parliamentary groups and deputies	10.9	5.9	5.9	7.5	3.0
Conference committee in the mediation between Bundestag and Federal Council	12.5	12.7	7.4	1.9	2.7
Promulgated without amendments	37.2	39.8	45.6	33.1	35.8

Sources: Schindler, I, 687; III, 551; IV, 825.

individual amendments (about seven per key decision). During the 11th and 12th Bundestags (1987–94) only every seventh bill provoked amending motions from an individual deputy.

The concertation of activities by the parliamentary groups is also obvious in the light of the *questions concerning the state of the art in pending legislation.* During the Grand Coalition (1966–69) the Liberal mini-opposition used this instrument because it was too weak in personnel to enter the debate with well formulated amendments. During the sixth legislature (1969–72), when the Christian Democrats had to work in the opposition for the first time, the questions were used as means to continually attack the new government, but were combined with amendments and complete counterbill propositions. The questions concentrated on foreign policy (50 per cent of the key decisions) and on educational policy (50 per cent) (see Table 3.11).

The number of questions concerning pending bills in educational policy may be explained by the high proportion of teachers in parliament. Foreign policy is an arena which is usually less transparent than others and invites

Table 3.11 Amendments of the opposition parties (in percentage of all motions for amendments among the 150 key decisions)

	1st	2nd	3rd	4th	Bundestag 5th	6th	7th	8th	8th	10th	11th	12th
No. of amendments	26	42	33	32	40	52	66	34	52	50	64	64

questions. Comparing the types of regulation, this instrument is used most frequently in cases of restrictive measures (33 per cent).

Two actors dominate the amending policy: the parties – especially the opposition – and the Federal *Länder*. The influence of the *Länder* as an autonomous legislator has decreased, but in terms of intergovernmental policy-making (*Politikverflechtung*) their influence on the national legislative process has increased. In many key decisions, such as gene technology (1990), the Länder showed up with dozens of amending motions.

The amending power of the opposition was greatest in the days of the fundamental opposition of the SPD under Schumacher, under the early Social Democrat–Liberal coalition (1969–76) and with the rise of new oppositions since 1983. Later, co-government of the opposition led to more constructive motions. Rifle-type amendments began to prevail over shotgun pressure or, in other words, unspecific amendments for amendment's sake. Comparing the policy fields the opposition was most active with amendments in educational policy (58 per cent) and economic policy (52 per cent). In terms of types of regulation the opposition was most active in less controversial fields, such as protective (57 per cent) and regulative measures (52 per cent) which involved little government spending and where the opposition could hope that its efforts would be rewarded by the adoption of the proposition by the coalition parties in power. In cases of controversial policies, such as restrictive measures, the opposition showed its flag in the debate, but was less active in using its amending power because of the low probability of success.

Strategies of the Oppositions

The opposition is not a notion in the Basic Law. Even in the parliamentary statutes it is inadequately dealt with. But contrary to the majority parliamentarianism in the UK the rights of the opposition are protected by provisions for the parliamentary groups in general and the parliamentary minorities in particular (Wollmann, 1970: 68f).

Legislation is considered to be the parliamentarians' main function. When the Christian Democrats went into opposition in 1969 – although they continued to consider themselves as the 'natural governmental party' – they transformed their frustration about the loss of power into legislative activities. Its 122 proposed bills constituted 21 per cent of all the bills during the sixth legislature (1969–72). The SPD opposition in the fourth legislature (1961–65) launched only 12 per cent of the bills introduced into the House and about less than 10 per cent of all the proposed bills in total (Veen, 1976: 49). In power after 1969, the SPD tried to slow down the procedure on oppositional bills with all the means at its disposal: 29 opposition proposals were accepted. Not all of them were important: 18 accepted proposals were technical regulations and distributive measures for very small groups.

German literature has accepted a typology on oppositions developed by Robert Dahl:

1   issue-oriented ad hoc opposition
2   cooperative opposition
3   competitive opposition.

Types 2 and 3 prevail in Germany in different blends. Cooperative opposition in fundamental questions (anti-terrorism laws, limiting asylum-seekers and immigration, labour market policy, German unity) coexists with competitive opposition in most other legislative areas. Issue-oriented ad hoc opposition is more common with the approach of elections: the smaller coalition partner tries to emphasize his own profile. Limited conflicts in the governmental coalition are increasing in the parliamentary debates as well as in the voting behaviour of the parties.

Parliamentary co-government of the opposition is sectoral and time-limited. It is most often found at committee level (cf. Chapter 3, pp. 37–47), especially in the Defence Committee (Berg, 1982: 253) in times of a crisis. In the plenary sessions co-government of the opposition is demonstrated most frequently by the rapporteurs of the committees. Sometimes the rapporteurs from the two principal parties emphasize the good cooperative climate and also try to preserve the committee consensus in the plenary debates. When conflicts arise in the public debate of the House, the opposition is sometimes reminded of the amount of cooperation it has already invested into a bill at committee level. When the 'federal financial support for students' law (1971) was discussed, the rapporteur of the governmental party addressed the opposition: 'I cannot imagine that you want to reduce your contributions in the committee work on the bill by not voting in favour of the final law' (Hauck, SPD, 6th BT, 24.6.1971: 7672A). This strategy was not always successful. Sometimes it was only in the plenary sessions that the opposition realized how little it had gained by the cooperation, as happened to the Christian Democrats in the discussion of the 'constitution of industrial enterprise' (1971) (6th BT, 10.11.1971: 8593A).

There are three motives for a cooperative opposition:

- The bill is *not controversial*. In environmental policy there is often no visible enemy. The reports are full of praise for the opposition (for example, Hirsch, FDP, 7th BT, 18.1.1974: 4684A).

- *Log rolling is possible.* Even a fundamental opposition, such as the SPD under Schumacher, was persuaded to cooperate in the necessary constitutional revisions for the rearmament laws by concessions in the codetermination issue in the iron and coal industries. The radical Communist opposition – at the time still represented in the German parliament – was the only group to denounce this kind of hidden agreement (1st BT, 19.7.1952: 10257C).
- *Lengthy negotiations and concessions in the substance of the bill.* In some cases, after long negotiations the opposition introduces a bill together with the government parties, as in the case of the 'structural reform of the health system' (1992). Here, using oppositional cooperation to patronize the government, which had shown a certain capacity to learn from the opposition since the last bill (1988) – celebrated as an event – proved to be a failure (12th BT, 9.12.1992: 10918C, 10917D). In other cases, as in the issue of the Maastricht Treaty (1992), the bill was introduced by the government, but co-sponsored by the largest opposition party, the Social Democrats, which tolerated, however, the dissent of their party's left wing (12th BT, 2.12.1992: 10831D, 10855A, 10875A).

Latent grand coalitions – excluding only the Green Party and the East German post-Communists (PDS) – are necessary in leading social issues, such as the 'reform of the retirement allowances system 92' (1989). While this compromise strategy makes a clumsy and fragmented system work, it has the drawback of deparliamentarizing decision-making in that the parliamentary groups and the coalitions' coordination committees are strengthened (Nullmeier and Rüb, 1993: 223). The steering process of the parties is already preceded by the civil servants who also have their own party loyalties and by the experts with different party affiliations.

In rare cases the cooperative opposition produces paradoxical results, as in the time of the coalition between the Social Democrats and Liberals. These parties usually disagreed on social policy issues, as in the 'reform of retirement allowances' (1972), and the coalition majority evaporated during the discussion of the bill. The Christian Democratic opposition took the project over in a modified form and cooperated with the Social Democrats in a kind of 'additive strategy' (Michalsky, 1984: 139). In boom periods the additive strategy can be successful because there is a possibility of distributing benefits to the clientele of all the major parties. In times of a slump, however, the cooperation of government and opposition has to reach an agreement at the expense of a dominant status group, as happened with the medical associations. In such cases the mediation round tables with the opposition are more important than the coalition committees. The agreements are usually time-limited as the parliamentary groups naturally have little inclination to fetter their hands for an entire legislative period (Diskussionsveranstaltung, 1994: 496). This type of cooperation with the opposition is necessary during periods when the opposition has a majority in the Federal Council. In these negotiations the Speaker of the opposition becomes more important than the leader of the smaller coalition partner. During the negotiations for a reform of the tax system (April 1997) Gerhard Schröder countered FDP leader Gerhard's interventions by asking a Christian Democratic minister, 'Do you really allow to be blocked by this five-percent-man?', alluding to the FDP's meagre election results.

The opposition has increased negotiating power when a previous bill has failed. The 'structural reform of the health system' bill (1988) was carried against the opposition (Perschke-Hartmann 1994: 95). In 1992 a new law was impossible without substantial cooperation from the SPD opposition, which was made possible by a common strategy of conflict against the status groups active in the field (Lauer-Kirschbaum 1994: 234f). The first attempt to regulate failed, but it was 'successful failure' because it led to a more durable second solution with the help of the opposition.

These examples do not diminish the role of the competitive opposition in the German Bundestag. One indicator for it is the statistics of the *calls to order* (Table 3.12). The 1st Bundestag (1949–53) and the 6th Bundestag (1969–72) were the heydays of offensive interventions. Schumacher, the leader of the SPD opposition, was excluded for three weeks from the sessions because he had called Adenauer 'a chancellor of the Allied powers'. Yet, compared to later interventions from the most aggressive deputies, such as Herbert Wehner (SPD) or Franz-Josef Strauss (CSU), this sounded rather moderate. The access

Table 3.12   Sanctions imposed in the German Bundestag

	8th BT 1976–80	Bundestag 9th BT 1980–83	10th BT 1983–87	11th BT 1987–90	12th BT 1990–94	1st–12th BT 1949–94
Calls to order	25	5	12	7	3	106
Critique from the Speaker	30	13	132	78	33	573
Exclusion from the floor	0	0	2	3	0	23
Temporary exclusion from the sessions	0	0	0	2	0	4
Interruption of sessions because of unruliness of the oppositions	0	0	0	0	0	0

Source: Schindler 1995: 558.

of new oppositions, such as the Green Party and the East German post-Communists (PDS), led to new verbal conflicts and unruly behaviour in the House, with a consequent increase in calls to order. The post-Communists were accustomed to strict order in the time of the GDR, and this was reflected in their moderate behaviour in a free parliament.

Less formal indicators for the competitiveness of the opposition are the figures for the *introduction of bills* (cf. pp. 29–36), voting behaviour (pp. 81–95) and the *use of the post-parliamentary instruments of control* of legislation (Chapter 4 generally).

The behaviour of the fundamental oppositions was no independent variable but codetermined by the established parties. When their speakers tried to discriminate and exclude the new oppositions in appeals to the 'parties that carry the state, which does not include the Green Party' (10th BT, 5.12.1986: 19803A) the new opposition's unruliness was almost programmed. Once accepted as part of the new opposition, the number of calls to order involving the Greens diminished drastically.

Among the normal instruments of the opposition the use of *questions* (by 90 per cent of all questioned), *interpellations* (84 per cent), *oral questions in the question hour* (70 per cent) and 'urgent' *questions* (more than 90 per cent) are a vested right (Schindler, 1995: 563; see also Table 3.13).

Since 1990 the old SPD opposition has been in the awkward position of having no uncontested leader because it has maintained its shortsighted strategy of exchanging its candidate for the chancellorship every four years (for example, Rau in 1986, Lafontaine in 1990. In between, Scharping as a party leader and in 1998, Schröder became SPD candidate for the chancellorship). The most visible Green politician, Joschka Fischer and the PDS intellectual Gregor Gysi were perceived as the most interesting opposition leaders by the media although neither were official leaders of their parties. In such a situation the traditional nostalgia of the left-wing SPD for a fundamental opposition is strengthened. In the debate on 'constitutional reform' (1994) there were controversies between Schäuble's (parliamentary group leader of the CDU–CSU) nationalism and Jochen Vogel's (SPD) 'constitutional patriotism' although, on the whole, the divergences were slight. Even the PDS did not advocate a socialist constitution but fought only for a 'radical democratic constitution'. It did not ask for 'a new Republic', but was satisfied with demagogical propositions, such as adding an East German and a female Chamber to the German Bundestag (12th BT, 30.6.1994: 20964D). Unlike in the first reunification of German territories by Bismarck in 1871, no new fundamental opposition was created, despite the fact that the more conservative politicians considered the PDS as a fundamental opposition. This perception had, however, consequences for the oppositional behaviour of the SPD in that the semi-fundamental oppositions

Table 3.13 Instruments of control in the German Bundestag

Instruments	8th BT 1976–80	9th BT 1980–83	10th BT 1983–87	11th BT 1987–90	12th BT 1990–94	1st–12th BT 1949–94
Petitions excluding mass petitions	48 846	29 749	49 118	52 528	81 881	478 103
Mass petitions	90 800	440 730	239 518	272 876	437 447	nd
Interpellations	47	32	175	145	98	938
	(70.2%)	(75.0%)	(84.2%)	(86.2%)	(85.7%)	(85.7%)
Questions	434	297	1 006	1 419	1 382	7 526
	(84.3%)	(84.1%)	(95.5%)	(98.5%)	(98.4%)	(98.2%)
Oral questions	11 826	4 971	7 208	4 134	4 215	70 581
	(64.1%)	(60.6%)	(65.9%)	(70.1%)	(64.9%)	(64.9%)
Urgent questions	49	13	41	39	57	639
	(100%)	(0.0%)	(82.9%)	(92.3%)	(nd)	(nd)
Written questions	11 641	9 413	15 836	16 117	16 665	79 361
						(nd)
Number of question hours	135	79	142	107	121	1 485
						(nd)
Actual debates	9	12	177	126	103	414
	(100%)	(66.7%)	(75.0%)	(50%)	(nd)	(nd)
Reports from cabinet sessions	–	–	3	32	44	89
Governmental declarations	19	16	49	38	35	298

Notes: The figures in brackets indicate the percentage use of the instruments of control by the opposition parties.
nd = no data.

Source: Schindler, 1995: 563 (in brackets the % of the opposition parties in the use of the instruments of control).

of the Greens and the post-Communists forced the party more often into the role of a cooperative opposition.

Voting on Bills

Charles de Rémusat has coined the *bon mot*, 'Unanimity is a proof of serfdom'. The more majoritarian a system – like the UK – the more monotonous is the voting culture. Research on voting therefore was fascinated by the US Congress which is characterized by little party discipline, and the abundant use of roll calls. However, even in the UK voting discipline has shown striking variations over time: when new policies entered the arena in the 1970s parliamentarians changed their behaviour and became more ready to defy discipline and risk a government defeat. In the more conservative 1980s MPs were more disciplined and only since 1992 has a new unruliness faced the whips (Melnish and Cowley, 1995). There have been certain parallel changes in voting behaviour in the German Bundestag.

The decision-making situation is normally clear: affirmative versus negative votes. In certain ambiguous situations, when the party cannot impose discipline on its members, a sequence of alternatives is voted. In such a situation, *rational choice* becomes complicated. During the vote on the abortion law (1992) the Speaker had to explain, 'as soon as one alternative gets a majority the other motions are not voted on any more' (12th BT, 25.6. 1992: 8224C). In a situation where the fifth preference does not necessarily wait until the end of the voting procedure tactical calculations become difficult. In this case, the women's inter-party motion was at the end and unexpectedly won a majority. The decision on the capital (Bonn or Berlin 1991) has given rational choice research an opportunity to demonstrate that Berlin won because of the sequence of alternatives. The Bonn lobby was stronger but it miscalculated its strategy during the vote on the five motions (Pappi, 1992). Rational politicians repeatedly calculate the risks in open voting situations. The most common strategy is the sudden withdrawal of a motion.

Party discipline (in German it sounds more coercive – *Fraktionszwang*) in a free representative system was difficult to accept – although since Burke's failure in Bristol, when he refused to accept mandates from voters of his party, everybody has known that an insistence on a free mandate can lead to non-re-election. Lutheran Protestant countries emphasize the free conscience even more than Calvinist or Catholic countries because it was a basic notion in Luther's theology. But the free conscience entered the constitution only in Lutheran countries (Denmark, §56; Germany, Art. 38.1). If we trust the surveys among deputies, party discipline is imposed only on the parties of political adversaries (53 per cent): only a small minority (24 per cent) admitted that party discipline also existed in their own party (Patzelt, 1996).

In some questions of *Weltanschauung* party discipline is suspended. When, in 1952, the conservative regional 'Deutsche Partei' introduced a motion for the restoration of capital punishment, none of the great parties – except the Social Democrats – demonstrated a party line. Sometimes the parliamentary groups test opinion in their meetings. Sometimes – as was the case with the abortion law – the SPD announces that it has not tried to direct its members by means of a consultative vote in the parliamentary group, not even when it involves a motion proposed by the SPD itself (12th BT, 25.6.1992: 8254C). Even when party discipline is not used by the parliamentary groups, adversaries are often convinced that undue indirect psychological pressure has been exercised by the more conservative party establishment. PDS representative Gysi even tried to blame East German women in the CDU who once were in favour of the GDR abortion law and later turned to the majority opinion among the Christian Democrats (12th BT, 25.6.1992: 8252D). When the Speaker, Rita Süssmuth (CDU), confessed that she would vote for the inter-party women's bill, conservative Christian Democrats attacked her and demanded her resignation as a Speaker. Even the more liberal CDU members were disgusted by this kind of intolerance (ibid.: 8324D).

Political correctness debates entered the German Bundestag when Gysi (PDS) asked the 527 men in the Bundestag to abstain and let the female deputies decide the issue (ibid.: 8253C). Since also in these controversial questions a roll call is normally demanded, the party has at least a control over the dissenters *ex-post facto*. The proposal of *voting apartheid* was rather demagogical and not quite in tune with the people's ideas about representation. Surveys show that only 10–13 per cent of women prefer to be represented by deputies of their gender (Rebenstorf and Wessels, 1989: 421). The psychological pressure on dissenters came to the surface when a second abortion bill (1994) was voted on, because the Constitutional Court had ruled that parts of the first solution were not in tune with the constitution. This time, Speaker Rita Süssmuth voted with her party. Now the leftist opposition – which had hailed her dissent two years ago – blamed her severely because she had allegedly bowed to party discipline (12th BT, 26.5.1994: 19990 C & D). Her own argument for this change of opinion was that she did not want to risk the Constitutional Court suspending the parliamentary decision once more – a rational and quite understandable line of argument.

Breach of party discipline in situations of roll call is carefully pondered and mounted by those deputies who dare to rebel against the party whips. In 1980 it was ruled in the statutes (§31) that deputies were allowed to give a 'personal declaration' of a maximum of five minutes before the vote. However, when the Green Party used this instrument as a means of obstruction the rules were changed to state that personal declarations were supposed to follow the vote. In 1989 the rule was liberalized again (GOBT §31,1) and the Speaker was given some discretion over whether he or she allowed personal declarations before the vote on a bill. Originally, personal declarations were rare occurrences (first legislature, 39; third legislature, 0). Since the access of new parties the number has increased to 296 personal declarations (11th Bundestag) (Schindler, IV, 1994: 600) (Table 3.13). The more controversial a bill the more it provokes personal declarations concerning voting behaviour. When party dissenters were isolated in their deviant voting behaviour a personal declaration has to appease the parliamentary group leader (for example, 6th BT, 10.11.1971: 8643B). Bills which were able to cause a conflict of loyalty between the deputy's party and his or her interest group affiliation, such as the 'structural reform of the health system' (1992), provoked dozens of personal declarations (12th BT, 9.12.1992: 10972D). The increase of these personal declarations is also the consequence of other variables, such as the growing populist responsiveness of the political class and the tendency to 'confess' which entered parliament with the Green and alternative deputies. In the long run, dissenting votes can undermine a parliamentary career, but they can also increase a politician's prestige when he or she carefully develops the reasons for dissenting from the party line, such as Hildegard Hamm-Brücher (1996: 280). But even this lady suffered sanctions from her parliamentary group only when she did not follow her party in 1982 to topple Chancellor Schmidt in a constructive vote of non-confidence.

Roll Call Voting as an Indicator of Conflict

With growing conflicts in a five-party system where majorities are more uncertain than they used to be in the former three-party cartel (1961–83) the number of roll calls has increased. The Green Party has frequently moved a roll call. This instrument is used as a means of control for the party establishment as a response to growing dissent in the parties. Only in three cases is voting transparent:

- on non-secret elections
- in roll calls
- voting by passing through different lobbies (*Hammelsprung*).

In the first 11 legislatures (1949 until the Reunification in 1990) there were 877 roll calls and 493 votes by passing through different lobbies.

The planning of party discipline in voting seems to be the easiest form of steering of parliamentary groups: no complicated networks of diverging interests have to be outmanoeuvred. The parliamentary group develops an integrative philosophy on the basis of a common programme: the threat of sanctions against dissenters is not the only means of achieving integration.

Most decisions are made by means of the normal anonymous voting procedure. The parliamentary minutes follow the style of the Speaker or his deputies who conduct the sessions. Some of them specify 'large majorities with x negative votes and y abstentions'. Some Speakers state only 'accepted'. The Bundestag statistics since the ninth legislature stopped listing 'controversially accepted laws' because their number were difficult to reconstruct from the minutes (Schinder, IV, 1994: 844f). I have preferred to

Table 3.14 Unanimous decisions

1st BT	1949–1953	19.3%
2nd BT	1953–1957	58.4%
3rd BT	1957–1961	63.7%
4th BT	1961–1965	71.0%
5th BT	1965–1969	71.1%
6th BT	1969–1972	70.2%
7th BT	1972–1976	70.5%
8th BT	1976–1980	61.9%
9th BT	1980–1983	59.6%
10th BT	1983–1987	16.4%
11th BT	1987–1990	19.8%
12th BT	1990–1994	nd

Source: Schindler, IV, 1994: 845f.

construct three rubrics: 'unanimous', 'large majority' (which includes many votes from the non-governmental parties) and 'majority' which normally encompasses the coalition parties and none or few dissenters from the opposition.

'Large majority' means limited conflict. The lower the number of unanimous decisions the greater the conflicts. As can be seen in Table 3.14, the first legislature started with 19.3 per cent unanimous votes on the bills in parliament rising to 71 per cent during the 4th and 5th Bundestags (1961–69), including the period of the Grand Coalition (1966–69). The proportion of unanimous decisions depends on the number of parties. The Communists and other groups were no longer represented in the second legislature so unanimity increased from 19.3 per cent to 58.4 per cent. When the Green Party entered parliament in 1983 unanimity went down from almost 60 per cent to 16.4 per cent (10th Bundestag, 1983–87). Unanimity is, however, limited in its capacity to indicate conflict and has to be reinforced by the two other rubrics 'large majority' and 'majority', because in times of *rapprochement* between government and opposition the lower level of conflict causes an increase of individual dissenting votes in the opposition party, as demonstrated by the SPD after Adenauer.

Unanimity is most likely in routine decisions and decreases in key decisions on crucial laws. Even in Italy in the period of 'polarized pluralism' the Communists carried three-quarters of the decisions together with the Christian Democrats. The German general parliamentary statistics (GESTA) lists for 1980–94 26.5 per cent of unanimous decisions on 'crucial laws' which correspond with my key decisions.

Roll call votes increased during the 1980s (see Table 3.15) because of

86 *The Legislator*

Table 3.15 Roll calls in the Bundestag

	8th BT 1976–80	9th BT 1980–83	10th BT 1983–87	11th BT 1987–90	12th BT 1990–94	1st–12th BT 1949–94
Roll calls	58	26	128	162	129	1006
Voting by passing through different lobbies	4	2	10	4	4	497
Personal declarations concerning the vote	31	26	154	296	nd	nd

Source: Schindler, 1995: 563.

declining margins of governmental majorities and growing fragmentation of the party system. Roll calls were rare under the Grand Coalition (1966–69) since the streamlining of parliamentary work by the two party giants was so perfect that roll calls were rarely needed. Nevertheless, the low number of roll calls did not mean an absence of conflicts. The more the giant organizations claimed unanimity, the more dissent was growing in the wings of the two coalition partners. In many cases, the two principal parties tolerated the dissent because their majority was so huge that they did not need every single vote from the governmental parliamentary groups. In some policy fields (foreign policy, educational and environmental policy) a small latent coalition between the Social Democrats and the Liberals was visible. The SPD tolerated a certain number of dissenters who voted with the Liberal mini-opposition as a trial balloon for future alternatives.

Roll call analysis in Germany is more difficult than in the United States for a number of reasons:

- In the United States the *number of cases* is larger and more equally distributed over the legislatures.
- *Homogeneity of voting* is more developed in Germany than in the United States (1955–88: 71–86 per cent in the House of Representatives and 66–85 per cent in the Senate) (Stanley and Niemi, 1990: 193).
- Deputies' *individual motivations* in correlation with social background data and regional data have a higher explanatory value in the United States than in Germany where party cohesion is the most dominant variable.

Quantitative roll call analysis frequently ends like an ancient Greek tragedy: the stage is full of dead bodies of falsified hypotheses. Most analyses conclude that correlations are weak. Early German studies of the Dolf Sternberger school (Wildenmann, 1955; Kralewski and Neunreither, 1963; Markmann, 1955) started from an anglophile liberal image of parliamentary government, hostile to the modern party state. Deviant voting behaviour was welcomed as a proof of freedom, until left wings drove the liberal scholars into the camp of those who hailed party discipline as a rampart against 'anarchy'.

Various explanations of dissenting voting on legislation have been offered:

- Gerhard Loewenberg (1967) in his seminal study on the Bundestag studied – in tune with his American socialization – the *social reasons* for deviant behaviour. Deputies with a background in the professions and in commerce show less dissent than deputies with agrarian and artisan backgrounds. Parliamentary group elites obey the party line more strictly than backbenchers. Deputies with an organizational background or who restrict their role to satisfy the needs of their constituency are more open to dissent. Functionaries of the lower party echelons also dissent more frequently in order to satisfy the requirements of their constituency party.
- Some studies emphasize the *differences of national systems* (Schwarz and Shaw, 1976). Behaviouralist studies normally point at the *political culture* rather than on the mechanics of the institutions. Common values (Hechter, 1987) explain the degree of voting dissent in various parliaments.
- In many recent studies, *institutions matter*. In majoritarian systems the size of the majority is a predictor of the degree of voting dissent (van Mechelen and Rose, 1986: 58). But when margins became narrow, even consensual democracies try to streamline voting behaviour. Oversized majorities in legislative decisions are, however, not always a proof of consensus between the parties, but rather an indicator that dominant interests have penetrated both major parties to an extent that deviant voting behaviour is minimized.
- An important correlation has been found in the *size of legislation*. When bills are fragmented into small portions in order to win majorities dissenting votes are minimized. This, however, applies more frequently to routine legislation than to key decisions.
- *Party control and calculation of chances for re-election* are two indicators that dominate the American discussion of voting behaviour. In Germany deputies' individual calculations of their chances of re-election is hardly an independent variable because party control is

essential. The number of safe constituencies is decreasing. In the eighth legislature (1976–80) the Christian Democrats still had 65 safe constituencies and the SPD 30. In the 13th Bundestag (1994–98) these decreased to 41 and 14 (Schindler, 1995: 553). An American conclusion would be that decreasing safety of constituencies further strengthens party discipline. However, in Germany, half the deputies entering parliament on the basis of a party list do not think in terms of re-election in their constituency, but have to consider their standing in the party conference which selects candidates on the *Land* level. Although the deputies who entered the Bundestag via the party lists seem to be even more dependent on their party, their voting behaviour does not show patterns which are different from the constituency representatives.

- In the United States the *length of mandates* correlate with the degree of independence in the voting behaviour of deputies. The continuity of representations makes deputies more independent of their party (Fiorina, 1977: 62). This has no parallel in Germany. With the exception of some party leaders, the party may even favour a change when a mandate seems to be too uncontested and too long.
- Whereas rational choice approaches emphasize the individual reasons for complying with party discipline, European research on parliaments concentrates instead on *ideological cohesion and group identity feelings* to explain the high degree of uniformity in voting behaviour. This does not exclude rational choice considerations: deputies behave 'as if' they were maximizing their benefits (Zintl, 1990: 274). Competition among parliamentarians is twofold: competition between one's own party and other parties, and competition with other members of one's own party for career opportunities.

    Quantitative studies found that, in Germany, professionalization and group identity feelings had the most predictive capacity to explain party discipline. Parliamentary socialization had little impact (Saalfeld, 1995: 218, 245).
- *Policy arenas and types of regulation* prove to have some impact on the homogeneity of voting in parliamentary party groups. The number of roll calls is highest in foreign and defence policy and in those decisions which cause the most conflict between parties (redistributive measures, 77.7 per cent; restrictive laws, 54.1 per cent – see Table 3.16.

    Unanimity in voting on bills was highest in environmental policy (54.7 per cent). More than half of all the key decisions (51.3 per cent) were decided on in competitive majority decisions. Among the types of regulation decisions by small margins prevail among restrictive

Table 3.16 Voting on bills according to types of regulation (%)

	Restrictive	Regulative	Extensive	Protective	Distributive	Redistributive	Total
Roll calls	54.1	42.2	47.0	34.2	18.7	77.7	41.3
Majority	70.8	48.4	58.8	51.5	40.6	55.6	51.3
Large majority	20.8	39.3	29.4	14.2	43.7	44.4	32.1
Unanimous decision	8.4	12.3	11.8	34.3	15.6	0.0	16.6
Dissent in parliamentary groups	33.3	42.3	52.9	17.1	9.3	44.4	29.3

Table 3.17 Voting on bills in policy fields (%)

	Foreign	Legal	Economic	Social	Construction	Education	Environment	Total
Roll calls	69.5	47.2	36.3	41.3	7.6	20.0	27.2	41.3
Majority	73.9	55.5	51.5	41.3	38.4	20.0	36.3	51.3
Large majority	17.5	30.5	36.3	41.3	23.0	60.0	9.0	32.1
Unanimous decision	8.6	14.0	12.2	17.2	23.0	0.0	54.7	16.6
Dissent in parliamentary groups	47.8	36.1	24.2	34.4	0.0	20.0	9.0	29.3

(70.8 per cent), extensive (58.8 per cent) and redistributive measures (55.6 per cent), as might be expected. Among the policy fields, foreign policy decisions are first among the roll calls (73.9 per cent), followed by legal (55.5 per cent) and economic policy (51.5 per cent) (see Table 3.17).

Between 'unanimous' and 'majority' lies a type which has been classified as 'large majority'. It includes decisions from the number of votes a coalition can mobilize (minimum 51 per cent) up to 99%. This type of decision indicates *cooperative opposition*. This happened in almost one-third of the key decisions (32.1 per cent) and dominated in educational policy (60.0 per cent), *social policy* (41.3 per cent) and among distributive (43.7 per cent) and regulative decisions (39.3 per cent).

Roll calls are not only scheduled in a final vote on a bill: they often take place in the second reading of bills. But this does not exclude the possibility that, in the final vote of the third reading, a large majority will endorse a law. This is true even of the highly conflict-prone redistributive decisions. Seven out of nine went through a roll call – and nevertheless were finally accepted with a 'large majority'. Roll calls stimulate publicity. Deputies try to avoid their names being mentioned as a dissenting voter in a vital issue of high interest even in their constituencies. Thus, majorities increase. Similar reasons can lead to the final compliance of the opposition which does not want to be blamed for the failure of an important bill – but before complying shows its flag in roll-calls with an independent, and maybe more far-reaching, concept for the solution of the problem.

The hidden legislative 'grand coalition' is not always so integrated that individual members of the parliamentary groups concerned would not try to veto a law which won a large majority by turning to the Constitutional Court. This happened in the case of the 'inter-state treaty' with the GDR (1990) and with the 'federal programme of consolidation' (1993). The 150 key decisions cannot, however, clarify all the questions. The high proportion of roll calls in the sample leads to an artificial correlation with dissent in the parliamentary groups. Moreover there are more conflicts of *Weltanschauung* among the key decisions than in routine legislation. This means that dissent and deviance from party discipline is naturally higher than normal.

Party Development and Legislative Periods

Percentages of conflict in 150 key decisions over time are only a small part of the story. Historical descriptive interpretation has to be added to make sense of the statistics. The tendency towards conflict is naturally high in periods of consolidation of democracy (first and second legislatures). The high number of 'large majorities' is meaningless unless we analyse the mechanisms of consensus-finding under the Grand Coalition (5th Bundestag). New conflicts arose under the conditions of Reunification (eleventh and twelfth legislature).

Over time there have been certain trends in the middle-range development of the legislative behaviour of the parties and these are described below.

The Adenauer era In the Adenauer era the Christian Democrats were highly unified around the chancellor in foreign and security policies. However, parts of the party had some difficulties in cooperating with the Social Democrats in social policy issues. In some cases ('creation of Federal Office of Labour', 'the law on refugees' (1953), 'Law on burden-sharing with the refugees' (1952)) some Christian Democrats did not follow the party establishment. Even in the security policy there was some dissent. Minister of Domestic Affairs Gustav Heinemann, who was imposed on a reluctant Adenauer by the Protestant wing of the party, rebelled against the rearmament of the Federal Republic and even left the party. He did not enter the opposition party SPD straight away, because he suspected that even the Social Democrats were not really pacifists and feared that, in this party, he would have to accept an 'Ollenhauer army' instead of an 'Adenauer army' (Ferdinand, 1985: 35). The Christian Democratic wings did not agree on the Anti-monopoly Law (1957) which explains the cumbersome procedure in passing this bill so dear to Minister of Economic Affairs Ludwig Erhard.

The Liberals in the Adenauer era had a double problem of cohesion: the nationalistic wing was reluctant to follow Adenauer's course of unconditional integration into the Western bloc; the wing emphasizing economic liberalism, on the other hand, was against the chancellor's almost 'social-democratic' politics of social security. National questions, such as the Saar statute (1955), the European defence community (1953) and the NATO Treaty (1955) led to revolts in the FDP, and party discipline was violated in social issues, such as 'codetermination in the steel and iron industry' (1951), the 'law on industrial relations scheme' (1952) or the 'burden-sharing law' (1952). In the Saar debate the Liberal leader Dehler – an anti-Nazi like Adenauer, but a nationalist – warned against Adenauer's trust in France, because of Germany's bad historical experiences 'since the annexations of Toul, Verdun and Nancy' (2nd BT: 3905D). In the discussion of the 'reorganization of the pension system' (1957) large factions of the Liberals dissented and the Social Democratic opposition carried the law (Hockerts, 1980: 435). In half of the roll calls (14 out of 27) on defence and foreign policy more than 10 per cent of the Liberals violated party discipline. In 1956 in Nordrhine-Westphalia the CDU Prime Minister Arnold was toppled by a vote of censure brought by the FDP and SPD. The 'Young Turks' among the Liberals (Döring, Mende, Schell and Weyer) provoked a counterrevolt. Some FDP-ministers (Blücher, Neumayer, Preusker and Schäfer) left the party and founded a liberal splinter group (the FVP). In 1957 Adenauer achieved an absolute majority at the polls. For the first time the FDP had a chance to practise its credo: 'no coalition with a party which has more than 50 per cent.'

In the Adenauer era the SPD came closest to the image of a highly integrated party, unified by ideology, an old tradition and discipline. The homogeneity of voting on bills at that time was far more the product of ideology than of sanctions against possible defectors.

The Grand Coalition The Grand Coalition developed new patterns of legislative behaviour (1966–69). The majority of the two giants – the CDU and the SPD – was so great that they could afford to be tolerant against dissenters. In 1968 the left wing of the SPD (54 deputies) voted against the 'emergency laws'. The CDU tolerated defectors in the voting on the reform of the penal law (1969) which depenalized homosexuality and the bill on 'wage payment in a case of illness' (1969). Integrated voting of the Grand Coalition was sometimes organized only in the final decision. It was no secret in the plenary debates that, in the committees, many Christian Democrats voted with the Liberal mini-opposition, as in the case of the 'law to promote the labour market' against the motions of the SPD (5th BT, 13.5.1969: 12909C).

Conversely, the Liberals' obstruction of social policies before the Grand Coalition was formed helped to encourage the cooperation of the giants. In 1965, when the CDU tried to launch the 'second law of property building' the Liberal coalition partner blocked it. During the debate a speaker from the SPD opposition mocked:

> No Social Democrat participated in the debate for the last two hours. We watch an internal conflict of the coalition, Mister Chancellor. I wonder, however, why your paedagogical efforts so far had no impact on your smaller coalition partner. (Leber, SPD, 5.5.1965: 9019B)

The coalition of Social Democrats and Liberals (1969–82) This coalition, in its turn, changed the voting behaviour of the parliamentary groups. The Christian Democrats developed into a fairly integrated opposition. Only in foreign policy was there a certain dissent under opposition leader, Barzel. Four CDU deputies voted in favour of the 'basic treaty with the GDR' (1973). The UN treaty was carried by many Christian Democrats. The treaties with Moscow and Warsaw got a broader majority due to the abstension of many

Christian Democrats. There were only nine CDU votes against the treaty with the Soviet Union and 16 against the treaty with Poland, the latter being carried by a minority to the Constitutional Court in Karlsruhe.

The hidden grand coalition in social policy was smaller, but continued to exist. The wing of the CDU close to the trade unions under Katzer voted in favour of the 'enterprise constitution' (1971) and the 'law on leave for pregnant women' (1979), whereas the conservative wing continued to fight against the law in the Federal Council, with the consequence that the conference committee (*Vermittlungsausschuss*) found no mediative solution – a rare occurrence.

The SPD, on the other hand, was affected by the leftist tendencies in the party resulting from the students' rebellion. When the SPD had to carry a number of restrictive measures against terrorism (1977, 1978) the conflicts came to the fore. Hansen, Coppik and two others – dubbed the 'gang of the four' – voted against the party line and increasingly marginalized themselves. The more the SPD came under double pressure – from the opposition and its own left wing – the more it tried to streamline the parliamentary group's voting behaviour. Opposition leader Barzel complained in the discussion on the 'enterprise constitution' (1971) that '… the coalition behaved in a rigorously stubborn manner. We experienced a voting machine. All arguments lost their sense' (6th BT, 10.11.1971: 8668D). Sometimes the strategy of a competitive coalition was illusory: during the sixth legislature when the Christian Democrats tried to learn how to behave as an effective opposition they bombarded the coalition with amendments and motions and vexated the government with their passionate speeches, but then, in the final stage, hoped for the continuity of cooperation between government and opposition – mainly by hoping for liberal defectors in the coalition. This calculation proved to be correct only in the case of very conservative liberals centred around the Baron von Kühlmann-Stumm and was compensated by left-wing Christian Democrats who abstained and did not follow their party leader in a fundamentally negative vote.

The era of the coalition of Christian Democrats and Liberals (1982–90 until German Reunification) This period demonstrated an exception to the rule that new oppositions are particularly cohesive. The SPD which had been the most disciplined party in parliament for a long time experienced a decline in its cohesion, especially in foreign and defence policy. Competition with a new opposition, the Green Party, gave the left-wing Social Democrats opportunities for dissenting along with the Greens. On the other side, the Christian Democrats, thanks to Chancellor's Kohl's organizational skills, remained remarkably unified in their voting behaviour. Kohl had already transformed the party during its period in opposition into a party with a strong membership and rising self-confidence, thereby giving it the traditional advantages of a social democratic mass party.

The FDP liberals were put in the awkward position of voting in a new coalition against measures which they had endorsed under the Social Democrat–Liberal coalition. When the new SPD opposition attacked the new and old governmental party, the FDP, its speaker in the debate on the 'reorganization of conscientious objection' (1982) countered the attacks on 'liberal treason' very skilfully:

> I am a cautious man, dear colleague, and collected at the computer the voting results of the last coalition. If you want, I will read the names of those in your parliamentary group which did not vote in favour of your law. (9th BT, 16.12.1982: 8892A)

The Green competitors irritated the Social Democratic opposition a good deal. Initially, the SPD did not view the Greens as potential partners for cooperation, but the Green Party falsified their negative attitude. Whereas the SPD in the imperial Reichstag voted against the government for 40 years, the Greens moderated their legislative behaviour after few years and stopped turning up at the Bundestag inappropriately dressed: for example, during the first swearing in of a Green minister at the *Länder* level, Fischer wore jogging shoes; during the second oath he came in a proper suit without a tie; in the third round he looked like others, only the tie was slightly more colourful. In October 1995 the Green Party had a vice president who directed the debates as a speaker. Antje Vollmer (Green Party) blamed a Green colleague who had found the whole process sickening:

> Nothing causes vomiting in this honourable House, and if someone has the feeling he must vomit he cannot say so because this is an unparliamentary expression which I do not tolerate. *Tempora mutantur!*

The transition from the Bonn to the Berlin Republic (1990–98) During this process the coalition of Christian Democrats and Liberals continued to exist, but the access of new parties and the new type of conflicts in a budding national state – not accepted by all the deputies – created new patterns of legislative behaviour. The SPD was torn to pieces in decisions on the 'reunification treaty' (1990), the federal electoral law (1990) and other bills. 'The economic and social union' of the two German states (1990) even caused 25 negative votes in the SPD (11th BT, 21.6.1990: 17281, 17355). The strain on the SPD caused by the Green co-opposition was not even mitigated by the fact that the West German Green Party failed to be represented in the 12th Bundestag because it missed its chance to find an ally for a list of coalitions. The Christian Democrats also had some problems with German Reunification: 13 CDU members voted against the 'reunification treaty' (1990). The SPD failed to vote unanimously in decisions on asylum-seekers (1993) and the 'structural reform of the health care system' (1992). In the twelfth legislature (1990–94) the PDS usually acted as the fundamental opposition unanimously voting against the reunification laws. This forced the SPD in some cases to reduce its own misgivings and to carry the Christian Democrats' legislation. In such cases as the 'investment and privatization law' the SPD helped the government by abstention because it did not approve the basic neocapitalist tendency of the bill. In questions of *Weltanschauung* ('capital Berlin' 1991, 'abortion' 1992, 1994) even the post-Communist PDS did not vote in full party discipline.

The times when the SPD, according to the Lowell index, reached an achieved 100 per cent (sixth and ninth legislatures) were gone. The Christian Democrats had a similar degree of cohesion in the ninth and the tenth legislatures (1980–87). Even the 93.6 per cent achieved by the CDU in the history of the Bundestag since 1957 and the 96 per cent homogeneity of the SPD up to the tenth legislature (1983–87), according to the Rice index, were no longer possible after Reunification (Saalfeld, 1995: 109). But on the whole – and compared to the United States – party discipline is still remarkable, and even among the Liberals never fell below 87 per cent (ibid.: 110f). There is therefore no justification for taking declining party discipline as a symptom of crisis. In some respects, the recent trends are a unique consequence of Reunification. In other respects, it could be said that Germany, which found it difficult after the Second World War to accept broadly tolerate deviant behaviour and learn to live with a higher degree of 'disorder', came more into line with other democratic political systems.

The Federal State and the Decision-making Process

Amendment Policy of the Federal Länder

As mentioned in Chapter 1, the American 'cosy triangles', in the German context, are instead 'uncosy pentangles', including the *Länder* and their representation. The participation of the *Länder* can be measured by three indicators:

1   the number of bills introduced by the Federal Council (see Chapter 3, pp. 29–37)

2   the participation of Federal Council members in the Bundestag debates (see Chapter 3, pp. 69–76)
3   the number of mediations by the conference committee on request of the Federal Council.

In comparative studies Germany is listed among the two-chamber systems. This is unavoidable in substance, but is nevertheless legally wrong: the Bundestag according to the Basic Law (Art. 77.1) is the only legislator. In many cases, its authority is not mitigated by the requirement of consent from the Bundesrat and this applies to more than 50 per cent of the bills. Even the conference committee can only attempt a mediating proposal which is not binding (Henseler, 1982: 851).

The bureaucratic nature of the Federal Council, comprising members of the *Länder* executive and the strength of bodies outside parliament based on the party state, from coalition committees to round tables with the opposition, have contributed to the deparliamentarization of the decision-making process. This development strengthened in the process of Reunification. Concerning the 'solidarity pact' (1993) for East Germany the Federal Government had to admit in the answer to a deputy's question, 'The closed round table for the solidarity pact was an informal meeting for political consensus-building which preceded the parliamentary legislative procedure' (12th BT: 4649). Some authors (Lehmbruch, 1976: 160) have postulated that the competition between the parties has been undermined by the competition of the *Länder*; the Reunification showed, however, that federalist competition is increasingly used for the party purposes (Abromeit, 1993: 12). Only in few decisions, as in the case of the constitutional reform, have *Länder* interests, independent of the party composition of governments, prevailed over party interests. In August 1994 the constitutional reform was rejected with the votes of all the 16 *Länder* which agreed that they wanted to extend their competences in legislation at this occasion. The Christian Democrats in power were forced to return to a former compromise with the Christian Democratic *Länder* governments, and Article 72 GG was changed. The federal competence of legislation was accepted 'so far as the creation of equivalent conditions of life on the Federal territory or the safeguarding of legal and economic unity...makes a federal regulation inevitable'. Even the SPD-governed *Länder* finally agreed because the opposition did not want to enter the electoral campaign under the stigma of having vetoed the constitutional reform (Batt, 1996: 95).

The further the legislative competence of the *Länder* declined the more active the federal units became in the national legislative process. Amendment proposals by the *Länder* are an important indicator of this attempt to intervene in the federal legislation. They are most visible in cases

Table 3.18 Types of coalition in the *Länder* in the 1990s

CDU–CSU-led governments	SPD-led governments
1 Christian Democrats without coalition Bavaria (6)* Saxony (4)	**4 SPD without coalition** Nordrhine-Westphalia until 1995 (6) Sleswig-Holstein until 1996 (3) Saar (3) Hamburg until 1994 (3) Brandenburg since 1994 (4) Lower Saxony 1994-1998 (6)
2 Christian Democrats and Liberals Saxony-Anhalt until 1994 (4) Thuringia until 1994 (4) Baden-Württemberg since 1996 (6)	
	5 SPD and Liberals Rhineland-Palatinate (4)
3 Grand Coalition – CDU-led with SPD Baden-Württemberg until 1996 (6) Berlin (4) Thuringia since 1994 (4) Mecklenburg-Pomerania since 1994 (3) Bremen since 1995 (3) *Option not yet used:* CDU–Green Party	**6 SPD and Green Party** Lower Saxony until 1994 and 1998 (6) Hesse (4) Nordrhine-Westphalia since 1995 (6) Sleswig-Holstein since 1996 (3)
	7 Traffic-light coalition (red-yellow-green) – SPD, FDP, Green Party Brandenburg until 1994 (4) Bremen until 1995 (3)
	8 Minority government – SPD tolerated by a small party Hamburg since 1994 (3) Statt-party Saxony-Anhalt since 1994 (4) Post-Communist PDS

*Numbers in brackets = number of seats in the Federal Council.

of governmental bills and less frequent in cases of parliamentary bills. Quite a few proposals from the *Länder* are not based on party interest because they are carried by *Länder* governed by different party constellations. When Lehmbruch (1976) wrote his book on the federal aspects of the party state he was confronted basically with two types of *Länder* government – CDU–CSU and Liberals, SPD and Liberals. In the meantime the coalition-building process is much more complicated (see Table 3.18). Originally there was one national coalition in Bonn and in the *Länder*. Since then, the Berlin republic has proliferated the political options in many respects. Significant changes in the party, system such as the decline of the Liberals (FDP), the regional veto position of the post-Communists (PDS) in East Germany, and the rise of the Green Party since 1983, have driven this development. Only the theoretically possible coalition of the Christian Democrats and the Green Party has so far not yet been tried.

Since the *Länder* have to vote uniformly – independent of the number of parties in government – the negotiations of the *Länder* are preceded by complicated negotiations among the coalition partners in one *Land*. The amendment motions are less affected, however, by questions of party symmetry than the final vote on a bill.

Which are the most active *Länder*? Originally, it seemed that the *Länder* with the clearest party profile are the rabble-rousers in the Federal Council. Bavaria (14.6 per cent) and Hesse (10.8 per cent) in the Social Democratic camp were the chief contenders (see Table 3.19). However, although both *Länder* are very active indeed, in the sample 150 key decisions they are not on top. The small number of *Länder* interventions (444) forces us, however, not to overrate the validity of this type of statistic. Some *Länder* distorted the sample by bombarding parliament with a whole battery of amending motions; others preferred to restrict their activity to motions in cooperation with other *Länder*. In East Germany, since the twelfth legislature (1990), the Länder made this a kind of rule in order to show their solidarity. Furthermore, the East German amendments can hardly be compared to those of the West German *Länder* because one legislature (1990–94) is too short to obtain valid data.

Table 3.19 **Amending motions of the West German *Länder* (1st–12th Bundestags) 1949–94 (%)**

Baden-Württemberg	18.9
Bavaria	14.6
Berlin	1.8
Bremen	6.0
Hamburg	9.6
Hesse	10.8
Lower Saxony	9.6
Nordrhine-Westphalia	8.3
Rhineland-Palatinate	8.3
Saar	4.0
Slesvig-Holstein	8.1
Total	100.0
	(no. = 444)

In East Germany, in 1990 Saxony leads among the key decisions, as might be expected. In West Germany Baden-Württemberg (18.9 per cent) is leading. Berlin, until 1990, was also not comparable because of its guest status in the German parliament and in the Federal Council and, in any case, normally moved matters which had an immediate connection with the city. The biggest *Land*, Nordrhine-Westphalia, was active only in the middle range. These figures denote attempts to influence legislation, but not influence itself. The big *Länder* had other instruments to make their influence felt at their disposal. Bonn was situated, after all, in the territory of Nordrhine-Westphalia and open to many informal influences and pressures, so that amendments to bills in the Bundestag were less important in Düsseldorf than for some other federal units.

A second indicator of activities in the national process of decision-making is the participation of members of the Federal Council (prime ministers and ministers) in the debates of the Federal Diet. Here, the number of *Länder* interventions has increased over time. In the first 12 legislators (1949–94) 691 interventions for all the decisions were counted. In the 9th Bundestag (1980–83) there were 50. In the 12th Bundestag (1990–94) this number had trebled to 159 (see Table 3.20).

Not all these interventions of *Länder* ministers in the Federal Council are true *Länder* initiatives. Some of them are pushed by interest groups who try to gain influence after failures to influence the committee work in parliament. *Länder* governments are more open to influences from the groups than the federal government. As an expert put it frankly in the debates on the law on chemicals (1980): '...the Laender governments are more obliged to their native industries...than the federal government to the national industry' (quoted in Damaschke, 1986: 139).

Table 3.20 **Number of contributions to the parliamentary debate by members of the Federal Council**

	8th BT 1976–80	9th BT 1980–83	10th BT 1983–87	11th BT 1987–90	12th BT 1990–94	1st–12th BT 1949–94
Number of contributions	68	50	72	77	158	691
Among them: reports for the conference committees	12	5	1	0	0	84

Source: Schindler, 1995: 64.

Consociationalism of the Länder versus Party Majority Democracy: The Role of the Conference Committees

Party majority democracy and consociational democracy among the units of the federation are not always clearly separated. During periods when the opposition has a majority in the Chamber or the *Länder* – as in the last phase of the Schmidt (SPD) and Kohl (CDU) governments – both principles are used in the same direction. The first conflict between the Bundestag and Federal Council arises about the question of whether a law needs the approval of the *Länder* chamber. The Federal Council tries to extend the number of bills needing approval of the Federal Council – even when the Federal Diet has a different perception. The struggle for the approval is a power struggle because it determines whether the Council can use its veto according to the constitution (Art. 77,4 GG) with a majority of two-thirds which can be overridden only by two-thirds of the Bundestag. In the first legislature the number of laws which needed approval amounted to 43 per cent; in the third it crossed the 50 per cent mark. Sometimes it soared to over 60 per cent (tenth and twelfth legislatures) but usually it oscillates around 55 per cent (Schindler, IV, 1994: 848, Stand XII: XXVI). The degree of dissent is sometimes considerable. In the eighth legislature (1976–80) the majorities of the two chambers had a different opinion on the requirement of approval in 26 cases, whereas the founding fathers had counted on about 10 per cent of dissent on this question. But this rise is the product of a paradox: the more unimportant legislation remaining with the competencies of the *Länder* becomes, the more stubbornly they defend their right to participate in the federal legislation. Federal Council approval is necessary when the implementation of federal laws requires the help of the *Länder* administration. The Federation has only a small administrative infrastructure, but the range of state activities is growing – despite loose talk on the declining steering capacity of the state (cf. Chapter 1). The implementation of regulations by the *Länder* originally was meant to be the exception but became the rule because regulation is increasingly combined with distribution of funds (Vierzig Jahre Bundesrat 1989: 184). Who decides in a case of conflict? The federal president can use his discretion when signing a bill, but he normally follows the line taken by the federal government. The last possibility of obstruction is the appeal to the Constitutional Court. Of the 13 cases in this sample two decisions occurred (abortion and the reorganization of conscientious objection) in which the Court ruled that the law needed the approval of the Federal Council. Despite these cases the Constitutional Court has not, however, generally tried to expand the right of approval of the Federal Council. Conflicts between the two chambers have often arisen when a law – which originally needed the

Council's approval – has been amended. The Constitutional Court tried to close this door of increasing competences of the Bundesrat when it ruled that amendments need the approval of the Federal Council only when they regulate an issue which in itself would need the endorsement of the chamber of the *Länder* (BVerfGE 37: 63).

Apparently two principles compete in the German federal system:

1 *The Federation has a duty to 'create equivalent conditions of life'* (before Reunification Article 72 GG even read: 'to guarantee uniform conditions of life'). Although this article is not mandatory it increases the Federation's motivation to regulate citizens' social life.
2 On the other hand, *the Länder have to preserve their interests*. They try to avoid obligations to contribute financially to equivalent life conditions, but at the same time they want to co-legislate on the national level.

Even when bills do not legally need Federal Council approval the *Länder* can attempt to veto a regulation after appeal to a conference committee. This happened only 26 times in the first 11 legislatures (1949–90). In 19 cases the veto was overruled by the absolute majority of parliament. During the first 11 legislatures the Federal Council tried to veto 88 bills. Eventually, after mediation, more than half these bills (48) became law (Schindler, IV, 1994: 848). The conference committee should be equidistant between the two chambers but, in reality, it became more of a Federal Council instrument (Kilper and Lhotta, 1996: 130). Reunification increased the number of actors from 22 to 32. The resulting increase in complexity necessitated pre-consultation of the *Länder* 'oligarchs' in round tables (Diskussionsveranstaltung 1994: 504).

The parties have sometimes used the conflicts over the conference committees for party strategy. In the debate on the 'second structural reform of the budget' (1981) the conference committee was accused of having organized the sabotage of parliament's competences and attempting to decide in non-public sessions (Conradi, SPD, 9th BT, 1973: 4269B & C). The conflict was brought before the Constitutional Court which did not agree with the complainant but admitted that, in this case, the procedure was 'close to the limit of the legally acceptable' (BVerfGE 72: 187ff).

No party can claim not to have used the Federal Council and the conference committees to gain advantages for party political purposes. The SPD started with this procedure at the time of the 'burden-sharing law' (1952), launching 40 amendments via the Federal Council and thereby making agreement difficult (Schillinger, 1985: 281f). When class politics leads to a clear polarization the Federal Council is the last goalkeeper before the Constitutional Court. Sometimes both instruments for vetoing were used against a bill, as in the case of the 'law on the promotion of apprenticeships' (1977).

Conflicts between the two chambers are mediated by conference committees. In about one-third (49) of the 150 key decisions the conference committees had to find a compromise between Bundestag and Federal Council. During the SPD-led government the proportion of vetos from the Bundesrat increased to 34.7 per cent. As can be seen from Table 3.21, in *foreign policy* the Federal Council rarely has a right to co-legislate (13.8 per cent). In *social policy* Federal Council interventions are below average (31 per cent). In *education* (60 per cent) and *economic policy* (39.3 per cent) the conference committees were most frequently active. Among the types of regulation the *extensive* (60 per cent) and the *protective* decisions (40 per cent) were the first target of the Bundesrat's mediation power. Oddly enough *redistributive* measures rarely necessitated the involvement of conference committees (22.2 per cent).

Despite the Federal Council's veto power, the Bundesrat is no graveyard for key decisions. The proportion of bills decided upon by the Bundestag, but not promulgated because the Federal Council did not agree, varied between 0.8 per cent (eleventh legislature) and 2.2 per cent (ninth legislature) (Schindler, IV, 1994: 848). The fact that economic issues and the extension of rights are the most common reason why conservative groups appeal to a conference committee strengthen the suspicion that the Council's veto power is sometimes also used for the parties' ideological purposes.

Table 3.21 Appeals to the conference committees (%)

Foreign defence	Legal	Economic	Social	Policy fields Housing and Construction	Education	Environment	Total
13.8	38.8	39.3	31.0	30.0	60.0	36.6	32.6

Restrictive	Regulative	Extensive	Types of regulation Protective	Distributive	Redistributive	Total
25.0	27.2	47.0	40.0	31.2	22.2	32.6

4 Control of Legislation

Judicial Review of Legislation

Legally, parliament can participate in the proceedings of the Constitutional Court in several ways:

- as complainant
- as defendant (§63, Law on the Constitutional Court)
- as co-complainant in a judicial procedure which the Bundestag has not initiated (§65.2, Law on the Constitutional Court).
- as witness or adviser (§94.1, §23.2 Law on the Constitutional Court).

The Court is in a strong position vis-à-vis the Bundestag. Parliament may have the first word, but the Constitutional Court has the last (Schneider and Zeh, 1989: 1655). Three types of proceedings prevail:

- judicial review of norms
- challenges to the law's constitutionality brought by citizens
- disputes between state agencies in front of the Court.

The sentences of the Constitutional Court can have serious *ex post facto* consequences for the legislation. They have, however, an impact even *ex ante* because the legislators frequently act in a kind of 'anticipatory obedience' to the Court. Oppositional threats 'to carry a bill to Karlsruhe' are quite normal in parliamentary debates.

Three indicators reveal the influence of the Constitutional Court on legislation:

1 the number of laws which have undergone judicial review
2 the number of laws invalidated by the Court
3 the preventive threat of carrying a case to Karlsruhe in the parliamentary debates.

Originally there was the possibility of asking the Constitutional Court for advice in cases of doubt on the constitutionality of a law. The Federal Construction Law (after long retardations promulgated in 1960) underwent this procedure, although serious doubts were articulated in the cabinet on this kind of procedure which was later abolished (Kabinettsprotokolle, vol. 4, 1988: 719).

Ex-post facto *Impacts*

The abstract control of norms – without a pending dispute – allows the most coherent examination of a law. This procedure is much rarer (end of 1994: 124 cases, 68 already decided) than the *concrete control of norms* (2901 cases, 931 decided and 1830 otherwise dealt with). This direct control of constitutionality is balanced by an indirect control in the case of a challenge of the law's constitutionality (*Verfassungsbeschwerde*) against a sentence of a lower court.

The 150 key decisions falsify a popular prejudice that the Constitutional Court is a cemetery of parliamentary laws:

- Since the fifth legislature (1965–69) the number of *laws declared null and void* has decreased. In this case the norm has to be substituted.
- A milder form of critique of the legislator is the sentence that a law is *incompatible with the Basic Law*, the constitution. In this case the legislator has various options by which to correct his work and the norm cannot be applied. The judgment on the 'law on allowances for the deputies' showed, however, that the room for manoeuvre is not much greater than in the case of a law being declared null and void (Landfried, 1996: 49).
- *The request to keep to a mode of interpretation of the law compatible with the constitution* apparently binds the hands of the legislators least. For innovative treaties (for example, Moscow, Warsaw, Maastricht) the Constitutional Court used to take resort to this kind of intervention. It respects the prerogative of parliament but, since there is no political questions doctrine (that is, refusal of a case because it is not judicial but political and thereby falling under the auspices of another institution) accepted in Germany, it means no furthergoing interpretation or amendment of the regulation is considered as constitutional. In such a case, the Court detailed instructions on which application of the law is the only legal one. This type of intervention is also increasing in other countries – for example, in France with the *déclaration de conformité sous reserve* (Favoreu in Landfried, 1988: 100).

In foreign policy the Court's impact is limited; in domestic decisions it can immobilize forthcoming amendment policy, as in the case of the codetermination judgments. In foreign policy issues the Court – normally liberal in matters of basic rights of the citizens – has sometimes shown a conservative attitude. If we compare judgments which renounced territories which were formerly part of the German Empire, the judgment of the Saar statute sounded as though it was expressing confidence in Adenauer's foreign policy, whereas the judgment on the treaty with the GDR sounded rather like a vote of censure against Brandt's *Ostpolitik*.

- Most of the key decisions which underwent judicial review were declared *compatible with the Basic Law*, among them far-reaching innovations such as the 'reform of the penal law' (1969) or the 'law for promoting the labour market' (1969).
- In rare cases the indirect control of norms on the basis of a challenge to the constitutionality of a law has led to the *squashing of the judgment of a lower court* (3 out of 108 judgments).

The Constitutional Court has intervened in the legislative process since 1951. If we look at the statistics of laws which have been declared null and void or incompatible with the Basic Law, a clear hierarchy of policy arenas is visible: social, finance and legal policy attract most of the interventions (Table 4.1). The key decisions which attracted the Constitutional Court's interventions (Table 4.2) is an indicator for legislative conflicts: 40 per cent of the key decisions were confronted with the Court. The Constitutional

Table 4.1 Policy fields in which laws were declared null and void or not compatible with the Basic Law (1951–91)

Social Policy	61
Tax and fiscal policy	35
Legal policy	29
Regulations among the state agencies	25
Economic policy	12
Transfer policy	9
Educational policy	7
Labour market policy	6
Health policy	4
Environmental policy	1
Military policy	1
Others	7

Sources: von Beyme, 1985: 268 and later calculations by Landfried, 1996.

108 The Legislator

Table 4.2 Key decisions in front of the Constitutional Court

	Foreign	Legal	Policy fields Economic	Social	Construction	Education	Environment	Total
Laws								
No.	12	17	9	12	4	4	2	60
in %	52.1	47.2	27.2	41.3	30.7	80.0	18.1	40.0
Judgments								
Later judgments								30 (27.7%)
Threat of the Constitutional Court in the parliamentary debate of bills which did not undergo judicial review								18 (12%)
Decisions								
Null and void	11.3	21.3	6.2	19.4	0.0	12.5	0.0	14.8
Incompatible with the Basic Law	5.5	18.7	25.5	3.8	20.0	37.5	66.6	19.4
Interpretation has to be strictly within the limits of the constitution	38.8	15.6	12.5	11.5	20.0	12.5	0.0	17.5
Compatible with the Basic Law	44.4	34.3	56.3	65.3	60.0	37.5	33.3	45.6
Squashed lower court judgments		9.6						2.7

Control of Legislation 109

Table 4.2 Key decisions in front of the Constitutional Court *(continued)*

	Restrictive	Regulative	Extensive	Protective	Distributive	Redistributive	Total
Laws (%)	33.0	42.4	64.7	31.4	40.6	33.3	40.0
Judgments (no.)	12	23	18	20	24	11	108
Decisions (%)							
Null and void	0.0	21.7	11.1	15.0	16.7	18.1	14.8
Incompatible with the Basic Law	0.0	30.4	0.0	35.0	25.0	9.1	19.4
Interpretation has to be strictly within the limits of the constitution	33.3	8.6	27.7	20.0	12.5	9.1	17.5
Compatible with the Basic Law	41.7	39.3	61.1	63.0	45.8	63.7	45.6
Squashed lower court judgments	25.0						2.7

Court issued 108 judgments concerning 60 laws. An important question is to what extent the oppositional parties use the Constitutional Court for their veto politics: 27.7 per cent of all the judgments preclude an action by the oppositions because they were issued in later legislatures. Later judgments normally add amendments to a law, although not necessarily only those parts which have recently been amended.

The Constitutional Court has hardly ever prevented a key decision, although the whole or parts of 14.8 per cent of the laws were declared null and void. In one-fifth of the cases (19.4 per cent) the law was declared as being incompatible with the Basic Law. The judgments containing a negative intervention against the legislator are most frequent in legal policy (21.8 per cent) and social policy (19.4 per cent). In both fields the opposition cannot be blamed for the interventions because the laws were passed with large majorities, thus including most of the votes of the opposition. The size of a majority does not protect, however, against unconstitutionality of a law (for example, the Party Law (1967). There were even unanimous decisions ('acceleration of the procedure for asylum-seekers' 1978) which failed to be accepted by the Court in Karlsruhe.

Extensive laws which created new rights and possibilities for the citizens most frequently underwent judicial review (64.7 per cent), followed by *regulative* measures (42.4 per cent). The latter were most frequently among those laws declared null and void (21.7 per cent), followed by the *redistributive* laws (18.1 per cent). *Protective* measures most frequently ended by being declared as incompatible with the Basic Law (35.0 per cent), although the decision in parliament in this type of regulation tended to be less conflict-ridden than others, since the federal units often drive the issue to the Court because they have to implement it and costs are involved. *Extensive* measures were most frequently earmarked with the clause that the interpretation has to be strictly within the limits of the Constitution (33.3 per cent). Judgments were squashed exclusively in legal policy.

Ex-ante *Impact of the Constitutional Court*

The *ex-ante* impact of the Constitutional Court has contributed to the fact that the legal control of a bill has been shifted from the Ministry of Justice to informal steering bodies (Schreckenberger, 1994: 339). In the parliamentary stage of the decision-making ex-justices of the Constitutional Court have often been invited to parliamentary hearings, not because they were experts on the substance of the law, but only to hear their opinion on the possible reactions of the Constitutional Court.

In many debates the threat to carry the issue to Karlsruhe is present – even in 12 per cent of those laws for which this ultimately did not happen. The 'Karlsruhe astrology' sometimes developed strange forms. Entire constitutional mandates were interpreted in some judgments. In other cases, opinions of judges were constructed without recourse to a specific decision (for example, 12th BT 30.6.1994: 20949C, 20958A). Overinterpretation of judgments are used to functionalize the Court. Individual phrases of judgments are discussed without evaluating the context and considering whether the phrase was taken from the basic reasons of a judgment or merely *obiter dicta* which are increasingly invading the Constitutional Court's judgment.

The *ex-ante* impact of the Constitutional Court has three variations in the parliamentary debates:

- threat and counterthreat in the struggle between parties
- hidden conflict in the governmental coalition
- the development of an inter-party consensus.

Threat and counterthreat in the struggle between parties Since Almond's and Verba's civic culture study, Germany has been renowned for her legalistic culture. Political conflict is unpopular. Most Germans would prefer to settle disputes by the courts. An early example of this attitude was exemplified by the conflict about the 'European defence community' (1954). The Christian Democrats tried to sue the SPD opposition. The Court turned this down (BVerfGE 2: 145). The SPD opposition tried to outlaw the treaty but the Court ruled that a bill – not yet passed by parliament as law – cannot be subject of judicial review (BVerfGE 1: 396). The Court, at this early stage of consolidation of democracy, had to teach the parties a lesson that the majority and the minority of parliament are not entitled to act as complainant and were directed back to the road of political settlement of disputes (BVerfGE 2: 144, 170f, 178) instead of asking for a preventive control of these norms which did not yet exist.

In later cases parliament began to perceive that the threat of the Court was no substitute for a political decision (9th BT, 26.5.1981: 2057B, 2058D). Sometimes the opposition's attempt to terrorize the government with these threats were met with humour, as in the case of the 'law on the promotion of vocational training' (1981):

> In the future each Federal minister will have to carry the Constitution day and night under his arm to make sure that not a minor paragraph of the bill can be found which serves as pretext that the Constitutional Court tries to enter into political decisions. (9th BT 1.10.1981: 3190A)

Threats by a conservative *Land*, like Bavaria, were countered with irony: 'They did not vote for the constitution, but they use it as a base to sue the government' (ibid.: 3195C).

The Green Party as a new opposition initially criticized the conservative judgments of the Constitutional Court but, as soon as they realized the usefulness of the strategy, they also used threats of the Court – even in matters which did not consider only the constitutionality of the bill, but also its feasibility (10th BT, 26.9.1985: 11923D). In other words, judicial activism was criticized, but invited when it seemed to benefit the Party's strategy.

Hidden conflict in the governmental coalition Occasionally a dissent in the coalition was rhetorically carried to Karlsruhe as in the case of the 'second law for fortune-building' for all citizens (4th BT, 5.5.1965: 9005D).

The development of an inter-party consensus In some cases, the interventions of the Constitutional Court were so substantial that an inter-party consensus grew in order to avoid repeated sanctions from the Constitutional Court, as in the case of the regulations of abortion (12th BT, 25.6.1992: 8241B, 9960ff). Opposition against the 'counter-captains of Karlsruhe' sometimes entered the debate (7th BT, 7.9.1975: 13885B, 12th BT, 26.5.1994: 19971C). Not all the cases where parliamentarians and their juridical experts launched constitutional defeatism against a bill ended up before the Court (for example, the 'law on chemicals' (1980). Moreover, experts were hardly ever unanimous even on the legal aspects. In a hearing on the 'codetermination bill' in December 1974 six experts thought that the bill was constitutional, whereas five others raised doubts on this (Minutes of the hearing, 19.12.1974: 36). Only rarely did a constitutional lawyer admit that 'all the jurists also conduct legal policy'.

In some cases the counterarguments against the anticipatory obedience to the Court were those of time: the Court in the meantime will have noticed that there had been a change in the legal mood of the population which it would be unable to ignore in a future decision (12th BT, 8250D). In other words, a historical change of values was set against the assumption of permanent values on the basis of a natural right doctrine in the Court.

When certain deputies took the Court judgment for granted without admitting the right of politicians to criticize them, the opposition made clear that it is close to the essence of democracy that even 'a criticism which turns out to be wrong has a right to be uttered' (H-J. Vogel: 8th BT, 8.6.1978: 7562C). In some of the crucial laws the constitutional misgivings were launched by the interest groups concerned. When the majority chose to ignore them (12th BT, 9.12.1992: 10915B) as in the case of the 'structural reform of the health system' (1992) it was a victory of the political decision, no longer intimidated by Court judgments which had been functionalized by vested interests.

The all-party consensus to agree on the necessity of political decisions against a narrow legalism sometimes developed because the Constitutional Court expanded its competences:

- The Court's *statement of facts* was increasingly transformed into a prognosis of future development (Philippi, 1972: 193).
- The Court developed a tendency to *regulate a whole complex* instead of confining itself to the issue at stake. The judgment on the 'allowances of the parliamentarians' (BVerfGE 40: 296) was thus transformed into an 'abstract review of a norm' even though only a very concrete challenge to its constitutionality was on the judges' table. The Court increasingly leaves judgments on legality and enters into the political feasibility of policies (Zeh, 1988: 199). There is a danger that the Constitutional Court starts from the assumption that it has greater wisdom than parliament, even in political matters.
- The Court judgments are full of restrictions for political actors in the future. The *obiter dicta* – which are only loosely related to the issue – are proliferating. Since the 1970s decisions more often appeal to the legislator that he must act. This was sometimes necessary to protect such human rights as in the 'equalization of legitimate and illegitimate children'. In many other key decisions, however, as in the party laws, the decisions on education, on abortion or in the 'basic treaty with the GDR' (1973), the sentences put parliament under a petty tutelage of the Constitutional Court.

Negative consequences of the expansion of competences of the Constitutional Court are:

- the *retardation of political decisions* because the legislator waits until the judgment is issued
- *further devaluation of the deputies' judgement*
- *strengthening of the influences of bureaucracies and parties outside parliament*.

In the 1970s judicial activism was directed against the Social Democratic government and caused much criticism. In the 1990s a series of judgments was directed against the conservative government and provoked wide criticism even among the most conservative constitutional lawyers who normally refrain from criticizing the Constitutional Court. The propaganda for a 'lean state' threatened to turn into a promotion of an 'opulent judicial review'. The waves of judicial activism and judicial restraint will probably never find a balance acceptable to all parties and politicians.

Control of the Feasibility of Legislation: Implementation by the Bureaucracy

Policy research in the last two decades has shifted from decision-making in central bodies to implementation. National decision-making seemed to be remote from the real problems of society which normally arise when a law is implemented. Quantitative research was no longer satisfied with measuring the *output* of the legislative process, but turned to the evaluation of the *outcome* in comparative perspective and the *impact* of regulations on a policy field. Whereas the French language resisted the new anglicism and tried to translate it with the circumscription *mise en action*, the German language easily accepted the term 'implementation'. The roots of the term indicate that the passing of a law does not automatically lead to good impacts. Implementation has been interpreted as 'implantation'. The law has to be implanted into a social environment – not always open to new regulations – and nurtured by the administration.

The statist bias of the older theories of state has been overcome. Goal-oriented steering programmes have replaced the traditional conditional programmes. The administration receives certain guidelines from the legislator, but it no longer simply executes some metaphysical 'will of the legislator'; it increasingly contributes to political decisions in its own right (Grimm, 1990: 300). The state has been reduced to the role of a mediator or supervisor and has lost its hierarchical priority over a functional subsystem which meets it on an equal footing as a bargaining partner with other social subsystems.

The bargaining is mostly done by the administration. Its direction in the negotiations varies widely, however, according to different policy issues. In the case of the 'code of construction law' (1986) its remit was extensive. In certain sub-issues, such as investment policy in the housing and construction sector, however, its discretionary powers were strictly limited (Schmidt-Assmann in Hoffmann-Riem and Schmidt-Assmann, 1990: 14). Generalizations, or even quantifications, of the implementation process are therefore hardly possible. Together with implementation research, evaluation has been emphasized (cf. Chapter 4, pp. 119–133). Implementation has the advantage in that its criteria of control are slightly more narrow than the overall evaluation of a law.

Implementation research has some feedback on legislation as a decision-making process. The programme of a bill (cf. Chapter 2, pp. 15–28) is no longer a static variable. The goals of a bill change according to the stage of the policy cycle. During the implementation phase certain interests have too little impact because the administration for the transformation of a law into social reality needs the cooperation of vested interests. Abstract norms have to be reduced to the realistic expectations of the citizens affected by a regulation (Mayntz, 1980: 240). This is an important caveat to legislation research which starts from a national 'central perspective' on the political problems of society.

Classical implementation research concentrated on regulative measures in a broader sense. It was limited to laws which need a certain administrative input. When norms are realized only through court judgments this is not normally called implementation. Symbolic legislation and laws which cannot be exclusively implemented by the national state, such as foreign policy agreements, are also not included in evaluation studies.

The implementation of the 150 key decisions cannot be studied by one author. The author has to rely on the empirical studies of administrative research. This reduces the number of interesting cases to far fewer than 150. We have to exclude the following:

- **Laws of symbolic policy**. These are not meant to be rigorously implemented (for example, the 'law on matrimonial violation', 1997).
- **Foreign policy decisions**. One can, of course, do research on whether all the clauses of the 'basic treaty with the GDR' (1973) were executed on both sides. But if the agreement was a success this was not exclusively due to the Federal Republic's implementation skills. Success in foreign policy often depends on more than two national actors.
- **Decisions which have never been applied**. This was fortunately the case with the 'emergency laws' (1968), which caused so much trouble in the decision-making phase.
- **Decisions which create new institutions**. The military ombudsman (1957) or the 'council of economic advisers' (1963) can be studied in its work. Whether the institutions prove to be feasible is, however, beyond the scope of a normal implementation study.
- **Decisions which are controlled by judicial review of courts of justice**. These include cases such as the reforms of the penal law (1973, 1974).

Studies on the implementation of key decisions are usually based on interviews with the implementing elites. Usually they are only half standardized and require the interviewer to have much detailed knowledge (Hucke and Wollmann in Mayntz, 1980: 222f). For these key decisions there are about a dozen studies available. One of the few findings that can be generalized seems to be that the implementators are more critical about the feasibility of a law than the citizens in general. Evaluation studies in a broader sense therefore normally come to more positive conclusions than implementation studies in a narrow sense. Another restriction of implementation studies is the local or regional limitation of their scope. The local study of policy does not allow the generalization of findings about, say, education or health reform bills over the whole country.

On the one hand, the feedback of implementation studies on legislation improves the bills and the amendment bills. On the other hand there is the danger of fettering the hands of the legislator by narrow considerations of what implementators think is feasible. The more technical details the control of efficacy involves, the less the reports on experiences in implementation are understood and used by the deputies concerned (Zeh, 1988: 207). Furthermore, administration is strengthened at the expense of legislators, and scientific technocrats – most of whom are not neutral but linked to vested interests – take priority over the political decision-makers.

The feasibility of laws is influenced by factors mostly beyond control of the deputies:

- The administrators are fully responsible for the *precision* of the formulation of a law which avoids ambiguities and contradictions.
- The feasibility is the more difficult to assess *the deeper a regulation enters into social relations* which are scarcely controllable by state agencies.
- Implementation often meets with a certain *resistance from organized interests* which was not expressed during the decision-making process. This was true of many environmental laws, because industry initially did not anticipate the consequences of a regulation, or the law did not anticipate the consequences of a regulation, or the law did not contain precise guidelines for implementation which were later added by a decree.
- The feasibility of a law depends on the *competence of institutions* to implement. The calculating of administrators' reactions seems to be fairly possible, but many regulations are carried through or supervised by para-statal institutions, *Länder* authorities or even by interest organizations of those who are affected by a norm.

Many laws are partly political symbols which become feasible only by amendments after the first experiences or by decrees regulating guidelines for implementation. This was the case in the 'federal law on immissions' (1974). The law contained laudable declarations on environmental protection. The concrete values for admitted emissions and immissions were, however, only regulated by a decree on the measurement of air pollution (Müller, 1986: 253). When 'codetermination' and 'representation of personnel' regulations are implemented, their feasibility depends on the social climate of the factories. In small enterprises with a paternalistic but benevolent patron the regulations do not function at all (Wagner, 1960: 143).

When decrees regulate the implementation the legislator has a certain right to participate in the formulations. Since the Weimar Republic there has been an established practice of appending reservation rights concerning the implementation decrees to laws. In 1958 the Constitutional Court endorsed this practice. Since 1963, these rights have been used less frequently and, for this sample of key decisions, they play a very limited role, with the exception of the 'law on economic stability' (1967) (List of reservation rights of the legislator in Schindler, IV, 1994: 931ff).

The process of German Reunification since 1990 showed the importance of analysing the actors responsible for the implementation of laws. The national legislator was overburdened. The federal administration had to hand over responsibilities to the *Länder* bureaucracies; in other cases it had to take over responsibilities normally vested in the federal units. But because the *Länder*, in cultural policy for instance, did not want to spend scarce resources on East Germany, the Federation took over. The process became a kind of 'Keynesianism of Reunification' – against the will of the actors involved (see Matrix 4.1).

In many fields the Federation set only a normative framework and left implementation to para-statal institutions, such as the Trusteeship Organization (*Treuhandanstalt*). In many arenas the organized interests have implemented the policies. Since the national state entered into a conflict on health policy with the organized interests of the physicians it left the reorganization of the health system in East Germany predominantly to the self-organization of the health sector. There were hardly any interest groups organized for the protection of the former GDR institutions and policies. In many arenas, the semi-sovereign state (*Katzenstein*) in Germany was overburdened in a double sense. On the one hand, Reunification developed into the 'hour of the executive', weakening the legislative branch in the process. On the other hand, the federal state was supposed to regulate so many matters at the same time that its activities became erratic and soon needed correction by means of amendments and acceleration laws (*Beschleunigungsgesetze*).

Self-regulation of society may smooth down conflict, but it is hardly able to promote innovative policies. The government in Bonn made it clear for those who wanted reforms that Reunification was not the opportunity to realize reforms which would not have been possible otherwise (Schäuble, 1991: 156). Reunification did not fundamentally change the policy-making

Matrix 4.1 Actors and goals in the steering process of German Reunification

		DOMINANT ACTORS		
		Statal	Para-statal	Interest Goals
GOALS	Preservation of GDR institutions and regulations	Cultural policy, protection of monuments, economic structural policy, educational system in East Germany	Active labour market policy, labour market regulation for the trusteeship institution (*Treuhandgesellschaft*)	Agricultural policy, wage policy, trade union policy for the preservation of jobs
	Transformation and import of West German institutions and regulations	Constitutional policy, developing the federal system, financial policy, legal policy (highly controversial: e.g. Western regulation of abortion), women's policy, civil servants' policy	Privatization policy, monetary policy, transformation of the Academy and the universities	Social security system, health research, investments of entrepreneurs
		RTV and radio policy	Transformation of large research units	

Source: von Beyme, 1994.

patterns, but gave rise to a certain autonomy of the implementing agencies. In periods of consolidation of democracies this is a common feature. In the early years of the Federal Republic, Germany had a kind of auxiliary bureaucracy run by the refugees' interest groups for the implementation of the 'burden-sharing law' (1952) (Schillinger, 1985: 285). The greatest degree of autonomy after Reunification was developed by the Trusteeship Organization and the Federal Office for the Labour Market in which certain interest groups play a major role (Blankenburg *et al.*, 1976: 258f). These para-statal institutions even developed a certain potential for resistance against parliament. The Federal Office of Labour frequently defended the status quo of labour market policies and changed the goals of certain laws such as the 'law for the promotion of labour' (1969) and the 'law on vocational training' (1969).

In some policy fields implementation from above, by the authorities, met with countervailing implementation *from below* (Wollmann, 1983: 192) which corrected certain unrealistic goals set by the legislator. The municipalities, as a lower echelon of state actors, opened ways and means for a less bureaucratic process of implementation in cases where hierarchical steering from above failed to attain its goals.

Implementation research tends not to concentrate on individual laws but to assess a whole network of regulations (laws and decrees). They have different qualities. Some are binding programmes for the implementing authorities, others encourage self-regulation of the subsystem (Blankenburg and Krautkrämer in Mayntz, 1980: 138f). There are laws of symbolic values, such as laws of environmental protection, which contain a nucleus of a programme which is highly acceptable to the great majority and therefore must be respected by organized interests. But there are more marginal regulations around this programme nucleus which have been opposed by the organized interests to an extent that even the nucleus of the programme has remained unfeasible – as in the air protection policy (Knöpfel and Weidner, 1980: 101f).

Control of Efficiency and Efficacy: The Stage of Evaluation

The autopoietic theory of systems – extremely hostile towards all kinds of actors' theory and highly sceptical towards any attempt of state intervention in social subsystems – talked about the 'noise of legislation'. Is legislation only noise without impact? Even Luhmann (1990b: 143) did not exclude the possibility of successful legislation and control of a problem area. 'Vaccination laws' are his classical example. Even some environmental laws have an impact. Most successful in this perspective are post-interventionist laws – reflexive laws which do not claim to have an impact in terms of a unilinear causal model. Social subsystems selectively use legislation for their own purpose – sometimes against the intentions of the national legislator, thus creating 'order from noise', according to the formula of Heinz von Foerster (1971: 17). Evaluation in this concept is the most important part of legislation because it is a highly reflexive self-observation of a subsystem.

Parliaments did not accept the esoteric vocabulary of system's theory of the autopoietic school, but accepted some of its ideas in substance. *Self-observation* is developed on a permanent basis. It does not suffice to prepare legislation carefully in the policy formulation stage which is normally done more cautiously in the administration than in parliament. Parliaments, because of their limited term expectation of a maximum of four years (in Germany) are devoted to the 'urgency of issues under time pressure', whereas the administration has a longer horizon, especially under German conditions where civil servants, as *Beamte,* have life tenure and cannot easily be dismissed or shifted from one authority to the other. Administrations are said to be more evaluation-oriented because implementation always includes the evaluation of the efficacy of a regulation. Evaluation on the parliamentary level, however, exceeds the evaluations at the implementation stage. Evaluation research is not so much interested whether a regulation is accepted and meets with little resistance but also asks what kind of impact the norms develop in a society. Evaluation is more interested in the intention of the legislator than implementation. The early treatises on legislation (Filangieri, 1798) even dealt with a normative picture of a well ordered society. Legal positivism in the nineteenth century therefore developed more rigorous criteria for the check of a law – with a rather schematic division of formal criteria and the substance of a law (Mohl, 1862: 375ff).

One of the formal criteria was the postulate that laws have to be brief. In 1910, 22 imperial laws were issued; during the twelfth legislature of the Bundestag (1990–94) 507 federal laws were passed. The federal register of laws in 1954 contained 532 laws; by 1984 it had already increased to 1684. The length of laws had tripled although the number of laws remained almost constant (Schreckenberger, 1994: 26). The tendency to issue more long and complex laws has been explained by the fragmentation of the German decision-making system. An international comparison shows, however, that majoritarian systems with a clear parliamentary sovereignty do not produce shorter and clearer laws (Van Mechelen and Rose, 1986: 35).

The basic criteria for the evaluation are efficiency and efficacy. *Efficiency* is frequently defined by the degree to which a law has been implemented. *Efficacy*, on the other hand, is a measure for the attainment of the legislator's goals and involves an assessment on the basis of a norm system (Weiss, 1974: 19). During the period when a positivist attitude dominated, analysis of facts and normative assessment was strictly separated. In recent policy analysis both converge in evaluation research.

Parliament's instruments for the evaluation of the legislative output have so far been underutilized (Zeh in Hellstern and Wollmann, 1983: 249). These are as follows:

- **Evaluation of petitions.** Per legislature approximately 40 000 petitions are sent to the Bundestag.
- **Systematic observation of the court judgments.** This is done much more thoroughly in the ministerial bureaucracy.
- **Evaluation of reports and commissions of inquiry.** See Chapter 2, pp. 22–8.
- **Study of scientific literature on legislation.**

Deputies are flooded with material. Even research carried out by policy-advising para-statal institutions have been criticized as unfeasible for the use of parliamentarians (Engholm, SPD, 9th BT, 1.10.1981: 3188C). Policy advice institutions have proliferated and parliamentarians, feeling unable to keep up with the production of reports, have developed the habit of pragmatically 'muddling through'. Goals have not been reached but lowered, with the result that nobody expects an 'ideal law', and parliaments are satisfied with relatively feasible laws (Karpen, 1986: 9). Even lawyers have become increasingly interested in the implementation of norms, but only penal law has developed a special discipline which inquires into the transformation of laws into social behaviour, such as criminology. Civil law so far has no equivalent, except in parts of the sociology of law. The social science approach in jurisprudence has raised interest in 'experimental legislation'. Originally this trend was combined with the positivistic illusion that the processes of the implementation of law can be investigated with the same precision as processes which are dealt with in the natural sciences (Beutel, 1957: 34). However, generally, the dogmatics in the tradition of Roman law on the European continent was more resistant in the long run to social science approaches than the case law orientation of the common law tradition.

Evaluation research developed more modest concepts of control of social life by law. Encompassing implementation of norms is possible only under totalitarian conditions (Zeh, 1988: 208) and the experience of totalitarian societies showed that plenty of behaviour deviating from the socialist norms existed even there. Complete feasibility presupposes complete knowledge of social processes – and this does not exist. Although we know fairly exactly the behaviour of norm addressees under conditions of routine legislation, innovative laws normally cause unknown reactions, as well as a transformation of a whole society – which has occurred in East Germany since 1990 – with huge coalitions of social losers who create forms of behaviour hitherto unknown.

The neo-Marxists in the 1970s were the first to claim that welfare state laws changed nothing. During the 1980s, unorthodox leftists (cf. Nahamowitz, 1985: 259) increasingly accepted that the 'welfare state illusion' was a Marxist exaggeration. In the 1990s the most ardent opponents of Marxism in the autopoietic school of system's theory were even more sceptical about the steering capacity of legislation than the neo-Marxists. Their scepticism had an equivalent in the political sphere: the retreat of the welfare state was not organized in major restrictive codifications but rather unspectacularly by means of small amendments to existing laws and laws which implemented the state budget (*Haushaltsbegleitgesetze*) (Schmidt, 1988: 88).

The federal government, in the network of competing social theories, has tried to improve the evaluation *ex post facto*. The Ministry of Domestic Affairs and the Ministry of Finance developed a catalogue of evaluation questions with 10 main questions (text in Grimm and Maihofer, 1988: 420–423). These are as follows:

1. Is action of the state necessary?
2. What are the main alternatives of legislation?
3. Is the Federation competent to act?
4. Do we need a law?
5. Do we need action now?
6. What is the extent of necessary regulation?
7. Can we consider a limit of time for the validity of a law?
8. Is the regulation understood by the citizens?
9. Is a regulation feasible?
10. Are the costs appropriate for the problem regulated?

If all these questions were always thoroughly examined this might be tantamount to an invitation to non-decision by the legislator.

Efficiency and Efficacy

Economic evaluation research has contributed to the dichotomy of efficiency and efficacy. Efficiency is close to the code of the economic system and asks whether a goal is reached with the minimum of costs. Efficacy, on the other hand, is the degree of attaining a goal. Efficiency prevails in implementation research (cf. pp. 114–19) and is measured in terms of *output*, whereas efficacy has to consider the *impact* and the *outcome* of a law (Seibel, 1984: 64). Some laws are respected without sanctions. Others, such as abortion regulations, are not respected by a large minority and a third group, such as anti-terrorism laws or regulations concerning asylum-seekers, are continually violated by a small group, first because of political opposition and, second, because those to whom the law is directed are largely ignorant of it and are smuggled in by criminal entrepreneurs. Laws are more inefficient the further they distance themselves from social life which is beyond state control.

There are no laws with 100 per cent efficacy. Even autopoietic sceptics about legislation admit that certain measures are highly successful, such as the vaccination laws (Luhmann, 1990b). Indeed the vaccination laws were so successful that they were repealed until new epidemics, introduced from the Third World, made it necessary to issue a new vaccination law. The efficacy of laws can be put on a scale. Three principal measurements are discernible:

1. Efficacy cannot be controlled or does not depend on the national legislator.
2. Efficacy exists only on a symbolic level.
3. Efficacy is limited by certain intervening variables (see Table 4.3).

Table 4.3 The efficacy of laws

I	**Efficacy not under control or does not depend on the national legislator**	
1	Laws so far not applied	emergency laws (1968)
		Saar statute (1955)
2	Laws with disputed goals	military service (1956)
		basic treaty with the GDR (1973)
		unification treaty (1990)
		decision on the capital (1991)
3	Success not dependent on the national legislator	all foreign policy decisions
		Maastricht Treaty (1992)
II	**Symbolic politics**	
4	Law as an appeal to the citizens	sanctions in cases of abortion
		matrimonial violation (1997)
5	Law which was meant to be efficient but made obsolete by the development	law on refugees (1953)
		law on economic stability (1967)
III	**Efficacy restricted by interviewing variables**	
6	Purely formal regulation according to norms from outside	equal opportunities for men and women (1980)
7	Half-hearted compromise	anti-monopoly law (1957)
8	Law full of contradicting goals	law on chemicals (1980)
		law on the regional order (1965)
9	Efficient law with many unexpected dysfunctional consequences which are difficult to control	housing laws
		promotion of labour law (1969)
		promotion of training (1976, 1977)
10	Efficient only after amendments and acceleration laws	most regulations of retirement allowances
		restrictions for asylum-seekers
11	Insufficient attainment of goal by too fragmented regulation	gene technology (1990)
12	Efficacy depends on the persons who run an institution	Council of Economic Advisers (1963)
		military ombudsman (1957)
13	Efficacy if the administration accepts the law	most protective measures
		environmental protection
		social help law (1961)
		protection of mothers (1951, 1952)
		regulation of weapons (1972)
		social services (1972)
		law on pharmaceutical products (1961)
14	Efficient when norm addressees cooperate	codetermination laws
		community service for conscientious objectors (1982)
15	Efficient after a change of values in the population	reform of penal law (1969, 1973)
		regulation of abortion

Accepted Failure: Symbolic Politics

Technocratic modernism initially accepted only efficiency as a favourable criterion of the evaluation of laws. Later, the modesty of post-modern theories was satisfied with the limited impact of symbolic measures. Since Bagehot we know that the dignified parts of the constitution serve symbolic functions of integration and are nevertheless as important as the efficient parts of the constitution. Some authors (for example, Schultze-Fielitz, 1988: 290) have listed halfhearted compromises among the symbolic uses of legislation. But the conflicting parties in such a case are not aware of the limited effects of a regulation. Quite often, in distributive legislation of social policy, conflicting goals have not always prevented a law from developing some efficacy. These compromise laws have a limited impact, but they are considered to be better than a non-decision. The 'law on economic stability' (1967) was another legislative compromise between the two major parties under the Grand Coalition. The responsible minister, Alex Möller (1978: 332), later called it a 'normative model of action' rather than a law. Norm addressees of this law were not so much the investors and economic actors but the government itself which appealed to a heterogenous coalition in order to encourage a unified economic policy. The function of appealing to state actors was renewed in the discussion of the Maastricht Treaty. Christian Democratic deputies were proud that the central European Bank according to Article 88 of the Basic Law – in its turn, an appeal to the European level – was obliged to respect the German principles of economic stability (12th BT, 2.12.1992: 10817D). The magic quadrangle of principles as a German economic ideology was elevated to the rank of constitutional provisions already by the Reunification Treaty (1990). In the constitutional amendments necessary to enable the acceptance of the Maastricht Treaty one of these four goals, 'primordial engagement for price stability', entered the Basic law.

In these examples the legislator intended an efficient law, despite the use of formulas which are more appropriate for symbolic politics. This also happened with some anti-terrorism laws. The success of initial measures was poor: only later did we find out that leading terrorists had been sheltered by the GDR. Success in fighting terrorism was thus guaranteed by inventing new 'crimes' in order to strictly control the left-wing scenario which, it was argued, served to increase the recruiting reservoir of terrorism. Some criminologists were shocked by the degree to which elements of the offence were criminalized (Sack/Steinert 1984: 234f). Sometimes restrictive reactions of the state risk creating the evil which they claim to fight, because the left-wing groups feel pushed into a criminal environment. De-escalation later was rarely possible – as in the offer of a crown witness regulation (1986).

Certain regulations were meant to be efficient but turned out to be symbolic politics because the legislator did not create the necessary preconditions for an implementation of the norm (Kindermann, 1988: 227; Blankenburg, 1977: 43). Gender equalization laws (1980) have often belonged to this category. 'Symbolic politics' became a battle cry of the oppositions, as in the case of the 'law on protection of embryos' (1990): 'This law has only symbolic meaning and leaves enough room for manoeuvring for research...' (11th BT, 24.10.1990: 18214B). It is not always easy to decide whether this reproach is justified. The legislator is not a unity. Some parts of the majority which voted for the 'equalization of men and women' (1980) were serious about it. Other parts agreed only on a symbolic level, hoping that it would never be implemented. In this instance, the European Court held that the German law was only a declaration because no sanctions were provided (NJW, 1984: 2022). In some cases symbolic politics has been necessary to mitigate the public mood which demanded action by the legislator via the media. The legislator anticipated that the regulations were not very effective but wanted to prevent self-help by social groups. Matrix 4.2 gives examples of intended and unintended symbolic legislation.

Indicators of the Efficacy and Efficiency of Laws

There are many indicators for the efficacy and efficiency of laws. The most important of them are:
1 the capacity and structure to regulate the policy field
2 the speed of legislative action
3 the innovative qualities of regulations
4 goal attainment of laws
5 degree of unintended dysfunctional secondary consequences
6 the possibility of implementing a regulation
7 acceptance of a norm by the citizens
8 frequency of amendments.

Matrix 4.2 Types of symbolic legislation

	Intended	Unintended	
		From the beginning	Developed later
Examples	Punishment of abortion Matrimonial violation	Structural reform of budgetary laws	Stability law Anti-monopoly Law Some environmental laws

The capacity and structure to regulate the policy field The key decisions of this study are concerned with *problems which can be regulated*. Doubts are, however, increasingly arising concerning new high-risk technologies. Many risks have not been regulated because they have not been recognized. Risks which are sufficiently known, on the other hand, often have unknown dysfunctional consequences. Unclear prognosis in the preparatory work of legislation normally leads to diffuse regulations which make a law inefficient. Even when risks seem to be calculable, regulation frequently is late because the foreseen damages have already happened. In such a dilemma the legislator is inclined to non-decision and handing the consequences of new technologies over to the executive (Wolf, 1991: 77).

The concepts of 'danger' and 'risk' have to be differentiated. Risk can incur similar damage as endangering events but the probability of it happening is rather low (Rabenstein, 1995: 80). Post-modern social movements developed a tendency to alarmism which – reinforced by the media – suggests that a collective hysteria is justified to demand far-reaching regulations against the risks. In the propaganda of risks it is almost always 'five minutes to twelve'. The legislators, as politicians, are in the habit of being sensitive and responsive towards these moods in the population as a compensation for the increasing distance of politics from everyday life due to the fact that fewer citizens are directly involved in conventional politics. But quite often they are frustrated by excessive alarmism in a 'democracy of moods' and try to play down the necessity for regulation. Even the Constitutional Court has recommended the application of a minimal notion of dangers and risks.

Many risky technologies are regulated in laws which do not have a single goal – protection against endangering events, as the Green Party normally postulates – but which also contain elements that try to encourage and support new technologies in the name of future economic prosperity. The conflict between competing fundamental rights (freedom of economic development and freedom from dangers and risks) is not easy to handle because the law has no clear answers which right should have priority in a pending case (Vitzthum and Geddert-Steinacher, 1992: 16).

Evaluation supplied feedback on legislation because recent laws increasingly inserted whole arsenals of 'duties to report' and prohibitions with exceptions of detailed authorizations. The goals of laws are more precisely indicated in laws since 1980, such as the 'law on chemicals (1980) and later laws on environmental protection. Such 'programmatic laws' are spreading. There are, however, still laws which ambitiously encompass a whole policy field, such as the 'Regional Development Plan' (1965) or the 'Code of Social Policy' (general part, 1975), which remain full of vague formulas.

Court judgments increasingly contribute to the elimination of contradictions of goals in the laws. Since the 'law on the nuclear industry' (1959), the goals of protection and of support for a new technology have been in competition. Judgments of the administrative courts (BVerwG, DVB1 1972, judgment on the Würgassen atomic power station) and of the Constitutional Court (BVerfGE 49: 89: 141ff) have prioritized the protective goals in new technologies in an attempt to prevent new technologies becoming impossible to develop and have ruled that a 'certain risk' to the citizens is inevitable in the interest of technological progress. The 'law on gene technology' (1990) also experienced this competition between economic and protective goals. However, in practice, the law developed more in the direction of technological and economic progress. Comprehensive regulations of the whole policy field were demanded by a number of *Länder*, but this would have required an amendment to the constitution and the approval of two-thirds of the Bundestag. Consequently, the legislator preferred to regulate some details in various laws, such as the 'law on gene technology' and 'embryonic protection' (1990). In such a fragmented legislation, protective goals fall short of the original expectations because many unregulated questions remain between the specialized laws.

The speed of legislative action This is a minor indicator for the efficiency of parliaments. The average law in our sample needed between 199 days (first legislation) and 266 days (seventh legislation). The seventh legislation (1972–76) was the time of a new, highly experienced opposition of Christian Democrats who had previously been in power for 20 years and was very efficient at disrupting the legislative plans of the Social Democratic and Liberal coalition. When the Green Party entered the Bundestag (tenth legislature 1983–87), legislation was again impeded by a new opposition. The smaller the opposition, the more efficient legislation tends to be in terms of speed, as could be seen during the Grand Coalition (1966–69) when laws needed only 209 days to pass the parliamentary stage (Table 4.4).

Speed is not only dependent on the strength of the opposition but also on the policy field and the type of legislative regulation. Amendment laws and protective and distributive measures shared by most deputies, but also the highly controversial foreign policy decisions – because of external constraints – normally pass more quickly than other projects.

The Statistical Office of the Bundestag calculates the time a law needs from the moment the bill is formally introduced into parliament until the promulgation of the law. This is a legalistic approach. A social science approach would rather count a much longer timespan from the declaration of a goal in the governmental declarations to the moment when the president promulgates the law. Study of the policy formulation stage has already

Table 4.4 The speed of legislation

Legislature	No. of days needed for passing a law
1st BT 1949–53	199
2nd BT 1953–57	214
3rd BT 1957–61	244
4th BT 1961–65	254
5th BT 1965–69	209
6th BT 1969–72	212
7th BT 1972–76	266
8th BT 1976–80	234
9th BT 1980–83	187
10th BT 1983–87	259
11th BT 1987–90	212

Source: Schindler, IV, 1994: 862.

shown (Chapter 2, pp. 15–28), that about half those problems which have been mentioned by the federal chancellor as an issue which needs legislative regulation is not passed as a law in the same legislature. The mentioning of a problem is often only a proof that it is established on the agenda. Many laws have not been announced by a governmental declaration. In these cases the birth of a bill could be considered the first time that an issue was the subject of interpellations or the moment when government was asked to prepare a law. This happened for the first time in the case of the 'law on students' scholarships' (1959), 3rd BT, vol. 43: 3627), when a law was declared as 'urgently needed'. Nevertheless the bill took ten more years to become a law. For this delay it was not the Bundestag but the *Länder* which insisted on the prior regulation of the financial reform that was to blame (Hofemann, 1975: 92).

The level of conflict in society over a bill is also a variable which influences the speed of legislation. The emergency laws (1968) had been pending since the introduction of military service (1956). Three ministers of domestic affairs presented projects, but only the Grand Coalition was able to solve the problem more than 12 years later (Oberreuter, 1978: 204ff). Insurance for the health care of elderly people (1993–94) was another example of an issue which needed more than a decade, even though scientists and the media continually put this issue on the agenda (Thiede, 1990: 281f).

The time factor was frequently reflected in the debates. Democracy is temporary power, and politicians develop a sense of time which deviates from that of the normal citizens (Riescher, 1994: 84ff). This leads to frequent criticism that four years for a legislature is a too short timespan. The key decisions, however, show that a five-year-legislature – so frequently demanded by experts – would solve only part of the problem. *Enquête* commissions are often trendsetters and demand legislative action. But, as in the case of the commission on 'chances and risks of gene technology' years passed until, all of a sudden, an initiative was taken because the issue became a topic in the electoral campaign. The coalition took its time, but later blamed the opposition for the delay (11th BT, 29.3.1990: 15953B) although the opposition's resistance was partly provoked by this tactical use of a speeded up procedure.

Normally, as in the case of the 'federal construction law' (1960) or the 'promotion of the city construction planning law' (1971) which came a decade too late, numerous additional incentives are needed to transform an issue on the agenda into a bill and into a law.

Speed as an indicator of efficiency is a rather problematic criterion. Many bills, such as the 'law on economic stability' were passed quickly, but the efficient legislative process did not prevent the law from becoming rapidly dated. The durability of a regulation is probably more important than the rapidity of the legislative process. The law on economic stability (1967) reacted to a small economic crisis of 1966 in a very efficient way. But in the crisis of 1973, which ushered into the era of structural unemployment hardly known in the 1960s, the law was unable to solve the problems. Increasingly, laws become outdated very quickly. In many instances, durability is traded for a law with a limited time of validity. Other regulations, such as the emergency laws (1968) are 'sleeping' regulations. The fact that they have so far not been needed is no proof that they will never be needed in the future.

The innovative qualities of regulations There was a time of planning euphoria under the Social Democratic and Liberal coalition led by Brandt (1969–74). Laws were meant to be *innovative.* Reform policy was considered to be more than piecemeal engineering. But, in certain periods, legislation was scarcely coherent and ill-prepared. The first legislature (1949–53) under Adenauer's government, for example, had to regulate very quickly an enormous number of problems because the old Nazi laws had to be repealed. Even in the second legislature (1953–57) the bulk of legislation was devoted to the consequences of the Second World War. There were some innovations, such as extensive laws (codetermination (1951, 1952)) and redistributive measures (for example, the 'burden-sharing law' (1952). Those measures which were innovative were the integration of the last groups not yet integrated in a system of retirement allowances (for farmers, 1957) and the distribution of the surplus to the underprivileged strata of society in the dynamization of the retirement allowances (1957).

130   The Legislator

During the eleventh and twelfth legislatures, the German Reunification again imposed unplanned legislative reactions to historical events. Again, important redistributive measures were taken (Fonds of German Unity, 1990; Solidarity Law, 1991, Federal Programme of Consolidation, 1993). But the innovation of the legislative acts was more remarkable than the carefully planned character of the bills.

The type of regulation determines the innovative or reactive character of legislation. *Extensive* and *redistributive* measures need careful preparation because they normally arouse resistance from large parts of society. *Restrictive* measures also provoke resistance, but they are usually rather reactive, especially in the sphere of anti-terrorism and limitation of immigration. *Regulative* laws are also usually reactive rather than innovative. *Distributive* and *protective* laws, on the other hand, lie somewhere between the poles of reaction and anticipatory innovation.

The dichotomy of reactive and innovative laws entered evaluation research in the time of reform euphoria under Willy Brandt's governments. This criterion is not always useful: there are certain laws which are reactive and nevertheless developed an innovative character, such as certain environmental laws.

Goal attainment   Not all laws can be expected to attain goals in the same way. Monofunctional laws have a greater likelihood of reaching their goals than multifunctional laws, especially when conflicting goals are contained, as in the Anti-monopoly Law (1957), the 'law for the promotion of the workforce' (1969) and most environmental laws with their compromises between the promotion of new technologies and the protection of the citizens. Some laws have been assessed in terms of their capacity to reach their goals. But, as in the case of the 'law on leaded fuel' (1971), the procedures of measuring the impact of the law are controversial (Schultz, 1983). In other cases a law admits too many exceptions, so that its capacity to attain its goal becomes increasingly doubted, as in the case of the Anti-monopoly Law (1957) (Hüttenberger, 1976: 296; Robert, 1976: 346). Some laws, passed with best intentions, even developed consequences against the intentions of the legislators (Kloepfer, 1982: 40). Others were celebrated as a great innovation, such as the 'burden-sharing law' (1952) which was said to have alleviated the conditions which resembled those of the Palestinian refugee camps in the Middle East. But, even without the law, the integration of the refugees would have been successful because of the economic boom in the 1950s. This boom, which rapidly equalized the income of refugees and native West Germans, contributed to the dysfunctional consequence that the refugee wage-earners themselves paid large parts of the transfers to their own group. Redistribution did take place, but less from the well-to-do West German citizens to the refugees (46 per cent of the transfers) and increasingly from the state budget (32.2 per cent of the transfers) (Schillinger, 1985: 289).

In other cases, the goals were attained but not in the intended way, as in the case of the 'law on students' scholarships' (1971) because the average scholarship remained below the income level of other students, and the students or their parents increasingly had to participate in paying the costs (Hofmann, 1975: 172). But, again, the experts were more critical than those concerned, as a study on the 'law of vocational training' (1969) revealed. Two-thirds of those interviewed were satisfied (Bundesminister, 1973: 196) but the experts criticized many deficits in the implementation of the law, from deficits in the theoretical basis of the training to a deficit of control in the factories and the clumsiness of the bureaucracy.

Evaluation research normally had three options with which to improve the goal attainment of laws:

- amendments to the law
- precision of regulating decrees concerning the implementation of the law
- reinforcing the control institutions.

The third instrument, increasing control, is normally the most controversial. In an era of neo-liberal *laisser faire*, the mood of the majority in parliament is directed against more state control. In the debate on the 'law against organized crime' (1992), even the post-Communists thought that more control would do more harm to society than a non-decision because organized crime would be shrewd enough to outmanoeuvre all the new controls (12th BT, 4.6.1992: 7828B & C). Other speakers knew that additional controls were likely to fail but nevertheless wanted their introduction because of the symbolic value of such a gesture (ibid., 7833B).

The degree of unintended dysfunctional consequences The minimization of unintended dysfunctional consequences is a further criterion of evaluation. Even successful laws can have unwanted dysfunctional consequences. Environmental laws, such as the 'law on chemicals' (1980) increased the bureaucracy, and the Federal Office of Accounts (*Bundesrechnungshof*) worried about the balance between protective values and the economic feasibility of the policy measure. Distributive laws, such as 'housing laws' (1950, 1951, 1952, 1955, 1963, 1965, 1973), the 'laws for the promotion of the workforce' (1969) or of vocational training (1976, 1977) were largely successful, but accompanied by a host of abuses. Increasing controls, however, would create a bureaucracy which could be more expensive than the costs of individual abuses of benefits for the underprivileged.

The possibility of implementing a regulation Implementation creates rules of its own for evaluation (cf. pp. 114–19). The prospects for implementation are most important for those laws for which bureaucracy has a wide discretion, as in the regulation of 'social security' (1961) or the 'protection of mothers' (1951, 1952). The implementing bureaucracy itself is most critical with respect to the large parts of a law which it has to supervise. In the case of the 'federal construction law' (1960) 72 of the administrative experts and 31 per cent of the practitioners in the case of 'promotion of city planning' urgently demanded far-reaching amendments of the respective laws (Schäfer and Schmidt-Eichstaedt, 1984: 351).

Acceptance of a norm by citizens The acceptance of a law has an increasing importance in the populist political climate of post-modern society. As politicians increasingly renounce steering by imperative orders, they contribute towards weakening the citizens' readiness to obey (Grimm, 1990: 297). The state is downgraded to the role of a mediator. Obedience is substituted by the voluntary acceptance of regulations. Public acceptance of a law is more important the larger the number of citizens concerned. Antiterrorism laws and regulation of immigration normally excite only intellectuals for humanitarian reasons, but social distribution laws mobilize wide acceptance or resistance. In some cases those concerned do not know the consequences of a bill and remain silent. They intervene only in the implementation stage, as with the 'law of protection against immissions' (1974) or the 'law on chemicals' (1980). Here, acceptance caused mobilization and countermobilization over certain questions of ideology. In regulations liberalizing the penal law, depenalizing homosexuality, reforming the conditions of imprisonment for capital punishment or regulation of abortion, the conservative majority argued that it is not the task of the law to promote a 'sexual' or a 'legal' revolution (5th BT, 9.5.1969: 12832D). When the reintroduction of capital punishment was refused (1952), the majority of deputies, even in the conservative parties, did not follow the majority of citizens but the decision was nevertheless finally accepted, even by the public.

Frequency of amendments The number of amendments is an indicator of the efficiency of evaluation (see pp. 137–94). It is an illusion that evaluation is only a scientific assessment which finally can be answered with either a 'yes' or a 'no'. Foreign treaties such as the Saar statute (1955) or the 'basic treaty with the GDR' (1973) scored highly as a law, but when strong minorities do not accept them, scholars are helpless because the minorities decide on the basis of a subjective value judgement. The traditional science of legislation hoped to develop a scientific basis for the unambiguous evaluation of laws. Filangieri (1798, Vol. 1: 101) demanded the office of a 'censor of legislation'. The liberal Robert von Mohl (1862: 376) – as a legal positivist – did not think that this idea would improve legislation, anticipating correctly that such an office would interfere with the balance between parliament and the executive. Luhmann (1972: 292) nevertheless fell back on a technocratic utopia in proclaiming the need for an 'office of legislation' which would collect all the information on contradictions in the applications of law. This proposal is a dream – and not even an acceptable one – because it would further weaken the competences of parliament.

To a certain extent parliament itself handles the problem of evaluation satisfactorily with the help of three institutions:

- Laws are increasingly subjected to the *duty to report*. In this sample of key decisions this can be applied to 24.6 per cent of all the laws. This instrument of control dominates in educational (80 per cent) and environmental (72 per cent) policies (Table 4.5).
- Another instrument of control is an *additional hearing* (4.6 per cent of the decisions in this sample). It is most frequently applied in legal policy (8.3 per cent).
- Parliament creates *special institutions for the control of legislation* in fields where its competence is limited. This instrument is used in 4.7 per cent of the decisions, most frequently in economic policy (12.1 per cent). The special institutions for control develop a tendency to increase their autonomy. This threatens 'parliamentary sovereignty', but is less dangerous than a super-authority of control for all the legislation.

Amendment of Laws

Amendment often result from the process of the three controls by the implementing authorities, the Constitutional Court and the institutions of evaluation. The American option of repealing a law is very rare and has happened only in routine legislation, such as vaccination laws. The normal consequence of control is an amendment of the law. Amending laws in Germany are not always unimportant laws (see Chapter 1). This is particularly true for the amendments to the constitution which ushered in major reforms, such as the 'financial reform' (21st amendment to the Basic Law), constitutional complaints (19th amendment), emergency laws (17th amendment). Even when a constitutional reform was ultimately more modest than expected, as in 1994 when the Basic Law was adapted to the needs of the reunification process, it was far from being a marginal law.

Table 4.5 Consequences of evaluation (%)

	Foreign	Legal	Policy field Economic	Social	Housing	Education	Environment	Total
Report	17.3	5.5	33.3	20.6	15.3	80.0	72.0	24.6
Additional hearing	4.3	8.3	3.0	–	–	20.0	9.0	4.6
Control by special institutions	–	5.5	12.1	3.4	–	–	–	4.7

Constitutional change in Germany can follow two competing routes:

- amendments to the constitution
- judicial review of laws by the Constitutional Court.

Although the first route is not easy because of the requirement of a two-thirds majority, the amendment procedure in Germany is less cumbersome than in the United States where a majority of states has to endorse the amendment.

In the first 11 legislatures up to Reunification, 36 laws amending the Basic Law were passed, including 119 amendments of Articles (list in Schindler IV, 1994: 1127ff). Some left-wing authors, such as Seifert, suspected that the country was treating its constitution as the 'general conditions of trade' in an economic enterprise. But there were not only restrictive amendments, as the leftists suspected, but also rather innovative measures, such as the introduction of second trials of appeal in political criminal acts (Art. 96.5), constitutional complaint by citizens (Art. 93.1 4a & b), the military ombudsman (Art. 45b), an emergency parliament in the framework of the emergency laws (Art. 53a) and the state goal declaration of 'protection of the environment' (Art. 20a). Other fundamental reforms legally were only amendments to the penal code (1969, 1973).

The motives for amendments developed from different sources, including the European Union and the Constitutional Court, from just a change of paradigm in the perception of a policy, as in labour market policy (1969, 1976, 1977) or from new scientific insights. Distributive laws had to be adapted almost every two years to the changing economic conditions. Protective decisions in environmental law revealed the problems of the issue only in the implementation phase and required quick amendments of the law. In some distributive regulations, interest groups discovered that they could participate and urged amendments which made their groups eligible for inclusion in the benefits, as in the case of laws on behalf of the refugees (1952, 1953) or on housing (1950, 1956, 1960).

In other instances the legislator, under pressure of time, has regulated a matter only halfheartedly and speculated on a forthcoming amendment as in housing policy (1950, 1956), where the financial aspects were regulated only six years after the key decision.

Political crises have led to frequent amendments. This was true in times of consolidation when acceleration laws speeded up the implementation process. Implementing bureaucracies have invited amendments as in the case of the 'law on pharmaceutic products' (1961, 1964, 1976) (Murswieck, 1983: 287). Amendments have also had to compensate the deficits of the original law, as in the case of the 'second law on the formation of property by the working population' (1965) because the first law did not include the participation of the social partners, such as trade unions and investors (4th BT, 5.5.1965: 9005). Parliamentarians are not always ready to follow the advice of the bureaucracy for the amendment of laws, because the majority never knows which new problems will be raised by the opposition on the occasion of a debate on amending a former regulation (Luhmann, 1969: 188). Nor are the experts always unanimous as to what extent a law has to be amended, as a survey among specialists on the Federal Construction Law (1960) revealed (Schäfer and Schmidt-Eisenstaedt, 1984: 349).

The frequency of amendments is not a proof of a bad law and the absence of amendments is no proof of a perfect regulation. In some cases innovative laws, such as the regulation of codetermination (1976) have created a certain balance of power so that the trade unions – far from being wholly satisfied – renounce further amendments because they are afraid that countermobilization for a less progressive regulation might grow stronger than their own lobby (Borgmann, 1986). The conservative initiative to impose 'neutrality in labour struggles on the Federal Labour Office' (1986, §116 'promotion of labour force law') had shown that, after the conservative backlash in the country, it was better not to invite further roll-back strategies by the employers' association.

The fragmentation of the decision-making process in the German 'semi-sovereign state' prevents many innovations which are possible in a majoritarian regime. However, it prevents major roll-back strategies of the conservative camp. The winner does not take it all – particularly not in the policy arenas.

5 Conclusion

The Bundestag is only a part of the legislator. Many other institutions – entitled or not by the constitution – are working together in a complicated network to pass a law. A study of parliament thus unintentionally amounts to a study on the whole political system. The network is not the decision-making centre, but it serves to minimize the transaction costs of political decisions (Benz, 1993: 200). The networks are in permanent danger of losing their auxiliary character and developing autonomy with regard to the institutions constitutionally empowered to decide. Para-parliamentary and non-constitutional steering bodies are becoming increasingly important – from the round tables of the coalition to the negotiations with interest groups or the prime ministers of the *Länder* in the chancellor's office. Networks are in fashion – everything under the sun is now dubbed a 'network' where former research stated 'influence' or 'communication'. Despite this boom networks do not have an autonomous existence as a medium of social control, as does the 'market' or the 'hierarchy', because their organizational structure remain vague and, when they are longlasting, hierarchical elements intrude into their non-hierarchical structures.

In the American context of a majoritarian system, the actors of networks are less intimately connected with each other. Organized clusters of interest are opposed like armies in trench welfare. Interests cooperate in networks of their 'camps'. Between the camps there is a kind of unpopulated space for fire attacks. 'The core is hollow' (Heinz *et al.*, 1993). Parliament is more than a framework for hostile networks, ratifying decisions taken elsewhere and serving as a rubber-stamp for bills. Parliament – in the personal union of party politicians, deputies and facilitators for organized interests – organize the coordination in a decision-making process. Parliament, despite its important symbolic functions, can no longer contribute to the *social integration of society* in Parsons' sense, but serves for the *systemic integration in society*. Even 'power', moderately used, is applied in the decision-making process. The mediating functions, however, require rather cooperation and negotiations because the power recourses are not directly at parliament's disposition but have to be provided for by the administration, in cooperation with para-statal institutions and organized interest groups in a network of 'liberal corporatism'.

Parliamentary democracy lives under the paradox that the capacity of the state to control society is decreasing, but the number of citizens who demand actions by the state is increasing. Even absolutist rulers would not have dared to intervene so frequently in the economy and certainly they would never have considered that 'matrimonial violation' ought to be regulated by law. Politics is a 'forum for action under conditions of trial and error' (Ladeur, 1995: 179). Parliament is most suited to serve physically as the 'forum' of tentative action under conditions of uncertainty.

The results of actions – in terms of laws – are mostly full of contradictions. In disputes about the logic of a law the 'legislator's will' is still invoked by jurists, although everybody knows that there was no uniform will of a legislator when the law was created. But despite the scepticism of autopoietic systems theory the state acts continuously, although the steering capacity of parliament is limited. To use a metaphor of navigation: the ship of the state does not precisely drop the anchors at the provided place, but it does not bob up and down on the same spot either. Autopoietic theories consider decisions under conditions of uncertainty, mostly as symbolic politics which are purely and simply reactions to the demands of citizens who think that 'the state should act'. If steering of the state is successful, parliament sets only a framework for action. In many cases, the details of controlling society is left to the courts and to the administration.

Law and politics are two subsystems of society which are closely related to each other and do not correspond to the image of self-regulating systems of autopoietic theories. *Endosymbiosis* – which are familiar within biological systems – seems to occur also in the life of systems (Wagner, 1996: 100). Symbiotic relations between systems are, however, more conflict-ridden than symbiosis among living organisms. With increasing steering capacity the symbiotic relationship between political decision-making and judicial review is, of course, becoming more narrow in post-modern society.

Although parliamentary democracy is similar in most continental European countries, it has developed in different directions according to the organization of policy networks and policy arenas. The German Bundestag developed towards a parliament where majorities and committees are decisive, whereas Italy, despite the development of a party state as in Germany, remained at the traditional level of an entrepreneurial parliament, in which parties and interest groups streamline their parentela and clientela relations (Liebert, 1995: 349). However, the network organization is not stable over time. After the consolidation of democracy in the Adenauer era corporatist elements were strengthened in the fifth legislature under the Grand Coalition (1966–69). But Germany was never so fully corporatist that parties no longer mattered. Concentration of interest groups' initiatives functioned best under the conditions of the Grand Coalition, and this shows that the control capacity of parties is decisive for functioning corporatist relations among the interest groups. Compared with the United States, the German system of decision-making is less polarized (Pappi *et al.*, 1995: 400). The steering capacity of parties is greater than in the United States. Vertical intergovernmental decision-making in the German system of federalism, in combination with corporatism, is absent from the American system.

Since Mancur Olson, the efficiency of legislation in terms of the number of laws has been deducted from the interest group regimes in various systems. In this perception overregulation derives from the growing influences of the interest groups (Gray and Lowery, 1995: 548) and leads to *parliamentary sclerosis*. But despite the growing number of interest groups and new social systems, the number of laws did not grow (cf. Table 1.3, p. 12). Theories, such as Wagner's law of growing state expenditures and the hypothesis of growing bureaucracies or shares of state ownership, proved to be wrong (cf. von Beyme, 1985a).

The analysis of the decision-making process in its stages cannot be described in terms of a computer programme. The chronological arrangement of chapters in this study is only a didactic scheme for the representation of the material. Only by comparisons with former and later stages of the decision-making process can the complexity of the process be represented.

In the *policy formulation stage* the media, the parties and the ministerial bureaucracy and their scientific advisers are the most important actors (Chapter 2). Only in agenda-setting are the media decisive. The agenda relevant for political action is still set by the parties. Steering bodies of the coalition, government and administration channel the issues which are established on the parliamentary agenda (Chapter 2, pp. 20–22).

In the *policy decision stage* government is the most important actor for the introduction of bills (Chapter 3, pp. 29–104). Behind the formal initiative there are, however, old and new actors, such as the Constitutional Court, the scientific policy advisory bodies or the European Union. Parliament is mostly limited to streamlining and clustering a variety of proposals. Committee work (Chapter 3, pp. 37–48) is most important for the selection of initiatives by the interest groups (Chapter 3, pp. 48–62).

The existence by interest group regimes means that Germany as a whole cannot be categorized as a corporatist country. In some arenas there are *symmetric dualisms* as in corporatist textbooks. Most often, class politics in Germany leads to *asymmetric dualism* (economic, housing and environmental policies). In some arenas there is even a *double corporatism* of the partners of class conflict as well as of major status groups (property owners versus tenants, privileged status groups versus clients of social groups and organizations of the damaged and handicapped underprivileged in society). Pluralism and corporatism in some arenas are competing as a model of interest representation. *Oligopolistic status group pluralism* prevails in almost one-quarter of the decisions. *Pluralism* with a great variety of interests and free access to many groups is fairly rare (12.7 per cent). The 'American' type of true pluralism with access even for promotional groups and weak new social movements is found only in a minority of policy decisions.

Policies do not determine politics – for example the political decision-making process – in the same way as Lowi (1964) developed as a hypothesis for the United States, although this does happen in economic policy with its preponderance of symmetrical and asymmetrical forms of corporatism. Promotional groups show their dominance in legal policy (76 per cent) in which few interests intervene and advocacy politics is demanded for underprivileged and hardly represented interests. There is an affinity between policy arenas and regimes of interest representation in only about one-third of the decisions – not a very strong correlation. Among the types of decision the connection between distributive and redistributive decisions and an oligopolistic type of status politics by powerful organizations is strong. True pluralism with a dominance of promotional groups is concentrated in the field of protective measures which regulates by distributing considerable amounts of transfers.

Pressure group politics in a literal sense is rare. It was common in the consolidation phase of the Federal Republic and revived during the students' rebellion. Trade unions in Germany were important influence-seekers but were very rarely lured onto the road of pressure and politically motivated strikes.

Mass petitions in Germany are not very common and their influence is minimal. More important is the participation of parliamentary elites in demonstrations in the country, as happened in the first two legislatures, under the Grand Coalition and after Reunification. The double strategy – in and outside parliament – has rarely been successful. It is mainly the new underprivileged groups that have tried it, such as the refugees after 1949, the students and intellectuals under the Grand Coalition and the new social movements since the Green Party entered parliament in 1983.

Interest groups intervene, unsolicited, with their demands and solicited by committees in *public hearings*. Public hearings give the impression of a rather symmetrical representation of interests. *De facto* the asymmetry is much greater. Since the fifth legislature almost two-thirds of all the key decisions (64 per cent) have been preceded by public hearings; in the first 12 legislatures (1949–94) 58 per cent of the crucial laws were accompanied by hearings. Hearings have been rare only in foreign and defence policy and are most frequent in educational, social and economic policies.

The *parliamentary debate* has important symbolic functions and, via amendments, also efficient impacts on legislation (see Chapter 3, pp. 69–76). Even the opposition has considerable influence in the decision-making process in Germany (see Chapter 3, pp. 76–81). The parliamentary debate is structured in a fairly hierarchical way. Individual deputies have had a diminishing weight in the debate since 1949. The parliamentary groups steer the debate. The visibility of the parliamentary elite depends on the specialization in policy arenas, on the type of decision and the personal style of the incumbents.

The *specialization* of deputies in certain policy fields leads to an increasing dominance of the elites, such as chairpersons of the committees, rapporteurs, the representatives of the parliamentary groups (*Obleute*) and the chairpersons of the working groups of parliamentary parties. The smaller the parties are the more multifunctional are the politicians. The battle over justice in the debate is regulated in a consociational way.

The *opposition* (see Chapter 3, pp. 76–81) oscillates between the ideal types of *competitive model* and the strategy of *cooperative co-government*. These strategies are tuned according to policy arenas and types of decision. A third type, the *ad hoc opposition*, is mostly used by the smaller parties in a governmental coalition. Consensus-finding between governmental coalition and opposition has developed different patterns: in times of boom when a surplus can be distributed the 'additive strategy' is chosen, which grants benefits for the clientela of both major parties. In a slump, conflict is more fierce. The two major parties still try to take as little from their clientela as possible and support a confrontation of major status groups dominating a policy arena. Health policy is the chief example of this.

The uncosy pentangle of the decision-making process contains the *federal units*, the *Länder*. The less competences in legislation on their level that remain, the more they intervene in the federal legislation. Indicators for this increasing interest in vertical intergovernment policy-making are the growing number of amendments proposed by the *Länder* via the Federal Council and the growing participation of Federal Council members in the parliamentary debates of the Bundestag (see Chapter 3, pp. 95–104). The most important indicator is, however, the number of key decisions which raised much controversy between parliament and the Federal Council that a conference committee had to mediate. This has happened in about one-third (32.6 per cent) of the key decisions, most frequently in educational, economic and legal policy. Extensive decisions, granting new rights to citizens, were most often submitted to mediation (47 per cent of the cases).

142 The Legislator

The interests of the *Länder* are frequently distorted for party political reasons. The patterns of coalitions in the *Länder* play a significant role. They are much more complicated than during the period of a three-party cartel (1961–83). Long-term changes in the party system, such as the decline of the Liberals, the rise of the Green Party and the regional veto position which the post-Communist PDS developed in East Germany after Reunification made the process of legislation less calculable and more clumsy.

Three forms of *control of legislation* have developed in Germany:

- control of judicial review of the Constitutional Court
- control of the feasibility of laws by the implementing administration
- the evaluation of laws by policy advisory institutions and parliament.

The most spectular control is exercised by the Constitutional Court because of a *post facto control* as well as an *ex ante anticipatory obedience* of the legislator (see chapter 4, pp. 105–14). Forty per cent of all the 108 key decisions issued were carried to the Court. Some of the decisions were pushed to the Court by the opposition, but 27 per cent of all suits were initiated after the legislature in which the law was passed, making it likely that other causes had transformed the issue into a complaint, without calculated action from the opposition.

The Constitutional Court is no graveyard of parliament key decisions. Only about one-sixth (14.8 per cent) of the crucial laws were declared null and void, most frequently in legal and social policies. Almost one-fifth of the cases were considered to be incompatible with the constitution (19.4 per cent). There is no correlation between the size of the majority which passed a law and the constitutionality of the law. Also, norms which have been decided on with the votes of the opposition have failed in front of the Constitutional Court. A third type of judgment which stipulates that a law has to be interpreted in conformity with the constitution is apparently the slightest critique of legislation. Nevertheless the consequences of such a judgment can be far-reaching. The legislation can be turned against the will of the legislator when the lower courts apply the law in an undesired way.

The anticipatory impact of the Court is also considerable. In almost all the laws which finally ended in front of it, the threat of the Court dominated the parliamentary debates and the discussions of the committee. Moreover, in 12 per cent of the cases which were *not* carried to Karlsruhe the threat of the Court was also used in the parliamentary debates. The opposition frequently functionalized 'Karlsruhe', the threat. However, when the Court invalidated laws which had been passed by both government and opposition – such as the party law (1967) or regulations on abortion – a parliamentary consensus grew to avoid another intervention from the Court. Complete anticipatory

Conclusion 143

obedience in front of the Court has never developed because the parties have always claimed the priority of political decision.

Control of the feasibility of laws by the implementing bureaucracy (see Chapter 4, pp. 114–19) can be studied only on the basis of existing case studies. The number of key decisions is reduced, because of laws which have never been applied (emergency laws), or because institutions which have been created *per se* do not depend only on the virtues of German implementators. The experts in the bureaucracy, in most cases, have been more critical of a law than the average citizen. The results of the implementation phase are difficult to generalize because many laws are implemented by para-statal institutions or even by social organizations. The experiences of implementation increasingly have a rapid feedback on decision-making because they are applied in the amendment process.

The scientification of legislation has increased (see Chapter 2, pp. 23–8). This is especially true of the evaluation phase (Chapter 4, pp. 119–33). There are no successful laws in absolute terms. Efficiency and effectiveness have been differentiated. In some cases both cannot be controlled or the laws are effective only in a symbolic sense (cf. Table 4.3, p. 123). The effectiveness of laws is determined by additional conditions or is distorted by dysfunctional consequences. In many instances, a law was made effective *ex post facto*, by amendments and acceleration laws. Implementators and controlling institutions deeply influence the effectiveness of laws. Some inefficient laws grow into efficacy when the citizens accept it step-by-step. Some laws which initially looked efficient turned out to be ineffective because the social and economic conditions changed, as in the cases of the law on economic stability (1967) or the Anti-monopoly Law (1957).

The criteria for effectiveness have been differentiated: some problems raised doubts whether regulation is possible at all, as in the case of high-risk technologies. Procedural efficiency (speed of legislation) can be important in problems where quick interventions of the state are required. The capacity of innovative legislation, the degree of laws, goal attainment, the impact of dysfunctional consequences, the possibilities of implementing a law and the need for amendments are further criteria. The most important of all of them is increasingly the acceptance which a law finds among the citizens, although this criterion implies a risk of populistic ad hoc legislation.

The Constitutional Court has imposed the duty of permanent evaluation on the legislators. Duties to report, public hearings on implementation and control by specialized institutions have more and more impact on the legislation.

The American policy cycle provides for an 'end of policy'. This is rare in the continental Europe with its Roman law tradition. Laws are hardly ever repealed, but rather amended and substituted by a new law which is really new only *de jure*. The frequency of amendments is no indicator for good or bad laws. Certain measures, such as distributive decisions, force parliament to an almost annual adaptation of laws. On the other hand, laws which have hardly ever been amended do not prove excellence, but rather the fact that consensus in that matter is difficult to reach, so that the major parties prefer to live with unsatisfactory compromises of the past rather than launch a new debate which may create unrest in society. The laws on codetermination in the industrial enterprises exemplify this attitude.

The presentation of the material along the phases of the policy cycle should not suggest that every actor was present in all the stages of legislation and its control. The relative weight of actors and institutions has shifted over time. The decision-making process is not a soccer game with a level and regular sized playing field, fixed rules and numbers of players. The game of decision-making in political networks more resembles the bizarre game in *Alice in Wonderland* where everything is continually varying – the size of the playing field, the rules and the numbers of players. The goal posts keep moving and the ball has a life of its own.

The genesis of a theory of legislation in the time of the Enlightenment (Bentham, 1789, Filangieri, 1798) inclined towards a perception of legislation as a rational machine. In post-modern times, legislation has been compared to 'a garden rather than a product manufactured by a machine' (van Mechelen and Rose, 1986: 89). To extend this metaphor we could compare legislation with a park in the time of Romanticism. Originally it had been designed as a symmetric rational French garden, but time has distorted the design by a wild organic growth which has transformed it into a romantic English park. The rational design is still in the statute books and in the cooperation of those institutions entitled to decide by the constitution. But by-gardens have grown in the parliamentary park – concertations, round tables, negotiations between the Federation and the *Länder* have created a by- and para-parliamentarianism which has grown over the constitutional machinery of legislation. From time to time, conservative formalists beg to prune all this wild growth, but they overlook the fact that, without it, the constitutional machinery would no longer work.

The classical division of functions – leadership (government and parliament) and implementation (bureaucracy) – is no longer valid. By spreading reflective law and conceptions of non-hierarchical self-control new para-statal and private actors have gained influence over the decision-making process. Even among the non-statal social actors, the weight of actors is not constant over time. The corporatist social partners have lost in weight. An occasionally anarchical neopluralism made a comeback after the imputed death of the pluralist model of interest mediation.

American intellectual battles over whether parliamentarians are oriented by policy goals or by calculations of their chances of re-election (Fiorina, 1977), have little importance for continental European parliamentary systems. Parliament in Europe has never corresponded to the model of American pressure group pluralism. Germany has one of the most established party states in the world, leaving individual deputies little room for manoeuvre (cf. von Beyme, 1995). The 'legislative Leviathan' has been rediscovered even in the United States: 'parties and parliamentary groups of parties matter' is the new American message. In a parliamentary system there was little to rediscover. Parties and their steering capacity has always been recognized as the very essence of effective legislation. When parties fail, the whole system falls into disorder. The final report of the commission of inquiry into constitutional reform analysing the governmental crisis of spring 1972 admitted: 'The Bundestag was non-existent for several months and was unable to fulfil its task as a leading institution and of controlling the government' (Beratungen und Empfehlungen, 1, 1976: 21). The commission recommended the right to self-dissolution of parliament as a way out of a deadlock situation, but this advice has never been followed by German constitutional reformers. The situation was not so much caused by deficits in the constitutional institutions but rather by a deadlock between the party camps.

German deputies are aware that party membership is the most important factor for their election (56 per cent). Only a minority (34 per cent) emphasize their role as individual actors (Patzelt, 1996). Professionalization and specialization is driven by the parliamentary groups. In the UK 35 per cent of MPs and in the US Senate 40 per cent of representatives were 'generalists' (Searing, 1987; Sinclair, 1989: 85f). Specialization is, however, presented through the influence of interest groups. Normally only leftists, newcomers in parliament and the parliamentary elites are generalists. Female deputies, mavericks and elder deputies showed the strongest specialization in parliament (Esaiasson and Holmberg, 1996: 300). The planning of parliamentary groups frequently pushes individual deputies towards certain specializations.

The German Bundestag has been called 'perhaps the most powerful legislative chamber in Europe' (Aberbach *et al.*, 1981: 231). The structure of the decision-making process in parliament has approached the American model, partly by direct imitation, partly by the development of functional equivalents. The Bundestag lacks the independent structure of congressional staff members – the 'unelected representatives'. The strength of the parliamentary groups prevents them from growing. Three models have been differentiated (Lees and Shaw, 1979: 401). The presidential system has developed strong committees with weak party control, whereas the UK model, on the other hand, has weak committees but strong control by one governmental party. Germany has combined both: strong committees and strong party control which has equivalents only in Scandinavia (Arter, 1984: 207). Other typologies define *elitist 'top-down' models* and *populist 'bottom-up' models*. The European *parliaments – with the exception of Italy – belong to the elitist model*.

As in Scandinavia, control by parties is essential (Esaiasson and Holmberg, 1996: 313), and the deputies give high priority to the parliamentary party groups, contrary to the liberal mystique of the 'free mandate' even non-socialist deputies consider themselves as a kind of party delegate. The decline of parties has affected party identification and party membership, but not party control in parliament. The old hypothesis, developed by Lord Bryce, about the decline of parliaments cannot be generally applied to continental Europe. Parliaments have experienced ups and downs. In the 1960s they were more active than before (Damgaard, 1992), despite the rise of the segmented state (Olsen, 1978). Since then, parliament has not suffered a decline, but the centre of gravity behind its decisional power has shifted.

Another typology differentiates active and reactive legislatures (Mezey, 1979: 36). In comparison with a model of an active parliament – for example, the US Congress – the Bundestag could be called 'reactive'. Yet, compared to most continental European parliaments – especially to the French parliament – the Bundestag is very active, if we do not measure activity by the rather superficial indicator of laws passed per year (in the 1980s; Germany 83; France 94; UK 62) (Döring, 1995: 598).

The power of 'co-powers' has grown (Oberreuter, 1981: 17). This has caused countermovements within parliament. The capacity of parliamentary self-steering has been strengthened by the parliamentary parties. An *oligarchical state of coalition parties* – with elements of *co-government of the opposition* – was the response to the decline of direct representation of constituencies by individual deputies. The party state has been increasingly criticized. It is time to recognize its positive role for the revitalization of parliamentary government.

The oligarchical party establishment is becoming more independent from the party members and voters, but compensates this autonomy by increasing *responsiveness*. Parties in power try to transform their programmes and party platforms into political reality (Klingemann *et al.*, 1994). This does not mean, however, that politicians always follow the changing fashions of the electorate's will. In most of the innovative legislation – for example, the vote against capital punishment (1952), reforms of penal law, emergency laws, national census and gene technology – the people's will, as documented in surveys, has deliberately been ignored. Social movements have been able to mobilize against a law, as in the law on a national census 1987 (1985), but the boycotts were followed only by 3 per cent of the population (although this is, however, enough to distort the results). In other fields which really interest a great majority of the voters (for example, the anti-terrorism laws, limiting the number of asylum-seekers) the legislator is adopting a reactive and populist attitude.

On the whole, parliament has skilfully balanced on the tightrope between the Scylla of populist *reactiveness* and the Charybdis of innovative *activism* without losing touch with the electorate. Nevertheless the normative literature on democracy has been dissatisfied with the results of the political process and has proposed letting people decide in subpolitical units – under conditions where organized interests and bureaucracies do not paternalize the 'people's will'. The danger that an extension of the decision-makers will lead to an inflation of demands for participation has not been overlooked (Schmalz-Bruns, 1995: 250). The torchbearers of subpolitization, such as Ulrich Beck (1993: 233), are aware that 'subpolitization may lead to a general powerlessness'. More successful was the maintenance of the central decision-making networks, but at the same time mobilizing *advocacy politics* for those groups unrepresented in central decision-making.

The new critical policy analysis has developed a holistic and normative appeal. But it did not claim to be able 'to improve the political institutions' (deLeon, 1993: 482). This in fact is precisely the dilemma: critical policy analysis and critical neo-institutionalism do not cooperate sufficiently. Even Habermas (1992: 211), in his theory of discourse, has recognized, in the 1990s, the dangers of delegating important issues to the subpolitical units because legislation still has the duty to guarantee the unity of rights and benefits in a society. 'Normative defeatism' (ibid.: 400) is spreading. Only some incurable leftists dream of 'another Republic'. The left-wing movement of the 1960s criticized positivist science for doubling reality instead of offering new normative vistas on a better society. In post-modern time this doubling of reality has penetrated normative political thinking – even communitarianism normally offers forms of community-building that already exist but pretends to develop a normative appeal for the future. 'Reflective democracy' is thus in danger of ending up with the modest image of a 'neighbourhood watch-group'.

Appendix: The 150 Key Decisions of the German Bundestag

Abbreviations

BR	Federal Council
BT	Federal Diet
BTcomm.	Committee of the Federal Diet
BVerfGE	Decision of the Federal Constitutional Court
C	consequences
Drs	printed matter
FLO	Federal Labour Office
I	initiative
ND	non-decision
nph	non-public hearing
ph	public hearing
procl.	proclaimed
R	reference
rc	roll call
S	scientific advice
V	vote

Restrictive

1st Bundestag (1949–53)

1   *Statute of occupation*, 19.3.1953
    procl.: 28.3.1954
    R: occupational forces
    I: government
    V: majority
    rc: 225:165:2 (versus SPD, KPD, many FU and independent deputies)

150   *The Legislator*

Regulative

2   *European community on coal and steel*, 11.1.1952
    procl.: 29.4.1952
    R: Europe
    I: government
    ph: 5–6.9.1951
    V: majority
    rc: 232:143.3

3   *European community on defence* (EVG), 19.3.1953
    procl.: 28.3.1954
    R: Europe
    I: government
    V: majority
    rc: 244:166:2 (versus SPD, KPD, 1 CDU, 1 FDP, some FU)
    BVerfGE: 1:281 of 19.3.1952 (conforming to the constitution)
    BVerfGE: 2:143 of 7.3.1953 (motion of CDU/CSU-parliamentary group versus SPD opposition turned down)

4   *Federal law on civil servants*
    (BBG) 2.6.1953
    procl.: 14.7.1953
    I: government
    V: large majority (versus KPD)
    BVerfGE: 11:203 of 14.6.1960 (§110 invalid)
    BVerfGE: 21:329 of 14.7.1967 (not conforming to the constitution)

Extensive

5   *Codetermination in the mining industry*, 10.4.1951
    procl.: 21.5.1951
    I: government
    V: large majority

6   *Law on industrial relations scheme*, 19.7.1952
    procl.: 11.10.1952
    I: 7 drafts by government, BT, CDU, SPD
    ph: 17.10.1950, 5.12.1950
    V: 4 rc – majority
    rc: 195:139:7 (versus SPD, KPD, some FDP, right-wing extremists)
    conference committee

Protective

7   *Law on returnees*, 27.4.1950
    procl.: 23.6.1950
    I: government
    V: unanimous

8   *Law on the protection of youth in public*, 17.10.1951
    procl.: 4.12.1951
    I: CDU-parliamentary group
    V: almost unanimous
    conference committee

9   *Law on the regulation of minimal labour conditions*, 22.11.1951
    procl.: 11.1.1952
    I: BT, SPD opposition
    nph: 19.4.1950 (experts)
    V: large majority (versus 4 votes)

10 *Law on the protection of mothers*, 12.12.1951
    procl.: 24.1.1952
    I: BT, SPD opposition
    hearing: 9.9.1950
    V: unanimous
    C: new version 27.4.1968
    BVerfGE: 38:213 of 13.11.1974 (not conforming to the constitution)
    BVerfGE: 52:357, 38/213 of 25.1.1972 in the version of 18.7.1967 (on §9, 16/1, clause 1, not conforming to the constitution)

Distributive

11 *Law on house building*, 28.3.1950
    procl.: 24.4.1950
    I: government, 1949: SPD bill
    V: almost unanimous (some abstentions)
    BVerfGE: 4:388 v. 23.2.1956 (conforming to the constitution)

12 *Federal law on pensions*, 19.10.1950
    procl.: 20.12.1950
    I: government
    V: almost unanimous (4 abstentions)
    BVerfGE: 17:62 of 24.7.1963 (§45.5 clause 1 invalid)

13 *Law on housing property*, 31.1.1951
procl.: 15.3.1951
I: BT, FDP
V: unanimous

14 *Law on premiums for house building*, 24.1.1952
procl.: 17.3.1952
I: BT, interparliamentary groups
nph: experts
V: unanimous
BVerfGE: 45:104 of 8.6.1977 (version 1975) (not conforming to the constitution)
BVerfGE: 48:104 (in the version of 1975) of 20.6.1978 (conforming to the constitution)

15 *Law on refugees*, 25.2.–25.3.1953
procl.: 6.5.1953
I: government
V: Amendment rc
final vote: large majority

Redistributive

16 Law on the equalization of burdens (LAG), 10.7.1952
procl.: 14.8.1952
I: government. 8.9.1950 request of BR on the initiative of a law 3.7.1951 hearing concerning credits vouched for by the Reich
V: 4 rc
final vote: majority, rc (209:144:11) (versus KPD, SPD, 11 right-wing extremists)
conference committee
BVerfGE: 11:64 of 4.5.1960 (conforming to the constitution)
BVerfGE: 15:32 of 4.5. 1960
partly invalid
BVerfGE: 19:370 of 18.1.1966 (invalid in changed version)

2nd Bundestag 1953–57

Restrictive

17 *Law on volunteers*, 18.7.1955
    procl.: 23.7.1955
    I: government
    V: majority (versus SPD)

18 *Amendment of the constitution. Restriction of some basic rights for soldiers*, 6.3.1956
    procl.: 19.3.1956
    I: BT
    V: large majority (versus 20 votes)

19 *Law on compulsory military service*, 6.7.1956
    procl.: 21.7.1956
    R: international politics
    I: government
    hearing of church representatives on conscientious objection 1.6./4.6
    hearing of military experts, 7.6.1956
    V: 5 rc
    final vote rc: majority – 269:166:20 (versus SPD, BHE)
    conf. comm.
    BVerfGE: 12:45 of 20.2.1960 (§25 of the law interpretation conforming to the constitution)
    BVerfGE: 74:78 of 3.12.1986 (conforming to the constitution)

Regulative

20 *Law on financial adjustment of the Länder*, 19.11.1954
    procl.: 27.4.1955
    I: government
    hearing 22.6.1954
    V: almost unanimous
    conference committee

21   *Saar statute*, 27.2.1955
     procl.: 24.3.1955
     R: international politics
     I: government
     A. majority rc 264:201:9 (versus SPD, FDP, majority BHE)
     BVerfGE: 4:157 of 4.5.1955 (conforming to the constitution)
     C: report concerning economic integration of the Saar 16.10.1958 III/1002

22   *NATO treaty*, 27.2.1955
     procl.: 24.3.1955
     R: international politics
     I: government
     V: majority; rc 314:154:2 (versus SPD, some FDP)

23   *Anti-trust law (BKG)*, 4.7.1957
     procl.: 27.7.1957
     R: demands of the allies
     1948 expert council
     I: government
     V: majority
     C: annual report, Federal Cartel Office
     ph: 8./9.12.1971 (novella); rc before final vote
     BVerfGE: 20:257, 64 of 11.10.1966 (§80 Abs. 2, clause 2, null and void)
     BVerfGE: 74:78 of 3.12.1986 (conforming to the constitution)
     C: testimonial of the Monopoly Commission 524b, new version 1974, report of the government every 2 years

24   *First skeleton law on civil servants (BRRG)*, 11.4.1957
     procl.: 1.7.1957
     I: government
     hearing of Federal Union of Municipal Central Organizations, 15.9.1955
     V: rc amendment SPD, FDP, BHE rejected (154:202:6)
     final vote: majority (abstentions in CDU, SPD)
     BVerfGE: 10:285 of 2.2.1980 (conforming to the constitution)
     BVerfGE: 21:329 of 11.4.1967 (Hamburg law on civil servants null and void)

25 *European Economic Community*, 5.7.1957
    procl.: 27.7.1957
    R: international politics
    I: government
    V: very large majority
    C: structural report on integration, semi-annual
    Decision: 22.2. and 28.4.1967

Extensive

26 *End of occupation regime*, 27.2.1955
    procl.: 24.3.1955
    I: government
    V: majority rc (314:157)
    BVerfGE: 12:281: 21.3.1961 (conforming to the constitution)
    BVerfGE: 14:1 of 6.2.1962 (conforming to the constitution)
    BVerfGE 18:353 of 16.2.1965 (conforming to the constitution)

27 *Law on representation of personnel*, 17.3.1955
    procl.: 5.8.1955
    I: government
    hearing: 20.9.1954, 7.2.1955 communal central organizations
    V: majority
    rc: 207:179:20
    conference committee
    BVerfGE: 28:295 of 26.5.1970 (conforming to the constitution)

28 *Law on equal rights for men and women in civil rights*, 3.5.1957
    procl.: 18.6.1957
    I: government/SPD, FDP
    motions
    ph and nph: farmers – 21.4.1955;
    women's organizations – 12.7.1954;
    V: unanimous
    conference committee
    BVerfGE: 19:177 of 16.11.1965 (interpretation conforming to the constitution)
    BVerfGE: 24:104 of 24.7.1968 (§45 of order of bankruptcy in the law is invalid)

Protective

29 *Child benefit and family equalization bill*, 14.10.1954
    procl.: 12.8.1954
    I: BT, CDU/CSU–SPD/FDP draft law on children's subsidies
    V: majority – several rc on 2nd reading
    3rd reading rc: 215:202:1 (versus SPD, FDP, BHE, DP)

30 *Federal law on rents*, 14.6.1955
    procl.: 27.7.1955
    I: government
    V: majority
    conference committee

31 *Military ombudsman*, 11.4.1957
    procl.: 26.6.1957
    I: government/SPD draft
    V: majority (versus SPD and BHE)
    conference committee

Distributive

32 *Law on agriculture*, 8.7.1955
    procl.: 5.9.1955
    I: BT: FDP/CDU–CSU, DP
    V: large majority (2 dissenting votes)
    C: advisory board, annual reports (agrarian report)

33 *Second law on house building and families' homes*, 4.5.1956
    procl.: 27.6.1956
    R: in 1st BT law not passed
    I: government/BT: CDU–CSU
    BT: SPD
    V: majority
    conference committee
    BVerfGE: 21:117 of 17.1.1967 (interpretation conforming to the constitution)

34   *Old-age insurance for farmers*, 29.6.1957
   procl.: 27.7.1957
   I: BT, CDU–CSU
   hearing: 6.5.1957
   V: large majority
   BVerfGE: 78:232 of 31.5.1988 (conforming to the constitution)

Redistributive

35   *Revision of pension scheme* (ArVNG), 21.1.1957
   procl.: 23.2.1957 (dynamic pension)
   I: government/SPD draft
   hearing: experts 5/12/21.9.1956
   S: advisory board
   V: large majority
   rc: 318:32:10 versus FDP
   a. DP majority
   C: family equalization institution
   BVerfGE: 14:28 of 11.10.1962 (interpretation conforming to the constitution of Art. 2 of law)
   BVerfGE: 11:50 of 5.4.1960 (§293 line 2) (conforming to the constitution); further decisions 1988, 1970, 1971, 1972, 1992 (conforming to the constitution)

3rd Bundestag 1957–61

Restrictive

1st ND: *Law on the revision of health insurance* (KVNG), 17.2.1960, 1st reading
   I: government; BT, SPD
   V: 9.2.1961 BT–C with consent of all parliamentary groups dropped bill (internal conflict in CDU–CSU)
   2nd I: BT, CDU–CSU
   splitting of field of regulation
   C: economic security of workers in case of sickness, unanimous, shortly before elections. See Decision 44

158 The Legislator

Regulative

36 *Peaceful use of nuclear energy (law on nuclear energy)*, 3.12.1959
    procl.: 23.12.1959
    I: government, FDP, SPD bills
    hearing: 15.–16.6.1959
    V: very large majority
    conference committee
    BVerfGE: 33:265; 34,139 and other decisions (conforming to the constitution)
    BVerfGE: 49:89 of 8.8.1978 (conforming to the constitution)
    C: report: decision 1.7.1976; report on decontamination 14.12.1978

37 *Federal law on house building*, 18.5.1960
    procl.: 23.6.1960
    I: government, FDP initiative finished
    R: testimonial
    BVerfGE: 3:407 of 16.6.1954 (competence of federal government)
    nph: 21.–28.1.1959
    V: large majority
    conference committee
    BVerfGE: 8.11.1959 (conforming to the constitution)

Extensive

2nd ND: *Referendum on nuclear rearmament of the army*, 13.6.1958
    I: BT, SPD opposition
    V: in 2nd reading rejected
    rc: 128:217.2 (2 FDP abstentions)
    C: majority endorses suit at BVerfGE versus Hessen
    BVerfGE: 7:367 of 27.5.1958 (interim order)

38 *Civil alternative service*, 2.12.1959
    procl.: 13.1.1960
    I: government
    A: unanimous
    conference committee

Protective

39 *Industrial safety for youth*, 19.5.1960
    procl.: 9.8.1960
    I: government, SPD draft
    hearing: 18.–19.6.1957
    V: 2nd reading 3 rcs; SPD amendment rejected (234:140:7) (5 CDU votes for SPD draft, 5 CDU abstentions)
    3rd reading: majority

40 *Law on the distribution of medicaments*, 17.3.1961
    procl.: 16.5.1961
    I: government, SPD draft
    hearing: experts of associations 22.4.1959
    V: unanimous
    conference committee
    C: control by Federal Health Centre

Distributive

41 *Law on savings premiums*, 19.3.1959
    procl.: 5.5.1959
    I: government
    V: large majority
    BVerfGE: 45:104 of 8.6.1977 (version of 1974 not conforming to the constitution)

42 *Handing-over of the shares on the VW-GmbH into private hands*, 16.3.1960
    procl.: 21.7.1960
    R: decision of Federal High Court in VW savers' lawsuit
    I: BT: Dr Adenauer, Dr Erhard Stücklen, Cillien, Elbrächter, Krone, Deist and comrades
    V: majority
    conference committee

160 The Legislator

43 *Law on income support* (BSHG), 4.5.1961
    procl.: 30.6.1961
    R: BundesverwGvL 78/54 of 24.6.1954
    I: government
    hearing: Association of the Blind 27.10.1960; experts 25.1.1961
    V: majority (193:150:2) (vote by division)
    conference committee
    BVerfGE: 22:194 of 18.7.1967 (§33 para. 2, §96 para. 1, null and void)
    BVerfGE: 30:47 of 15.12.1970 (interpretation conforming to the constitution of §26 para. 1)
    BVerfGE: 37:154 of 7.5.1974 (conforming to the constitution)
    BVerfGE: 61:18 of 23.6.1982 (conforming to the constitution)
    C: report acc. §126C, every 4 years,VII/654)

44 *Insurance of workers in case of sickness (continued pay)* (amending law), 31.5.1961
    procl.: 12.7.1961
    I: BT, CDU–CSU/FDP finished
    hearing: 19.3.1958; 14.4.1961
    V: large majority (versus FDP)
    conference committee

45 *Law on child benefits*, 29.6.1961
    procl.: 18.7.1961
    I: government
    V: almost unanimous (2 dissenting votes, 2 abstentions)

4th Bundestag 1961–65

Regulative

46 *Council of economic advisers*, 26.6.1963
    procl.: 14.8.1963
    I: BT, CDU–CSU, FDP
    hearing: 12.6.1963
    V: unanimous

47 *Treaty on the ban of nuclear weapons*, 5.6.164
   procl.: 29.7.1964
   R: international politics
   I: government
   V: unanimous

48 *Regional development plan*, 12.2.1965
   procl.: 8.4.1965
   I: BT, Dr Schmidt ao (CDU–CSU, FDP, SPD) government
   hearing: 22–23.4.1964
   BVerfGE testimonial on competence of federal government
   V: almost unanimous (4 dissenting votes, 2 abstentions)
   C: report on original development decision of 6.3.1963; first report 1966; reports every 2 years, later every 4 years

Extensive

49 *Reduction of government control in housing* (amending law), 27.6.1963
   procl.: 29.7.1963
   I: BT, SPD opposition
   V: majority (versus SPD, draft converted by CDU amendments)

Protective

50 *Law on foreign immigrants* (AuslG), 12.2.1965
   procl.: 28.4.1965
   I: government
   V: unanimous
   conference committee
   BVerfGE: 38:52 of 16.7.1974 (interpretation conforming to the constitution)
   BVerfGE: 49:168 of 26.9.1978 (conforming to the constitution)
   BVerfGE: 50:167 of 17.1.1979 (conforming to the constitution)
   BVerfGE: 76:1 of 12.5.1987 (conforming to the constitution)
   BVerfGE: 54:341 of 2.7.1980 (interpretation conforming to the constitution of §38 AuslG)

Distributive

51 *Law on the revision of accident insurance* (UVNG), 6.3.1963
    procl.: 30.4.1963
    I: BT, CDU–CSU
    hearing: municipal central organizations
    25.10.1962, 29.11.1962, 6.12.1962; experts 10.5–14.6.1962; further hearing in non-leading committee of Social policy 15.2.1962
    V: almost unanimous
    C: report on accident prevention
    annual, Art. 1; decision 30.4.1963
    BVerfGE: 23:12 of 19.12.1967 (conforming to the constitution)

52 *Law on housing subsidies*, 27.6.1963
    procl.: 29.7.1963
    I: BT, CDU–CSU, FDP
    V: majority (versus SPD)

53 *Federal law on child benefits* (BKGG), 6.3.1964
    procl.: 14.4.1964
    I: government
    joint hearing: 25.4.1967
    V: unanimous
    BVerfGE: 22:29 of 24.5.1967 (conforming to the constitution)
    BVerfGE: 29:71 of 14.7.1970 (partly null and void)
    BVerfGE: 30:355 of 23.3.1971 (interpretation conforming to the constitution)

54 *Law on the revision of the final date for the reduction of government control in housing*, 30.6.1965
    procl.: 24.8.1965
    I: government
    V: unanimous

Redistributive

55 *2nd wealth formation of employees* (VermBG), 5.5.1965
    procl.: 1.7.1965
    I: government/FDP and SPD drafts
    hearing: 25.2.1965
    V: almost unanimous (3 abstentions)

5th Bundestag 1965–69

Restrictive

56 *Emergency laws*
(17th amendment to Basic Law), 30.5.1968
procl.: 24.6.1968
R: allied reserved rights
I: BT; CDU, SPD
ph: 9/16/30.11.1967/14.12.1967
V: majority
rc: 384:100:1 (versus FDP, 54 SPD, 1 deputy of FDP opposition pro)
BVerfGE: 30:1 of 15.12.1970 (interpretation conforming to the constitution)

Regulative

57 *Law on economic stability*, 10.5.1967
procl.: 8.6.1967
I: government
ph: 5/19/20.10.1966
V: large majority
C: council on economic situation, annual reports according to §9
annual report on economic situation

58 *Party law*, 28.6.1967
procl.: 24.7.1967
I: BT: CDU/CSU, SPD, FDP
ph: 21.4.1967
V: large majority
BVerfGE: 24,300 of 3.12.1968 (not conforming to constitution)
BVerfGE: 41:399 of 9.3.1976 (not conforming to constitution)
C: commission

59 *Financial reform/cooperative tasks in the federal system* (21st amendment to Basic Law), 11.12.1968
procl.: 12.5.1969
I; government;
BT, CDU, SPD, FDP
ph: 27.6.1968, 3.–4.10.1968;
municipal central organizations 14.11.1968, WRK president testified
V: large majority
conference committee: twice
C: §6 structural plan of cooperative tasks, regional economic structure, annual agrarian structure and coastal protection
Decision: 11.2.1982 and 3.5.1984 annual

Extensive

60 *Constitutional complaint, right of resistance* (19th amendment to Basic Law), 11.12.1968
procl.: 29.1.1969
I: BT, SPD with FDP opposition
question to BVerfG of judiciary committee 29.3.1968
V: large majority

61 *Reform of penal law*
(1.StRG §175) (2.StRG), 9.5.1969
procl.: 25.6.1969
I: BT: FDP deputies Dehler and comrades
ph: 28.2.1966; 1./2.3.1966; 23.5.1966;
Association of the Prevention and Compensations of criminal offences eV 31.5.1967; experts of the commission offences of the Federal Law Society and the German Judicial Association 28.3.1968; Commission on Imprisonment 27.2.1969
V: large majority
rc: 255:61
rc: 314:2:1 some CDU dissenters each time
BVerfGE: 28:386 of 9.6.1970 (§14 Abs. 1 StGB; §27b Abs. 1) (conforming to the constitution)

Protective

62   *Law on the promotion of employment*, 13.5.1969
     procl.: 25.6.1969
     I: BT: SPD and several deputies/government
     ph: 21–23.6.1967 ao
     nph: 6–7.3.1968
     V: unanimous
     BVerfGE: 34:338 of 13.3.1973 (conforming to the constitution)
     BVerfGE: 42:176 of 10.7.1984 (not conforming to the constitution)
     BVerfGE: 60:68 of 10.2.1982 (conforming to the constitution)
     BVerfGE: 61:138 of 19.10.1982 (conforming to the constitution)
     C: according to §239 AFG report until end of 1972; VII/403
     decision of 9.12.1983
     until 1985, X/3659

63   *Law on vocational training BBiG*, 12.6.1969
     procl.: 14.8.1969
     I: BT: CDU and FDP (in opposition)
     ph: 21–23.6.1967
     V: large majority
     BVerfGE: 72:278 of 14.5.1986 (not conforming to constitution)
     C: report of experts' commission concerning costs of extra scholastic vocational training

Distributive

64   *Law on promotion of vocational training*, 26.6.1969
     procl.: 19.9.1969
     I: BT: FDP 21.12.67, SPD 26.6.68, CDU 27.11.68
     ph: 24.4.1969; ministers of education 3.6.1969
     V: almost unanimous (1 dissenting vote, 1 abstention)
     BVerfGE: 72:9 of 12.2.1986 (not conforming to the constitution) ao (3) decisions (conforming to the constitution)

166 *The Legislator*

Redistributive

65 *Continued pay in case of sickness*, 12.6.1969
    procl.: 27.7.1969
    I: BT, CDU, SPD (separately 18.3.1969)
    ph: 29.4/5.5.1969
    V: majority
    rc: 388:38:7 (versus FDP, some CDU abstentions)
    BVerfGE: 48:227 of 26.4.1978 (§14 not conforming to Art. 3, line 1, Basic Law)

6th Bundestag 1969–72

Restrictive

66 *Gun-control law* (WaffG), 22.6.1972
    procl.: 19.9.1972
    I: BR: HH, BW, HB, NS, NRW
    V: unanimous
    BVerfGE: 44:308 of 10.5.1977 (conforming to the constitution)
    C: §42 report, once until 31.12.1982

Regulative

67 *Law on economic support of hospitals*, 1.3.1972
    procl.: 29.6.1972
    I: government; BT: CDU, FDP,
    SPD drafts
    ph: 3.5.1971
    V: majority (versus CDU) (several abstentions in the CDU)
    conference committee
    C: report, once until 1975; decision 1.3.1972, VI/3082

Extensive

68 *Law on industrial relations scheme*, 10.11.1971
    procl.: 15.1.1972
    I: government
    ph: 24/25.2/13/14.5.1971
    V: several rcs with CDU amendment
    final vote: majority rc (264:212:4) (Katzer and 21 CDU deputies pro versus 2 FDP, 4 CDU abstentions)
    conference committee
    BVerfGE: 42:133 of 11.5.1976 (conforming to the constitution)
    BVerfGE: 46:73 of 11.10.1977 (conforming to the constitution)
    BVerfGE: 47:191 of 14.2.1978 (conforming to the constitution)

69 *Treaty with the Soviet Union*, 17.5.1972
    procl.: 23.5.1972
    I: government
    V: majority
    rc: 248:10:238 (CDU–CSU-abstentions, 9 CDU, 1 FDP dissenting votes)
    BVerfGE: 40:141 of 7.7.1975 (interpretation conforming to the constitution)

70 *Treaty with the PR of Poland*, 10.5.1972
    procl.: 23.5.1977
    I: government
    V: rc (248:17:231) majority (CDU–CSU abstentions, 16 CDU-dissenting votes)
    BVerfGE: 40:141 of 7.7.1975 (interpretation conforming to the constitution)

Protective

71 *Law on protection against aircraft noise*, 16.12.1970
    procl.: 30.3.1971
    I: BT, SPD, FDP/draft CDU–CSU
    V: unanimous
    conference committee
    C: report; decision 16.12.1970, 17.4.1975

72 *Law on waste disposal*, 2.3.1972
procl.: 7.6.1972
I: government
ph: 8/9/29.11.1971
V: unanimous
conference committee
C: report; decision 2.3.1972, VII/1760

73 *Law on the avoidance of air pollution* (Law on leaded fuel BzBlG), 24.6.1971
procl.: 5.8.1971
I: government
ph.: 2–8.2/8.3/14.6.1971
V: unanimous
C: report: decision 2.3.1970, VII/1760

74 *Law on the promotion of social auxiliary services*, 26.1.1972
procl.: 17.4.1972
I: BT, CDU opposition
ph.: 23.9.1970
V: unanimous

75 *Law on the protection of animals*, 21.6.1972
procl.: 24.7.1972
I: government
ph: 8.2.1972
V: unanimous
BVerfGE: 36:47 of 2.10.1973 (not conforming to the constitution)
BVerfGE: 48:388ff of 20.6.1978 (§8, line 2, not conforming to the constitution)
C: report on the state of the law
§16d in version of 18.8.1986 every 2 years

Distributive

76 *Law on the promotion of urban development* (StBFG), 16.6.1971
    procl.: 27.7.1971
    R: report on urban development
    I: government, CDU dissenting draft
    ph: 16/23.4/10.12.1970; experimental games 25/26.3.1971
    V: 2nd reading: 2 rcs; 3rd reading: almost unanimous, some abstentions
    conference committee
    C: regular report on urban development, VI/1497; VII/3583

77 *Federal law on the promotion of students* (BAföG), 24.6.1971
    procl.: 26.8.1971
    I: government
    ph: 10.5.1971; 22.10.1975
    V: large majority (no abstentions)
    BVerfGE: 71:146 of 6.11.1985 (not conforming to constitution)
    C: report §35 BAföG every 2 years; VII/2697 16.6.1986 every two years

78 *Law on the promotion of graduates* (GraFöG), 24.6.1971
    procl.: 2.9.1971
    I: government, CDU draft
    ph: 20.10.1975
    V: almost unanimous
    conference committee
    C: report

79 *Law on the revision of the law on house building* (WoBauÄndG 1971), 11.11.1971
    procl.: 17.12.1971
    I: government, CDU deputies' draft
    V: unanimous

Appendix   169

Redistributive

80 *Law on the reform of pensions* (RRG 1972–flexible retirement age), 21.9.1972
procl.: 16.10.1972
I: government
ph: 17.1.1972
V: 2nd reading: rc,
CDU amendment (CDU got opening of pension schemes for self-employed persons and housewives with flexible retirement age through)

final vote rc: almost unanimous
(1 FDP abstention, Dr Diemer-Nicolaus)
C: report on financial consequences for handicapped persons

7th Bundestag 1972–76

Restrictive

81 *Structural law on the budget* (HStruktG) (drastic savings), 5.11.1975
procl.: 18.12.1975
I: government
nph: committee 13: youth
22.10.1975/German league of cities
German society of hospitals
nph: 22.10.1975; committee 4 domestic affairs
nph: committee 7 finance 16.10.1975
ph: committee 18 education 22.10.1975
committee 8 budget, renunciation for the benefit of experts committee
V: 2nd reading: CDU amendment
rc: rejected; 3rd reading: rc majority (223:168:0)
conference committee
C: report on the revision of the Grafög 24.11.1977

82 *Law on the fight against terrorists*, 24.6.1976
   procl.: 18.8.1976
   I: government BT, SPD, FDP (united);
   7 drafts, CDU dissenting draft
   nph.: 2.4.1976
   V: majority (versus CDU–CSU)
   conference committee

Regulative

83 *UN membership*, 10.5.1973
   procl.: 6.6.1973
   R: international politics
   I: government
   V: majority
   rc: 364:121:0 (versus large parts of CDU–CSU)

84 *Basic treaty with the GDR*, 10.5.1973
   procl.: 6.6.1973
   I: government
   V: majority
   rc: 268:217:0 (4 CDU deputies voted with the government)
   BVerfGE: 36:1 of 31.7.1973 (interpretation conforming to the constitution)

85 *Social law code* (SGB general part), 19.6.1975
   procl.: 13.12.1975
   I: government
   V: unanimous
   1 abstention
   conference committee
   C: report on §§13–15 and §17; decision 19.6.1975; §141 line 4 report on draft of the amounts of the contributions in mandatory health insurance

Extensive

86 *University skeleton law* (HRG), 12.12.1974
procl.: 26.1.1976
R: BVerfGE: 35,79 of 2.5.1973 NC decision
I: government
ph: 5/26.3.1971; 28.2/25.3.1974; 25.6/1.7.1974
V: majority (versus CDU–CSU, 4 abstentions in coalition)
conference committee
BVerfGE: 43,292 of 8.2.1977 (partly null and void)
BVerfGE: 62:117 of 3.11.1982 (interpretation conforming to the constitution)
ph: 5.12.1984 (revision) 15/16./24.4.1985
C: report on selection talks decision of 10.12.1986

87 *First reform of matrimonial law* (1.EheRG), 11.12.1975
procl.: 14.6.1976
R: 4 BGH decisions
I: government
ph: 2/9.6.1975
V: several rcs on amendment
rc: majority (228:192:0)
conference committee
BVerfGE: 47:85 of 21.2.1977 (conforming to the constitution)
BVerfGE: 53:224 of 28.2.1980 (conforming to the constitution)

88 *Codetermination law* (MitbestG), 18.3.1976
procl.: 4.5.1976
R: BVerfGE: 50:290 of 1.3.1979; report by experts' commission on co-determination; decision 14.6.1967 with budget law, VI/334
I: government 1974
ph: 16.10.1974/7.11.1974; 19.12.1974
V: majority rc (389:22:1)
BVerfGE: 33:303 and 43,291 of 8.2.1977 (interpretation conforming to the constitution)

Protective

89 *4th reform of penal law* (sexual penal law) (4. StrRG), 7.6.1973
    procl.: 23.11.1973
    R: special commission reform of penal law
    I: BT, SPD, FDP
    ph.: 23/24/25.11.1970
    V: majority rc (247:233:9) (versus CDU–CSU)
    conference committee

90 *5th reform of penal law* (§218 abortion) (5. StrRG), 20.4.1974
    procl.: 18.6.1974
    R: BVerfGE: 39:1 of 25.2.1975 (statement of being partly null and void, order)
    I: BT, SPD, FDP
    ph: 10/11/12.4.1972
    V: majority rc (247:233:9)
    conference committee
    BVerfGE: 88:203 of 28.5.1993 (not conforming to the constitution)
    C: report on the experience of §218 StGB decision of 21.3.1974
    Drs 8/2454 21.3.1975 Drs VIII/3630

91 *Federal law on the protection against immissions* (BImSchG), 18.1.1974
    procl.: 15.3.1974
    I: government
    ph: 14.6.1971; 22.5.1973
    V: 2nd reading amendments rejected; 3rd reading unanimous
    ph: 2nd revision 21.1.1980
    BVerfGE: 75:329 of 6.5.1987 (conforming to the constitution)
    C: report on the protection against immissions every 4 years; decisions of administrative tribunals

92 *Law on the protection of the environment* (BNatSchG), 3.6.1976
    procl.: 20.12.1976
    R: drafts of the 6th and 7th BT government 30.5.1972
    I: BRat, Rh.-Pf., S-H.
    ph: 23.9.1974; 3.10.1974
    V: unanimous
    conference committee
    ph: 16.4.1976

174 The Legislator

93 *Revision of the law on the distribution of medicaments*, 6.5.1976
procl.: 24.8.176
I: government
ph: 23.4.1975; 14.5.1975
V: unanimous
conference committee
ph: 23.4.1986;
report; decision of 6.5.1981, IX/1355

94 *Federal law on data protection* (BDSG), 10.6.1976
procl.: 27.1.1977
R: BVerfGE 1BvL 1963 of 16.7.1969 (decision on micro census)
I: government (6th BT: dep. Dichgans, Hirsch and others)
ph: 6.5.1974; 31.3.1976
V: large majority
conference committee
C: data protection commissioner
ph: 24.6.1985; 21.4.1986; 28/29.4.1986

Distributive

95 *Reform of corporation tax* (EGKStRG), 10.6.1976
procl.: 6.9.1976
R: EC-guideline
I: government
ph: 3.12.1975; 5.5.1976
V: majority
C: separation of 3rd law on tax reforms

96 *Law on the promotion of apprenticeships* (APlFG), 30.6.1976
procl.: 7.9.1976
I: BT, SPD, FDP; dissenting draft CDU–CSU
ph: 23.6.1976
V: rc CDU amendment rejected in final vote: majority conference committee: no attempt at reconciliation
BVerfGE: 55:276 of 10.12.1980 (not conforming to the constitution)
C: report on age limited decision of 8.2.1985 until 1988

Appendix 175

Restrictive

97 *Law on the curbing of costs of health insurance* KVKG (cost savings 1978: 42 Mio DM) 12.5.1977
procl.: 27.6.1977
I: government
ph: 23./24./25.3.1977
V: majority rc (241:205:0) (versus CDU-CSU) conference committee
C: concerted action in the health system Art.2, §6

98 *Law on communication inconfinement* 29.9.1977
procl.: 30.9.1977
I: BT, by all the parliamentary groups
V: majority rc (371:4:17) versus Coppick, Hansen, Hattmann, Thüsing, SPD and 12 SPD- and 5 FDP- abstentions: Matthäus-Maier, huchardt, Eimer ao)
BVerfGE: 46:1 of 4.10.1977 (motion for interim order rejected)
BVerfGE: 49:24 of 1.8.1978 (conforming to the constitution)

99 *Fight against terrorists* (amendment of penal law) (observation of defenders, separating pane) 16.2.1978
procl.: 14.4.1978
R: EC-Parl., decision
I: government
V: majority rc (245:244:0) (versus CDU and 4 SPD-leftists, Hansen ao) conference committee

100 *Law on speeding up proceedings for asylum seekers* amnd. Verw. GO. 23.6.1978
procl.: 25.7.1978
I: BT, FDP, SPD
V: unanimous
BVerfGE: 54:341 of 2.7.1980 (court sentence invalidated)
BVerfGE: 56:216 of 25.2.1981 (court sentence invalidated)
ph: 12.3.1982

101 *Monitoring law* (amnd. of law on restriction of privacy of correspondence, postal and telephone secrecy) 8.6.1978
procl.: 13.9.1978
R: BVerfGE: 30:1 of 15.12.1970;
I: government (draft 7th BT)
V: almost unanimous, 1 abstention

176 *The Legislator*

Extensive

102 *Equal rights for men and women at the working place*
25.6.1980 procl.: 13.8.1980
R: EC: report on Art.119 EEC-treaty 8.12.1966 Drs. V/1177, 27/10/1977 Drs. VIII/1002 from 1969 on every 2 years, from 1980 on every 3 years
decision: 25.6.1980 Drs. X/14
I: government
ph: 27.2.1980
V: gr. majority

Protective

103 *Revision of the law on conscientious objection* (KDVNG), 27.5.1977
procl.: 13.7.1977
I: BT, SPD, FDP
ph: 16.1.1980
V: majority rc (241:226) (versus CDU, parties voted unanimously)
BVerfGE: 48:127 of 13.4.1978 (null and void)
C: duty to report

3rd ND: *Revision of the law on conscientious objection* (KDVNG), 4.7.1980
rejected
R: BVerfGE 13.4.1978
I: BT, SPD, FDP
V: rc (210:217:1) rejected by majority (10 SPD deputies voted against alternative draft 4.7.1980)
I: BT, CDU–CSU
V: rc (193:252:0) rejected

104 *Law on chemicals* (ChemG), 25.6.1980
procl.: 16.9.1980
R: EC-guideline
I: government
ph: 3/4.3.1980
nph: 23.4.1980 on problem of secondary registration in subcommittee
V: almost unanimous (1 dissenting vote: Gruhl, independent, 1 abstention)
C: report after 4 years; decision of 25.6.1980

Distributive

105 *Law on tax reduction and promotion of investments*, 6.10.1977
  procl.: 4.11.1977
  R: council of economic advisers; testimony
  I: BT, SPD, FDP
  ph: 4.5.1977; 28.9.1977 (tax package)
  V: majority rc (219:206:0) (versus CDU, unanimous vote)
  conference committee: BT rc (422:0:0)

106 *Law on the promotion of apprenticeships*, 7.10.1977
  procl.: 23.12.1977
  I: BR, Hamburg
  V: majority
  conference committee
  BVerfGE: 55:274 of 10.12.1980 (not conforming to the constitution)
  ph: 7.6.1978

107 *Law on maternity leave*, 10.5.1979
  procl.: 25.6.1979
  I: government, CDU dissenting draft
  V: majority rc (268:126:1) (CDU divided, Blüm ao pro, 1 SPD abstention: Simonis)
  conference committee: no agreement proposal
  C: report on maternity leave; decision of 25.10.1979, IX/1210

4th ND: *Law on the protection of youth*, 23.5.1980
  R. BVerfGE 22,180; 18.7.1967
  I: BR, BaWü, BT-A 13 rejected; BR: rejected
  C: new government initiative
  V: majority (versus CDU)
  conference committee

178 *The Legislator*

9th Bundestag 1980–83

Restrictive

108 *Law on the proceedings of asylum* (AsylVfG), 14.5.1982
   procl.: 16.7.1982
   R: BVerfGE 30.6.1981; 1BvR 147/80; 1BvR 181/182/80
   BVerwG: 15.5.1981
   I: BT, SPD, CDU, FDP
   ph: 12.3.1982
   V: majority
   conference committee
   BVerfGE: 65:76 of 12.7.1983 (reversal of an administrative tribunal judgment)
   BVerfGE: 78:7 of 2.2.1988 (conforming to the constitution)
   BVerfGE: 86:280 of 2.6.1992 (interpretation conforming to the constitution)
   C: ph 14.2.1990

Regulative

109 *Census laws 1983*, 2.12.1981
   procl.: 25.3.1982
   R: EC guideline, report of data protection ombudsman
   I: government
   V: unanimous
   conference committee
   BVerfGE: 61:1 of 15.12.1983 (partly null and void)

Extensive

5th ND: *Law on the liability of the state*, 18.2.1982
   I: BT, SPD, FDP
   V: majority
   BR: consent denied (duty to consent according to promulgation and BR)
   BVerfGE: 61:149 of 9.11.1982 (null and void)

Protective

110 *Law on the promotion of vocational training* (BerBiFG), 1.10.1981
 procl.: 22.12.1981
 R: BVerfGE 2BvF 3/77 of 10.12.1980
 I: government
 V: majority
 conference committee
 BVerfGE: 72:278 of 4.5.1986 (not conforming to constitution)
 C: report on vocational training

111 *Revision on the law of conscientious objection* (KDVNG), 16.12.1982
 procl.: 28.2.1983
 R: ND 8th BT, BVerfGE 48,128
 I: BT, CDU, FDP, SPD – alternative draft
 ph: 8.12.1982
 V: majority rc (260:213:4)
 BVerfGE: 69:1 of 24.4.1985 (interpretation conforming to the constitution)
 ph: 2nd amendment 8.12.1988
 C: report, Art. 6, line 1 until Dec. 1985 X/3936

Distributive

112 *Law on social security for artists* (KSVG), 16.5.1981
 procl.: 27.7.1981
 R: NE 1980
 I: BT, SPD, FDP
 ph: 28/29.11.1979
 V: majority
 conference committee: BR rejection
 I (1981): BT, SPD, FDP
 V: majority
 nph: 18.3.1981
 BR: consent denied
 procl.: 1.8.1981
 BVerfGE: 75:108 of 8.4.1987 (interpretation conforming to the constitution)
 C: report on the social protection of self-employed artists 30.4.1971; 1.7.1976 Drs 7/5524; 22.5.1980 Drs 8/4006; 26.5.1981 Drs 9/429; until 1987

180 *The Legislator*

10th Bundestag 1983–87

Restrictive

113 *Neutrality of the Federal Labour Office in case of labour disputes* (§116 AFG), 20.3.1986
procl.: 15.5.1986
I: government
ph: 6.2.1986
V: majority rc (264:210:0)
BVerfGE: 4.7.1995 (interpretation conforming to the constitution)

114 *Law on the fight against terrorists*, 12.1986
procl.: 19.12.1986
I: BT, CDU, FDP
ph: 14.11.1986
V: majority (versus SPD and Greens)

Regulative

115 *Party law* (amend.) Part G, 1.12.1983
procl.: 22.12.1983
R: BVerfGE: 2BvF 1/57 of 24.6.1958; 1/78 of 24.7.1979; 1/65 of 19.6.1966; 1,3,5/67 of 3.12.1968; experts' commission
I: BT, CDU, FDP
ph: 9.11.1983
V: majority rc (416:26:11) (versus Greens, some abstentions in the SPD)
BVerfGE: 73:40 of 14.7.1983 (partly not conforming to the constitution)
BVerfGE: 85:264 of 9.4.1992 (not conforming to the constitution)
C: ph 21.11.1988

116 *Census law* 1987, 26.9.1985
procl.: 8.11.1985
R: BVerfGE: 65:1 of 15.12.1983
I: government (costs 715 Million)
ph: 17.4.1985
V: large majority (abstentions among Greens and some SPD deputies)

117 *Construction code*, 23.10.1986
procl.: 8.12.1986
I: government
ph: 12.3.1986 (experimental game); 14.4.1986
V: majority

Extensive

6th ND: *Codetermination in the mining industry, further validity*, rejected 16.1.1986
I: BT, SPD opposition
V: majority rc (168:201:0)

Protective

7th ND: *National objective: environmental protection* (36th amendment of Basic Law), rejected 16.1.1986
I: BT, Greens
V: majority

8th ND: *Law on nursing care insurance*, rejected 1.7.1986
I: BR, Hessen
V: BR, rejection

118 *Law on waste disposal* (4th amend.) (AbfG), 18.6.1986
procl.: 27.8.1986
I: government, Greens dissenting draft
ph: 30.9.1985
rc: 11.4.1986 on amendment of parliamentary groups
V: majority (versus SPD)

Distributive

119 *Law on the promotion of employment* (BeschFG), 19.4.1985
procl.: 26.4.1985
I: government (additional costs FLO 5 million 1985; 10 Million following years)
ph: 16/17.1.1985
V: majority rc (248:182.1) (versus SPD and Greens, 1 SPD for the majority)
C: report on educational aids; decision of 16.12.1982, X/357

182 *The Legislator*

9th ND: *Law on the reform of pensions*, rejected 21.6.1985
I: BT, SPD
ph: 28.2.1985; 13.3.1985
V: 2nd reading, rejected without debate

120 *Law on pensions for survivors and on maternity leave* (HEZG), 21.6.1985
procl.: 11.7.1985
R: BVerfGE: 39:169
I: government, SPD dissenting draft, rejected
ph: 28.2.1985
V: 1st reading 2 rc, amendment
SPD and Greens rejected (191:229:4) (24:205:0); 3rd reading, majority

11th Bundestag 1987–90

Restrictive

121 *Law on the reform of the health system* (GRG) (3rd versions on reform, saving of 14 billion DM), 25.11.1988
procl.: 20.12.1988
R: concerted action 'health',
commission of inquiry
I: government, BT, identical CDU, FDP
ph: 22/23.10.1987, 12/13/26 11.1987, 16–28.6.1988
V: 1st reading: rc on amendment of opposition; 3rd reading: majority, rc (241:207:2)

122 *Internal safety* (amend.) (StGB, StPO) (state witness regulation, ban on wearing masks at demonstrations), 21.4.1989
procl.: 9.6.1989
R: BVerfGE: 1BvR 233/81, 1BvR 341/81
I: government
ph: 30.11.1988
V: majority rc (209:150:1)

123 *Law on the reform of pensions 1992*, (RRG 1992), 9.11.1989
procl.: 18.12.1989
R: BVerfGE: 1 BvL 22/84; 1 BvL 71/86; 1 BvL 8/87 of 9.11.1988; federal social courts 17.11.1987; Advisory Social Council
I: government, BT, CDU, SPD, FDP brought together
ph: 26/28.4.1989
V: 1st reading: several rcs on Green amendment; 1st amendment rc (45:316:7) (10 SPD-votes for the amendment) majority; 3rd reading: large majority (some abstentions in SPD)

124 *Law on the revision of the penal law* (25th StrÄndG) (bugging operation), 20.6.1990
procl.: 20.8.1990
R: BVerfGE: 66:116 of 25.1.1984
I: BT, CDU, FDP
V: majority (versus Greens)

Regulative

125 *6th revision of the law on foreign trade* (export controls), 1.6.1990
procl.: 20.7.1990
I: government
ph: 23.10.1989
V: majority

126 *Unification treaty*, 20.9.1990
procl.: 23.9.1990
I: government, BT, identical CDU, FDP (brought together)
V: large majority rc (440:47:3) (13 CDU-dissenting votes, Czaja, Windelen ao; Greens dissenting
votes; 1 CDU, 1 SPD, 1 Green abstentions
BVerfGE: 82:316 of 18.9.1990 (not conforming to the constitution)
BVerfGE: 85:360 of 10.3.1992 (null and void, Art. 38, line 3, Satz 1 EV)
BVerfGE: 86:81 of 12.5.1992 (conforming to the constitution)

184 *The Legislator*

Extensive

127 *Federal law on elections* (amendment to the treaty of 3.8.1990 with the GDR), 5.10.1990
procl.: 8.10.1990
I: BT, CDU, FDP
V: large majority (versus Greens, PDS and 2 SPD)
BVerfGE: 82:323 of 29.9.1990 (partly null and void)

Protective

128 *Law on the regulation of gene technology*, 29.3.1990
procl.: 20.6.1990
R: Commission of inquiry into opportunities and risks of gene technology
ph: 18.9.1985; 24.2.1988
I: government
V: majority rc (201:145:2) (versus some SPD and 1 FDP, Hamm-Brücher)
C: report on legal regulations of gene technology XI/3908

129 *Law on data protection*, 31.5.1990
procl.: 20.12.1990
R: BVerfGE 65:1 of 15.12.1983, census law judgment
I: government, dissenting draft SPD, Greens
V: majority rc (205:170:0)
conference committee

130 *Law on the protection of embryos* (ESchG), 24.10.1990
procl.: 13.12.1990
I: government
ph: 9.3.1990
V: majority
C: cabinet report on artificial insemination of human beings XI/1856

Distributive

131 *Law on investments in the GDR* (DDRIG), 31.5.1990
procl.: 26.6.1990 (reduced tax receipts of 705 Million DM)
I: BT, CDU, FDP government
V: large majority (versus Greens)

Redistributive

132 *Federal treaty with the GDR*, 21.6.1990
procl.: 25.6.1990 (GDR-budget balanced by 'Fonds German Unity' 1990 22 billions; 1991 35 billions)
I: government, BT, identical CDU, FDP
V: large majority rc (445:60:1)

12th Bundestag 1990–94

Restrictive

133 *Law on the fight against drug trafficking* (OrgKG), 4.6.1992
procl.: 22.7.1992
I: BRat: Bavaria, Ba Wü
SPD Böhme and comrades, Däubler-Gmelin and comrades
V: almost unanimous

134 *Revision of asylum proceedings*, 5.6.1992
procl.: 30.6.1992
I: BT, CDU, SPD, FDP
ph: 18.3.1992
V: majority rc (286:188:15) (versus PDS, B 90, 5 SPD deputies)

135 *Structural law on health protection* (GRG), 9.12.1992
procl.: 21.12.1992
I: BT, CDU, FDP government
ph: 23–25.9.1992
V: large majority rc (455:54:21) (versus PDS, B 90,12 CDU, 5 SPD, 15 FDP)

136 *Law on asylum proceedings*, 26.5.1993
procl.: 27.7.1993
R: EC, Schengen agreement
I: government
ph: 11–24.3.1993
V: majority rc (496:198:1)
(versus several SPD votes 4 FDP
Baum, Hirsch and others, PDS and B 90)
BVerfGE:

186 *The Legislator*

Regulative

137 *Decision on the capital,* 20.6.1991
procl.: 26.4.1994
I: BT, individual groups of deputies
ph: 12.6.1991
V: majority for Berlin rc (338:320) (parliamentary groups split, decisive: PDS, B 90 pro)

138 *Maastricht treaty,* 2.12.1992
procl.: 28.12.1992
R: EC
I: government
ph: 18.9.1991
V: large majority rc (543:16:8) (versus PDS, 2 SPD, abstentions: majority B 90, 6 SPD, 2 CDU)
BVerfGE: 89,155 of 12.10.1993 (interpretation conforming to the constitution)

139 *Law on the revision of broadcasting,* 26.11.1993
procl.: 28.12.1993
I: government
V: large majority (without debate) (versus 3 dissenting votes, 2 abstentions, PDS)

140 *Law on the reorganization of postal service* (PTNeuOG), 29.6.1994
procl.: 14.9.1994
I: government, BT, identical, joint bill by parliamentary groups
nph: 2/3/13/14/20/21/28.4.94 of the 3 companies
V: majority rc (472:93:21) (requirement of two-thirds majority)

141 *Reform of the Basic Law* (GG Art. 3, 20a, 20b, 28, 29, 72, 74, 75, 76, 77, 80, 87, 93, 118a, 125a), 6.9.1994
procl.: 27.10.1994
I: BT, CDU, SPD, FDP
ph: 9
V: many rcs versus amendments; final vote large majority rc (622:3:4) (versus 2 CDU, PDS abstentions)
conference committee

142 *Law on the reorganization of the railroads* (ENeuOG), 2.12.1993
procl.: 30.12.1993
I: Reg; BT, identical CDU, FDP
ph: draft of Greens withdrawn
V: large majority rc (558:13:4) (versus PDS, B 90 abstentions) (requirement of two-thirds majority)

Extensive

10th ND: *Law on the introduction of referenda, Referendum in the Basic Law*, rejected 30.6.1994
I: BT: B 90
ph: 13.6.1991
V: large majority

Protective

143 *Law on the protection of pregnant women and families* (SFH (§218)), 25.6.1992
procl.: 27.7.1992
R: BVerfGE 39:1 of 25.2.1975 Unification treaty Art. 31,4
I: BT 7 drafts, 5 of parties SPD, FDP, CDU, B 90 draft of deputies
ph: 13/14/15.11. and 4/6.12.1991
V: 7 rcs of which 6 rejected, motion of group Wettig-Danielmeier ao accepted. rc (355:283:16) (versus CDU majority, 3 FDP, 2 SPD, 2 PDS)
BVerfGE: 86:390 of 4.8.1992 (interpretation conforming to the constitution)
BVerfGE: 88:203 of 28.5.1993, (interim order, not conforming to the constitution)

144 *Law on gene technology* (1st amend.), 1.10.1993
procl.: 21.12.1993
R: EC
I: government; BT, identical CDU, FDP
ph: 3.2/12.10.1988; 24.2.1988
V: majority rc (286:188:15) (versus SPD, PDS, B 90)
conference committee

145 *Law on nursing care insurance* (PflegeVersG), 20.10.1993
procl.: 26.5.1994
R: report on questions of neediness of care decision of 10.12.1992 X/1943
I: government, BT, CDU, FDP identical SPD, PDS drafts
ph: 6.9.93 BT committee law, 21.1.92 BT committee labour 3.6.92, 16.9.93, 17.9.93
V: 2nd reading rc: SPD amendment rejected; final vote: majority rc (322:223:7)
conference committee: 2
BVerfGE: 91:320 of 7.12.1994 (interim order rejected)

146 *Law on the protection of pregnant women and families* (SFH amendment), 26.4.1994
procl.: 21.8.1995
R: BVerfGE: 88:203 of 28.5.1993
I: BT, CDU–CSU, FDP, SPD and 2 drafts of individual deputies
V: majority rc (264:260:26) (versus many CDU, SPD, PDS, 2 FDP, B 90 and some abstentions in CDU–CSU)

Distributive

147 *Law on the elimination of obstacles in privatization of companies and promotion of investments*, 15.3.1991
procl.: 22.3.1991
R: Unification treaty
I: government; BT, identical CDU–CSU
ph: 5.3.1991
V: majority (versus PDS, abstentions in SPD, B 90)

Redistributive

148 *Law on solidarity with East Germany*, 14.5.1991
procl.: 24.6.1991
I: government
BT, identical CDU, FDP
V: majority (versus opposition parties)

149 *Law on the implementation of the federal consolidation programmes* (FKPG), 27.5.1993
procl.: 23.6.1993 (state and old *Länder* debited with 43.3 billion DM, new *Länder* 53.1 billion DM credited)
R: BVerfGE 86:148 of 27.5.1992
I: government
V: SPD amendment; rc (225:382:7) rejected
final vote: large majority, some dissenting votes, 1 abstention

150 *Compensation and equalization law* (EALG), 20.5.1994
procl.: 27.9.1994
I: government
ph: 15/16.9.1993; 2.2.1994
V: SPD amendment rejected; rc (114:273:13) (pro 1 CDU, 4 B 90)
final vote: majority rc (245:141:11)
conference committee

Bibliography

Aberbach, J.D. et al. (1981), *Bureaucrats and Politicians in Western Democracies*, Cambridge, Mass.: Harvard University Press.

Abromeit, H. (1993), *Interessenvermittlung zwischen Konkurrenz und Konkordanz*, Opladen: Leske & Budrich.

Ammermüller, M.G. (1971), *Verbände im Rechtssetzungsverfahren*, Berlin: Duncker & Humblot.

Appold, F.W. (1971), *Die öffentlichen Anhörungen des Deutschen Bundestages*, Berlin: Duncker & Humblot.

Armingeon, K. (1986), *Die Bundesregierung zwischen 1949 und 1985*, ZParl., pp. 25–40.

Arter, D. (1984), *The Nordic Parliaments: A Comparative Analysis*, London: Hurst.

Bachrach, P. and Baratz, M. (1994), 'Decisions and Non-Decisions', *APSR*, pp. 632–42.

Baron, D. 'A Sequential Choice Theory Perspective on Legislative Organisation', *Legislative Studies Quarterly*, 1994: 267–296.

Batt, H. (1996), *Die Grundgesetzreform nach der deutschen Einheit*, Opladen: Leske & Budrich.

Baumgartner, F. and Jones, B. (1993), *Agendas and Instability in American Politics*, Chicago: Chicago University Press.

Bechmann, G. (ed.) (1993), *Risiko und Gesellschaft: Grundlagen und Ergebnisse interdisziplinärer Risikoforschnung*, Opladen: Westdeutscher Verlag.

Bechtold, W.E. et al. (1977), 'Agenda Control in the 1976 Debates. A Content Analysis', *Journalism Quarterly*, pp. 674–681.

Becks, U. (1993), *Die Erfindung des Politischen*, Frankfurt: Suhrkamp.

Beneviste, G. (1977), *The Politics of Expertise*, (2nd edn) San Francisco: Boyd & Fraser.

Bentham, J. (1789), *The Principles of Morals and Legislation*, (2nd edn 1961), New York: Hafner.

Benz, A. (1993), 'Politknetzwerke in der Horizontalen Politikverflechtung' in D. Jansen and K. Schubert (eds). *Netzwerke und Politikproduktion*, Marburg, Schüren, pp. 185–204.

Benzner, B. (1989), *Ministerialbürokratie und Interessengruppen. Eine empirische Analyse der personellen Verflechtungen zwischen bundesstaatlicher Ministerialorganisation und gesellschaftlichen Gruppeninteressen in der Bundesrepublik Deutschland im Zeitraum 1949–1984*, Baden-Baden: Nomos.

Beratungen und Empfehlungen zur Verfassungsreform (1976), *Schlußbericht der Enquête-Kommission. Verfassungsreform des Deutschen Bundestages. Part 1: Parlament und Regierung*, Zur Sache 3, Bonn: Presse- und Informationszentrum des Deutschen Bundestages.

Berg, H.-J. (1982), *Der Verteidigungsausschuß des Deutschen Bundestages*, Munich: Bernhard and Graefe.

Beutel, F.K. (1957), *Some Potentialities of Experimental Jurisprudence as a New Branch of Social Science*, Lincoln, Nebraska.

Bundesbericht Forshung (1998) Bonn.

Bundesminister für Bildung und Wissenschaft (ed.) (1973), *Das Berufsbildungsgesetz in der Praxis. Eine Repräsentativbefragung von Auszubildenden*, Bonn.

Cox, G.W. and McCubbins, M.D. (1993), *Legislative Leviathan. Party Government in the House*, Berkeley: University of California Press.

Cox, G.W. and McCubbins, M.D. (1994), 'Party Government in the House. Bonding, Structure and the Stability of Political Parties', *Legislative Studies Quarterly*, pp. 215–31.

Damaschke, K. (1986), *Der Einfluß der Verbände auf die Gesetzgebung. Am Beispiel des Gesetzes zum Schutz vor gefährlichen Stoffen (Chemikaliengesetz)*, Munich: Minerva.

Damgaard, E. (ed.) (1992), *Parliamentary Change in the Nordic Countries*, Oslo: Scandinavian University Press.

DeGregorio, C. and Snider, K. (1995), 'Leadership Appeal in the US House of Representatives Comparing Officeholders and Aiders', *Legislative Studies Quarterly*, pp. 491–511.

deLeon, P. (1993), 'Demokratie und Policy-Analyse' in A. Héritier (ed.), *Policy Analysis*, Special issue of *Politische Vierteljahnesschrift* No. 24, Opladen: Westdeutscher Verlag, pp. 171–85.

Demmler, W. (1994), *Der Abgeordnete im Parlament der Fraktionen*, Berlin: Duncker & Humblot.

Diskussionsveranstaltung der Deutschen Vereinigung für Parlamentsfragen (1994), *Informelles Verfahren der Entscheidungsvorbereitung zwischen Bundesregierung und Mehrheitsfraktionen*, ZParl., pp. 494–507.

Döhler, M. (1990), *Gesundheitspolitik nach der 'Wende'*, Berlin: Sigma.

Döring, H. (ed.) (1995), *Parliaments and Majority Rule in Western Europe*, Frankfurt: Campus/New York: St Martin's Press.
Esaiasson, P. and Holmberg, S. (1996), *Representation from Above. Members of Parliament and Democracy in Sweden*, Aldershot: Dartmouth.
Ferdinand, H. (ed.) (1985), *Beginn in Bonn. Erinnerungen an den ersten Deutschen Bundestag*, Freiburg: Herder.
Filangieri, G. (1798), *La scienza della legislazione*, 9 vols, Catania: La Magna 1833.
Fiorina, M.P. (1977), *Congress. Keystone of the Washington Establishment*, New Haven: Yale University Press.
Fromme, F.K. (1996), 'Wer bestimmt?', *FAZ*, 14 February, p. 1.
Gill, B. (1991), *Gentechnik ohne Politik*, Frankfurt: Campus.
Görlitz, A. (1995), *Politische Steuerung*, Opladen: Leske & Budrich.
Görlitz, A. and Voigt, R. (1985), *Rechtspolitologie*, Opladen: Westdeutscher Verlag.
Götting, U. and Hinrichs, K. (1993), 'Probleme der politischen Kompromißbildung bei der Absicherung des Pflegfallrisikos', *PVS*, pp. 47–71.
Gray, V. and Lowery, D. (1995), 'Interest Representation and Democratic Deadlock', *Legislative Studies Quarterly*, pp. 531–32.
Green, D.P. and Shapiro, I. (1994), *Pathologies of Rational Choice Theory. A Critique of Applications in Political Science*, Chapter 6: 'Legislative Behavior and the Paradox of Voting', New Haven: Yale University Press, pp. 98–146.
Grimm, D. (ed.) (1990), *Wachsende Staatsaufgaben – sinkende Steuerungsfähigkeit des Rechts*, Baden-Baden: Nomos.
Grimm, D. and Maihofer, W. (eds) (1988), *Gesetzgebungstheorie und Rechtspolitik*, Opladen: Westdeutscher Verlag.
Habermas, J. (1992), *Faktizität und Geltung*, Frankfurt: Suhrkamp.
Hauck, R. (1990), *Der Wasserträger. Erinnerungen und Erkenntnisse eines Bundestagsabgeordneten 1965–1987*, Marburg: SP-Verlag.
Hechter, M.A. (1987), *Principles of Group Solidarity*, Berkeley: University of California Press.
Heinz, J.P. et al. (1993), *The Hollow Core. Private Interests in National Policy Making*, Cambridge, Mass.: Harvard University Press.
Hellstern, G.M. and Wollmann, H. (eds) (1983), *Experimentelle Politik – Reformstroh-feuer oder Lernstrategie?*, vol. 1, Opladen: Westdeutscher Verlag.
Hellstern, M. and Wollmann, H. (eds) (1984), *Handbuch der Evaluationsforschung*, vol. 1, Opladen: Westdeutscher Verlag.
Henseler, P. (1982), 'Möglichkeiten und Grenzen des Vermittlungsausschusses', *NJW*, H.16, pp. 849–094.

Hereth, M. (1969), *Die parlamentarische Opposition in der Bundesrepublik Deutschland*, Munich: Olzog.

Hereth, M. (1971), *Die Reform des Deutschen Bundestags*, Opladen: Leske & Budrich.

Herzog, D. et al. (eds) (1993), *Parlament und Gesellschaft*, Opladen, Westdeutscher Verlag.

Hirner, M. (1993), 'Das Parlament im Netzwerk gesellschaftlicher Interessen' in D. Herzog et al. (eds) *Parlament und Gesellschaft*, Opladen: Westdeutscher Verlag, pp. 138–83.

Hockerts, H.G. (1980), *Sozialpolitische Entscheidungen im Nachkriegsdeutschland. Alliierte und deutsche Sozialversicherungspolitik 1945–1957*, Stuttgart: Klett-Cotta.

Hofemann, K. (1975), *Ziel- und Erfolgsanalyse sozialer Reformprogramme am Beispiel des Berufsbildungsförderungsgesetzes*, Köln: Diss.

Hofman, G. and Perger, W.A. (1992), *Richard von Weizsäcker im Gespräch*, Frankfurt: Eichhorn.

Hoffmann-Riem, W. and Schmidt-Aßmann, E. (eds) (1990), *Konfliktbewältigung durch Verhandlungen*, vol. 1, Baden-Baden: Nomos.

Hohn, H.W. and Schimank, U. (1990), *Konflikte und Gleichgewichte im Forschungssystem*, Frankfurt: Campus.

Ismayr, W. (1990), *Berichte der Bundesregierung im Prozeß parlamentarischer Willensbildung*, ZParl, pp. 553–59.

Ismayr, W. (1992), *Der Deutsche Bundestag*, Opladen: Leske & Budrich.

Ismayr, W. (1996), 'Enquête-Kommissionen des Deutschen Bundestages', *APuZ*, B 27, pp. 29–41.

Johnson, N. (1979), 'Committees in the West German Bundestag' in J.D. Lees and M. Shaw (eds), *Committees in Legislatures: A Comparative Analysis*, London: Martin Robertson, pp. 102–47.

Jordan, G. and Richardson, K. (1983), 'Policy Communities. The British and European Style', *Policy Studies Journal*, pp. 603–15.

Jordan, G. and Schubert, K. (1992), 'A preliminary ordering of policy network labels', *European Journal of Political Research*, pp. 7–27.

Kaase, M. and Schulz, W. (eds) (1989), *Massenkommunikation*, Sonderheft 30 KZfSS, Opladen: Westdeutscher Verlag.

Die Kabinettsprotokolle der Bundesregierung, vol. 3 *1950*, vol. 4 *1951* (1988), vol. 5 *1952* (1989), vol. 6 *1953* (1989), vol. 7 *1954* (1993), Boppard: Harold Boldt.

Karpen, U. (1986), 'Zum gegenwärtigen Stand der Gesetzgebungslehre in der Bundesrepublik Deutschland', *ZG*, pp. 5–32.

Kather, L. (1964), *Die Entmachtung der Vertriebenen*, vol. 1, Munich: Olzog.

Kevenhörster, P. and Schönbohm, W. (1973), 'Zur Arbeits- und Zeitökonomik von Bundestagsabgeordneten', *ZParl.*, pp. 18–37.
Kewenig, W. (1970), *Staatsrechtliche Probleme parlamentarischer Mitregierung am Beispiel der Arbeit der Bundestagsausschüsse*, Bad Homburg: Vahlen.
Kilper, H. and Lhotta, R. (1996), *Föderalismus in der Bundesrepublik Deutschland*, Opladen: Leske & Budrich.
Kindermann, H. (1988), 'Symbolische Gesetzgebung' in D. Grimm and W. Maihofer (eds), *Gesetzgebungstheorie und Rechtspolitk*, Opladen: Westdeutscher Verlag, pp. 222–45.
Klingemann, H-D. *et al.* (eds) (1982), *Parties, Policies and Democracy*, Westview: Boulder, 1994.
Kloepfer, M. (1982), *Chemikaliengesetz. Gesetz zum Schutz vor gefährlichen Stoffen*, Berlin: Duncker & Humblot.
Knöpfel, P. and Weidner, H. (1980), 'Normbildung und Implementation: Interessenberücksichtigung in Programmstrukturen von Luftreinhaltungspolitiken' in R. Mayntz (ed.), *Implementation politischer Programme*, Königstein: Athenäum *et al.*
Knoke, D. and Pappi, F-U. *et al.* (1996), *Comparing Policy Networks. Labor Politics in the U.S., Germany and Japan*, Cambridge: Cambridge University Press.
König, T. (1992), *Entscheidungen im Politiknetzwerk*, Wiesbaden: DKV.
Kralewski, W. and Neunreither, K. (1963), *Oppositionelles Verhalten im ersten Deutschen Bundestag*, Köln, Opladen: Westdeutscher Verlag.
Krehbiel, K. (1991), *Information and Legislative Organization*, Ann Arbor: University of Michigan Press.
Kems, B. (1979), *Grundfragen der Gesetzgebungslehre*, Berlin: Duncker & Humblot.
Ladeur, K-H. (1995), *Postmoderne Rechstheorie. Selbstreferenz, Selbstorganisation, Prozeduralisierung*, (2nd edn), Berlin: Duncker & Humblot.
Landfried, C. (ed.) (1988), *Constitutional Review and Legislation. An International Comparison*, Baden-Baden: Nomos.
Landfried, C. (1996), *Bundesverfassungsgericht und Gesetzgeber*, (2nd edn), Baden-Baden: Nomos.
Lattmann, D. (1981), *Die lieblose Republik. Aufzeichnungen aus Bonn am Rhein*, Munich: Kindler.
Lauer-Kirschbaum, T. (1994), 'Kollektivverhandlungen und Selbstverwaltungskonsens: Interessenegoismus und Gemeinwohlorientierung in der Entwicklung und Reform der gesetzlichen Krankenversicherung' in B. Blanke (ed.), *Krankheit und Gemeinwahl. Gesundheitspolitik zwischen Staat, Sozialversicherung und Medizin*, Opladen: Leske & Budrich, pp. 207–44.

Lees, J.D. and Shaw, M. (ed) (1979), *Committees in Legislatures: A Comparative Analysis*, London: Martin Robertson.

Lehmbruch, G. (1976), *Parteienwettbewerb im Bundesstaat*, Stuttgart: Kohlhammer.

Leyden, K.M. (1995), 'Interest Group Resources and Testimony at Congressional Hearings', *Legislative Studies Quarterly*, pp. 431–39.

Liebert, U. (1995), *Modelle demokratischer Konsolidierung. Parlamente und organisierte Interessen in der Bundesrepublik Deutschland, Italien und Spanien (1948–1990)*, Opladen: Leske & Budrich.

Loewenberg, G. (1967), *Parliament in the German Political System*, Ithaca, Cornell UP.

Loewenberg, G. et al. (1985), *Handbook of Legislative Research*, Cambridge, Mass.: Harvard University Press.

Lohmar, U. (1975), *Das hohe Haus*, Stuttgart: DVA.

Lompe, K. et al. (1981), *Enquête-Kommissionen und Royal Commissions*, Göttingen: Schwartz.

Londregan, J. and Snyder, J.N. (1994), 'Comparing Committee and Floor Preferences', *Legislative Studies Quarterly*, pp. 233–66.

Lowi, T. (1964), 'American Business, Public Policy, Case Studies, and Political Theory', *World Politics*, pp. 677–715.

Luhmann, N. (1969), *Legitimation durch Verfahren*, Neuwied: Luchterhand.

Luhmann, N. (1972), *Rechtssoziologie*, 2 vols, Reinbek: Rowohlt.

Luhmann, N. (1990a), *Soziologische Aufklärung 5*, Opladen: Westdeutscher Verlag.

Luhmann, N. (1990b), 'Steuerung durch Recht? Einige klarstellende Bemerkungen', *Zeitschrift für Rechtssoziologie*, pp. 142–6.

Mann, S. (1994), *Macht und Ohnmacht der Verbände. Das Beispiel des Bundesverbandes der Deutschen Industrie e.V. (BDI) aus empirisch-analytischer Sicht*, Baden-Baden: Nomos.

Marcinkowski, F. (1993), *Publistik als autopoietisches System*, Opladen: Westdeutscher Verlag.

Marin, B. (ed.) (1990), *Governance and Generalized Exchange. Self-Organizing Policy Networks in Action*, Frankfurt/Boulder, Col.: Campus/Westview.

Markmann, H. (1995), *Das Abstimmungsverhalten der Parteifraktion in deutschen Parlamenten*, Meisenheim: Hain.

Mayntz, R. (ed.) (1990), *Implementation politischer Programme*, Königstein: Athenäum et al.

Mayntz, R. (ed.) (1983), *Implementation politischer Programme II*, Opladen: Westdeutscher Verlag.

Mayntz, R. and Neidhardt, F. (1989), 'Parlamentskultur. Handlungsorientierungen von Bundestagsabgeordneten – eine explorative Studie', *ZParl.*, pp. 370–87.

Mayntz, R. and Scharpf, F.W. (eds) (1973), *Planungsorganisation. Die Diskussion um die Reform von Regierung und Verwaltung des Bundes*, Munich: Piper.
Melnish, D. and Cowley, P. (1995), 'Whither the "New Role" in Policy Making? Conservative MPs in Standing Committees 1979 to 1992', *The Journal of Legislative Studies*, **1** (4), pp. 54–75.
Mezey, M.L. (1979), *Comparative Legislatures*, Durham: Duke University Press.
Michalsky, H. (1984), 'Parteien und Sozialpolitik in der Bundesrepublik Deutschland', *Sozialer Fortschritt*, pp. 134–41.
Michels, R. (1989), *Soziologie des Parteienstaats*, (4th edn), Stuttgart: Kröner, 1989.
Mill, J.S. (1861), *Utilitarianism, Liberty, Representative Government*, London: Dent Everyman's Library, 1960.
Mohl, R. von (1862), 'Die Abfassung der Rechtsgesetze' in *Staatsrechte, Völkerrecht und Politk*, Tübingen: Laupp, new edn vol. 2, Graz: Styria, pp. 375–691.
Möller, A. (1978), *Genosse Generaldirektor*, Munich: Droemer Knaur, 1978.
Müller, E. (1986), *Innenwelt und Umweltpolitik. Sozial–liberale Umweltpolitik – (Ohn)macht durch Organisation?* Opladen: Westdeutscher Verlag.
Müller, T. (1977), *Die Haltung der Parteien in der Bundesrepublik Deutschland zu den Problemen von Strafe und Strafvollzug*, Frankfurt: Lang.
Müller-Rommel, F. and Pieper, G. (1991), 'Das Bundeskanzleramt als Regierungszentrale', *APuZ* B 21/22, pp. 3–13.
Münch, R. (1991), *Dialektik der Kommunikationsgesellschaft*, Frankfurt: Suhrkamp.
Murswieck, A. (1983), *Die staatliche Kontrolle der Arzneimittelsicherheit in der Bundesrepublik und den USA*, Opladen: Westdeutscher Verlag.
Nahamowitz, P. '"Reflexives Recht". Das unmögliche Ideal eines postinterventionistischen Steurungskonzepts', *Zeitschrift für Rechtssoziologie*, pp. 29–44.
Naschold, F. (1967), *Kassenärzte und Krankenversicherungsreform. Zu einer Theorie der Statuspolitik*, Freiburg: Rombach.
Neidhardt, F. (ed.) (1994) *Öffentlichkeit, öffentliche Meinung, soziale Bewegungen*, Opladen: Westdeutscher Verlag (special issue 34 KZfSS).
Noll, P. (1973), *Gesetzgebungslehre*, Reinbek: Rowohlt.
Nowka, H. (1973), *Das Machtverhältnis zwischen Partei und Fraktion in der SPD*, Cologne: Heymanns.
Nullmeier, F. and Rüb, F.W. (1993), *Die Transformation der Sozialpolitik: vom Sozialstaat zum Sicherungsstaat*, Frankfurt: Campus.

Oberreuter, H. (1978), *Notstand und Demokratie*, Munich: Vögel.
Oberreuter, H. (ed.) (1981), *Parlamentsreform*, Passau: Passavia.
Offe, C. (1975), *Berufsbildungsreform. Eine Fallstudie über Reformpolitik*, Frankfurt: Suhrkamp.
Olsen, J. (ed.) (1978), *Politisk organisering*, Bergen: Universitetsforlaget.
Pappi, F-U. (1992), Die Abstimmungsreihenfolge der Anträge zum Parlaments- und Regierungssitz am 20. Juni 1991 im Deutschen Bundestag', *ZParl.*, pp. 405–412.
Pappi, F-U. et al. (1995), *Entscheidungsprozesse in der Arbeits- und Sozialpolitik*, Frankfurt: Campus.
Patzelt, W.J. (1993), *Abgeordnete und Repräsentation. Amtsverständnis und Wahlkreisarbeit*, Passau: Rothe.
Patzelt, W.J. (1996), 'Deutschlands Abgeordnete im Profil. Die Volksvertreter sind besser als ihr Ruf', *ZParl.*, 3, pp. 462–502.
Perschke-Hartmann, C. (1994), *Die doppelte Reform. Gesundheitspolitik Von Blüm zu Seehofer*, Opladen: Leske & Budrich.
Petermann, T. (1994), 'Das Büro für Technikfolgen-Abschätzung beim deutschen Bundestag: Innovation oder Störfaktor?' in A. Murswieck (ed.), *Regieren und Politikberatung*, Opladen: Leske & Budrich, pp. 79–99.
Philippi, K-J. (1972), *Tatsachenfeststellungen des Bundesverfassungsgerichts*, Cologne: Heymanns.
Puhe, H. and Würzberg, H.G. (1989), *Lust & Frust. Das Informationsverhalten des Deutschen Abgeordneten*, Cologne: Infomedia.
Rabenstein, K. (1995), *Die Diskussion über die Novellierung des Gentechnikgesetzes 1991–1993*, Hamburg: unpublished diploma-dissertation.
Rebenstorf, H. and Weßels, B. (1989), 'Wie wünschen sich die Wäler ihre Abgeordneten?', *ZParl.*, 3, pp. 408–24.
Rehfeld, D. (1981), 'Enquête-Kommissionen in der Bundesrepublik Deutschland', in K. Lompe et al., *Enquête-Kommissionen and Royal Commissions*, Göttingen: Schwarz, pp. 181–200.
Richter, M. and Müller, A. (1966), *Der Kampf um die Krankenversicherung 1955–1965*, Bad Godesberg: Verlag der Ortskrankenkassen.
Riescher, G. (1994), *Zeit und Politik. Zur institutionellen Bedeutung von Zeitstrukturen in parlamentarischen und präsidentiellen Regierungssystemen*, Baden-Baden: Nomos.
Rose, R. (1984), *Understanding Big Government*, London: Sage.
Rosewitz, B. and Webber, D. (1990), *Reformversuche und Reformblockaden im deutschen Gesundheitswesen*, Frankfurt: Campus.
Saalfeld, T. (1995), *Parteisoldaten und Rebellen. Fraktionen im Deutschen Bundestag 1949–1990*, Opladen: Leske & Budrich.

Sack, F. and Steinert, H. (1984), *Protest und Reaktion. Analysen zum Terrorismus 4/2*, Opladen: Westdeutscher Verlag.
Sarcinelli, U. (ed.) (1994), *Öffentlichkeitsarbeit der Parlamente*, Baden-Baden: Nomos.
Schäfer, F. (1982), *Der Bundestag. Eine Darstellung seiner Aufgaben und seiner Arbeitsweise*, (4th edn), Opladen: Westdeutscher Verlag.
Schäfer, R. and Schmidt-Eichstaedt, G. (1984), *Praktische Erfahrungen mit dem Bundesbaugesetz*, Melle: Knoth.
Schatz, H. (1970), *Auf der Suche nach neuen Problemlösungsstrategien: die Entwicklung der politischen Willensbildung im Deutschen Bundestag*, Meisenheim: Hain.
Schatz, H. (1973), 'Auf der Suche nach neuen Problemlösungsstrategien: die Entwicklung der politischen Planung auf Bundesebene' in R. Mayntz and F.W. Scharpf (eds) *Planungsorganisation. Die Diskussion um die Reform von Regierung und Verwaltung des Bundes*, Munich: Piper, pp. 9–67.
Schäuble, W. (1991), *Der Vertrag. Wie ich über die deutsche Einheit verhandelte*, Stuttgart: DVA.
Schillinger, R. (1985), *Der Entscheidungsprozeß beim Lastenausgleich 1945–1952*, Munich: Scripta Mercaturae.
Schindler, P. *Datenbuch zur Geschichte des Deutschen Bundestages I 1949 bis 1982*, Bonn (1983); *II 1980 bis 1984*, Baden-Baden: Nomos (1986); *III 1980 bis 1987*, Baden-Baden: Nomos (1988); *IV 1983 bis 1991*, Baden-Baden: Nomos (1994).
Schindler, P. (1995), 'Deutscher Bundestag 1976–1994: Parlaments- und Wahlstatistik', *ZParl.*, 4, pp. 551–66.
Schmalz-Bruns, R. (1995), *Reflexive Demokratie*, Baden-Baden: Nomos.
Schmidt, M.G. (ed.) (1988), *Staatstätigkeit*, Opladen: Westdeutscher Verlag (PVS-special issue 19).
Schmitt, H. (1987), *Neue Politik in alten Parteien*, Opladen: Westdeutscher Verlag.
Schmölders, G. et al. (1965), *Das Selbstbildnis der Verbände*, Berlin: Duncker & Humblot.
Schneider, H-P. and Zeh, W. (eds) (1989), *Parlamentsrecht und Parlamentspraxis*, Berlin: de Gruyter.
Schönbach, K. et al. (1994), 'Oberlehrer, oder Missionare? Das Selbstverständnis deutscher Juristen' in F. Neidhardt (ed.), *Öffentlichkeit, öffentliche Meinung soziale Bewegungen*, Opladen: Westdeutscher Verlag, pp. 39–161.
Schönbauer, G. (1983), *Wirtschaftsmitbestimmung im politischen Entscheidungsprozeß*, Frankfurt: Lang.
Schreckenberger, W. (1992a), 'Veränderungen im parlamentarischen Regierungssytem. Zur Oligarchie der Spitzenpolitiker der Parteien' in

K.D. Bracher et al. (eds), *Staat und Parteien. Festschift für Rudolf Morsey*, Berlin: Duncker & Humblot, pp. 133–53.

Schreckenberger, W. (1992b), 'Der Regierungschef zwischen Politk und Administration' in P. Haungs et al. (eds), *Civitas. Widmungen für Bernhard Vogel zum 60. Geburtstag*, Paderborn: Schöningh, pp. 603–14.

Schreckenberger, W. (1994), 'Informelle Verfahren der Entscheidungsvorbereitung zwischen der Bundesregierung und den Mehrheitsfraktionen: Koalitionsgespräche und Koalitionsrunden', *ZParl.*, pp. 329–46.

Schröder, H.J. *Gesetzgebung und Verbände*, Berlin: Duncker & Humblot.

Schulz, B. (1983), *Effizienzkontrolle von Umweltpolitik. Eine integrierte ökonomisch–ökologische Analyse am Beispiel des Benzinbleigesetzes*, Frankfurt: Haag & Herchen.

Schulz, C. (1984), *Der gezähmte Konflikt. Zur Interessenverarbeitung durch Verbände und Parteien*, Opladen: Westdeutscher Verlag.

Schulze-Fielitz, H. (1984) 'Das Parlament als Kontrolle im Gesetzgebungsprozeß' in H. Dreier and J. Hofmann (eds) *Parlamentarische Souveränität und technische Entwicklung*, Berlin: Duncker & Humblot, pp. 71–124.

Schulze-Fielitz, H. (1986), 'Fallstricke der Gesetzgebungsstatistik', *Zeitschrift für Gesetzgebung*, (4), pp. 364–8.

Schulze-Fielitz, H. (1988), *Theorie und Praxis parlamentarischer Gesetzgebung – besonders des 9. Deutschen Bundestages (1980–1983)*, Berlin: Duncker & Humblot.

Schüttemeyer, S. (1986), *Bundestag und Bürger im Spiegel der Demoskopie*, Opladen: Westdeutscher Verlag.

Schüttemeyer, S. (1989), 'Öffentliche Anhörungen' in H-P. Schneider and W. Zeh (eds) *Parlamentsrechts und Parlamentspraxis*, Berlin: de Gruyter, pp. 1145–59.

Schwarz, J.E. and Shaw, L.E. (1976), *The United States Congress in Comparative Perspective*, Hinsdale, Ill.: Dryden Press.

Schweitzer, C.C. (1979), *Der Abgeordnete im parlamentarischen Regierungssystem der Bundesrepublik*, Opladen: Leske & Budrich.

Searing, D. (1987), 'New roles for postwar British politics: ideologues, generalists, specialists and the progress of professionalization in Parliament', in *Comparative Politics*, vol. 22, pp. 431–53.

Sebaldt, M. (1992), *Die Thematisierungsfunktion der Opposition*, Frankfurt: Lang.

Seibel, W. (1984), *Die Nutzung verwaltungswissenschaftlicher Forschung für die Gesetzgebung*, Munich: Minerva.

Sinclair, B. (1989), *The Transformation of the U.S. Senate*, Baltimore: Johns Hopkins University Press.

Smith, R.A. (1995), 'Interest Group Influence in the United States Congress', *Legislative Studies Quarterly*, pp. 89–139.
Smith, S.S. and Deering, C. (1984), 'Committees in Congress', *Washington Congressional Quarterly*.
SPD außerordentlicher Parteitag Bad Godesberg 1959, Bonn: SPD-Vorstand.
SPD Parteitag Nürnberg 1968. Protocoll, Bonn: Vorstand der SPD.
Stammer, O. et al. (1965), *Verbände und Gesetzgebung. Die Einflußnahme der Verbände auf die Gestaltung des Personalvertretungsgesetzes*, Cologne: Westdeutscher Verlag.
Stand der Gesetzgebung des Bundes, *Bonn, Deutscher Bundestag, Bundesrat, Gruppe Datenverarbeitung*, 7 legislature 1988 – 12 legislature 1995, Baden-Baden: Nomos.
Stanley, H.W. and Niemi, R.G. (1990), *Vital Statistics on American Politics*, Washington DC: Congressional Quarterly Press.
Sturm, R. (1988), *Der Haushaltsausschuß des Deutschen Bundestages*, Opladen: Leske & Budrich.
Sturm, R. (1989), *Haushaltspolitik in westlichen Demokratien*, Baden-Baden: Nomos.
Thaysen, U. (1976), *Parlamentarisches Regierungssystem in der Bundesrepublik Deutschland*, (2nd edn), Opladen: Leske & Budrich.
Thiede, R.F. (1990), *Die gestaffelte Pflegeversicherung*, Frankfurt: Campus.
Töller, A.E. (1995), *Europapolitik im Bundestag. Eine empirische Untersuchung zur europapolitischen Willensbildung im EG-Ausschuß des 12. Deutschen Bundestages*, Frankfurt: Lang 1995.
van Mechelen, D. and Rose, R. (1986), *Patterns of Parliamentary Legislation*, Aldershot: Gower.
van Waarden, F. (1992), 'Dimensions and Types of Policy Networks, *EJPR*, pp. 29–52.
Veen, H-J. (1976), *Opposition im Bundestag. Ihre Funktionen, institutionellen Handlungsbedingungen und das Verhalten der CDU/CSU-Fraktion in der 6. Wahlperiode 1969–1972*, Bonn: Eichholz-Verlag.
Vetter, J. (1986), *Die Parlamentsausschüsse im Verfassungssystem der Bundesrepublik Deutschland*, Frankfurt: Lang.
Vierzig Jahre Bundesrat (1989), Baden-Baden: Nomos.
Vitzthum, W. Graf and Geddert-Steinacher, T. (1992), *Standortgefährdung. Zur Gentechnikregelung in Deutschland*, Berlin: Duncker & Humblot.
Vitzthum, W. Graf (1993), 'Zur Gentechniknovelle 1993', *Zeitschrift für Gesetzgebung*, pp. 236–47.
Vogel, H-J. (1996), *Nachsichten. Meine Bonner und Berliner Jahre*, Munich: Piper.

von Beyme, K. (ed.) (1979), *Die großen Regierungserklärungen der deutschen Bundeskanzler von Adenauer bis Schmidt*, Munich: Hanser, 1979.
von Beyme, K. (1983), 'Neo-Corporatism. A New Nut in an Old Shell?', *IPSR*, pp. 173–96.
von Beyme, K. (1985), 'The Role of the State and the Growth of Government', *IPSR* pp. 11–34.
von Beyme, K. 'Verfassungsgerichtsbarkeit und Policy Analysis' in Christian Broda et al. (ed.), (1985b), *Festschrift für Rudolf Wassermann zum 60. Geburtstag*, Neuwied: Luchterhand, pp. 259–77.
von Beyme, K. (1988), 'Politik und wissenschaftliche Information der Politiker in modernen Industriegesellschaften' in K. von Beyme, *Der Vergleich in der Politikwissenschaft*, Munich: Piper, pp. 347–68.
von Beyme, K. (1994), 'Verfehlte Vereinigung – verpaßte Reformen? Zur Problematik der Evaluation der Vereinigungspolitik in Deutschland seit 1989', *Journal für Sozialforschung*, pp. 249–69.
von Beyme, K. (1996), *Die politische Klasse im Parteienstaat*, (2nd edn), Frankfurt: Suhrkamp.
von Beyme, K. and Offe, C. (eds) (1996), *Politische Theorie in der Ära der Transformation*, Opladen: Westdeutscher Verlag (PVS special issue 26, 1996).
von Foerster, H. (1971), *Observing Systems*, Seaside, Cal.: Intersystems Publications.
Wagner, G. (1996), 'Differenzierung als absoluter Begutt', *Zfs*, pp. 89–212.
Wagner, H.R. (1960), *Erfahrungen mit dem Betriebsverfassungsgesetz*, Köln: Bund.
Weiss, C. (1974), *Evaluierungsforschung*, Opladen: Westdeutscher Verlag.
Wellenstein, A. (1992), *Privatisierungspolitik in der Bundesrepublik Deutschland*, Frankfurt: Lang.
Wessels, B. (1987), 'Kommunikationspotentiale zwischen Bundestag und Gesellschaft. Öffentliche Anhörungen, informelle Kontakte und innere Lobby in wirtschafts- und sozialpolitischen Parlamentsausschüssen', *ZParl.*, pp. 285–311.
Wessels, B. (1991), 'Vielfalt oder strukturierte Komplexität. Zur Institutionalisierung politischer Spannungslinien im Verbände- und Parteiensystem in der BRD', *KZfSS*, pp. 454–75.
Wiesenthal, H. (1981), *Die konzertierte Aktion im Gesundheitswesen*, Frankfurt: Campus.
Wildenmann, R. (1955), *Partei und Fraktion*, Meisenheim: Hain.
Willems, H. et al. (1993), *Soziale Unruhen und Politikberatung. Funktion, Ergebnisse und Auswirkungen von Untersuchungskommissionen in den USA, Großbritannien und der Bundesrepublik*, Opladen: Westdeutscher Verlag.

Wolf, R. (1991), 'Zur Antiquiertheit des Rechts in der Risikogesellschaft' in U. Beck (ed.), *Politik in der Risikogesellschaft*, Frankfurt: Suhrkamp, pp. 378–423.

Wollmann, H. (1970), *Die Stellung der Parlamentsminderheiten in England, der Bundesrepublik Deutschland und Italien*, Den Haag: Nijhoff 1970.

Wollmann, H. (1983), 'Implementation durch Gegenimplementation von unten? Zur sozialen und räumlichen Selektivität der Wohnungspolitik und ihrer Implementation' in R. Mayntz (ed.) *Implementation politischer Programme II, Ansätze zur Theoriebildung*, Opladen: Westdeutscher Verlag, pp. 168–96.

Zeh, W. (1984), *Wille und Wirkung der Gesetze. Verwaltungswissenschaftliche Untersuchung am Beispiel des Städtsbauförderungsgesetzes, Bundesimmissionsschutzgesetzes, Fluglärmgesetz und Bundesausbildungsförderungsgesetzes*, Heidelberg: R. v. Decker/G. Schenk.

Zeh, W. (1988), 'Vollzugskontrolle und Wirkungsbeobachtung als Teilfunktion der Gesetzgebung' in D. Grimm and W. Maihofer (eds), *Gesetzgebungstheorie und Rechtspolitik*, Opladen: Westdeutscher Verlag, pp. 194–210.

Zeh, W. (1989), 'Theorie und Praxis der Parlamentsdebatte in H-P. Schneider and W. Zeh (eds) *Parlamentsrecht und Parlamentspraxis*, Berlin: De Gruyter, pp. 917–37.

Zimmermann, M. (1982), *Machtfaktor Chemische Industrie*, Karlsruhe: BBU-Verlag.

Zintl, R. (1990), 'Probleme des individualistischen Ansatzes in der neuen politischen Ökonomie' in G. Göhler *et al.* (eds), *Die Rationalität politischer Institutionen*, Baden-Baden: Nomos, pp. 267–87.

Zintl, R. (1992), 'Kooperation und Aufteilung des Kooperationsgewinns bei horizontaler Politikverflechtung' in A. Benz *et al.* (eds), *Horizontale Politikverflechtung*, Frankfurt: Campus, pp. 97–146.

Index

abortion 29, 57, 100, 112, 118, 122, 123, 125
Adenauer, Konrad 7, 16, 20, 21, 60, 63, 71, 73, 74, 91 f., 107, 129
administration 12, 13, 15, 27, 33, 37, 40, 63, 68, 114–119, 120, 137 f., 143
advisory committees and experts 23–25, 37, 64, 68
agenda-setting 15–22
agricultural policy 36, 38, 61, 118
allied powers 34–36, 48, 59
amendment laws 3, 127, 131, 132–133, 143, 144
amendments to bills 3, 43, 45, 65, 74, 116, 117
antimonopoly policy 91, 123, 125, 130, 143
antiterrorism laws 7, 32, 50, 56, 64, 72, 77, 122, 123, 124, 132, 147
armament regulation 55, 123
asylum seekers 32, 50, 72, 77, 110, 122, 123

backbenchers 69–71, 74, 87
bills (introduction of) 29–37, 69, 79, 139
Brandt, Willy 66, 73, 107, 129, 130
budgetary policy 45, 52, 101, 121, 125

cabinet 16, 21, 22, 59, 63, 74
capital punishment 82
CDU-CSU (Christian Democrats) 27, 40, 41, 57, 75, 76, 78, 83, 92, 96, 97, 124, 127, 129
chancellor 17, 21, 22, 29, 71–74, 91–95, 128
chemicals (laws on) 52, 60, 63, 68, 123, 126, 131, 132
civil servants 46, 49, 63, 78, 119 f.
class politics 4, 16, 34, 49–62, 66, 139
coalition agreement 20–22, 43

coalition (governmental) 7, 18, 20–22, 29, 39, 43 f., 63, 68, 78, 96–99, 137
codetermination (Mitbestimmung) 26, 34, 45, 51, 59, 68, 73, 77, 91, 112, 117, 123, 129, 136, 144
committees (parliamentary) 4, 17, 24, 33, 37–51, 63–69, 75, 129, 145 f.
conference committees 5, 96, 100–102, 141
conscientious objection 56, 94, 100
consociationalism 32, 33
constitutional court (Karlsruhe) 12, 13, 18, 24, 25 f., 36 f., 38, 69, 83, 90, 100, 101, 105–114, 117, 127, 133, 135, 142 f.
constitutional reform 42, 48, 60, 70, 80, 96, 118, 135
construction policy 5, 25, 31, 40, 49–51, 61, 62, 67, 89, 103, 106, 107, 108, 114, 129, 132, 134, 136
corporation 8, 45, 49, 50, 52–59, 139–141
Council of Economic Affairs (Sachverständigenrat) 40, 123

DDR/East Germany 29, 34, 49, 54 f., 74, 94 f., 107, 113, 115, 117, 121, 124, 129 f.
debates in parliament 69–81, 105, 141
distribution 5–7, 46–62, 67, 89, 102, 103, 109, 130
drug law 42

economic policy 5, 26, 35, 45, 46, 47, 49–51, 61, 62, 65, 66, 67, 76, 89, 90, 102, 103, 107, 108, 117, 118, 129, 134, 141, 143
educational policy 5, 35, 45, 46, 47, 49–54, 61, 62, 66, 67, 73, 76, 86, 89, 90, 102, 103, 107, 108, 134, 141
elites (parliamentary) 7 f., 10, 11, 40–42, 69, 70, 72–74, 87, 141

embryonic protection 127
emergency laws 7, 19, 33, 74, 123, 128, 129
environmental policy 5, 15, 25, 27, 34, 35,
    46, 47, 53, 54, 60, 61, 62, 66, 67, 73,
    86, 89, 102, 103, 107, 108, 116 f., 118,
    126, 130, 131, 134, 135, 139
Erhard, Ludwig 22, 26, 91
European Union/European Community 24,
    34–36, 37, 91, 111, 125
evaluation (of laws) 114, 116, 119–133
experimental games 23

family policy 12
Federal Bank 40
Federal Council (Bundesrat) 18, 29, 30, 39,
    45, 46–48, 54, 95–103, 141 f.
Federal Labour Office 91, 136
federalism 2, 29–31, 45–48, 58 f., 73, 75 f.,
    95–103, 116
financial policy 22, 65, 101, 128, 133
foreign policy 34–36, 37, 46, 47, 49, 50, 51,
    61, 62, 66, 71–73, 74, 86, 89, 90, 91,
    92 f., 102, 115, 132

gene technology 7, 25, 44, 45, 68, 127
Genscher, Hans-Dietrich 71
government 12, 30–33, 43 f.
governmental declaration 20–22, 127
Grand Coalition (1966–69) 3, 19, 21, 32,
    33, 39, 46, 49, 72 f., 75, 85, 86, 90, 91,
    92, 124, 127, 138
Green Party 15, 16, 30, 32, 39, 49, 70, 79,
    80, 84, 85, 93, 94, 98, 112, 127

health policy 54, 55, 72, 84, 112, 117, 118,
    128
hearings 22, 23, 40, 48, 58, 63–69, 110–112,
    133, 140 f.
hierarchy 10, 45, 73, 87, 119
housing policy 5, 32, 49, 61, 62, 67, 103,
    114, 131, 134, 135, 139

immigration policy 7, 132
implementation 1, 7, 18, 114–119, 122, 125,
    133, 143
interest groups 7–9, 22, 34, 40–42, 44–62,
    63–69, 116, 119, 135, 137, 138, 143
intergovernmental decision-making 59, 75

judicial review 2, 105–114, 115, 120, 125,
    127, 142 f.

Kohl, Helmut 30, 54, 71, 74, 93 f., 100
KPD (communist party) 18f., 59

labour policy 22, 32, 77, 118, 123, 130, 135
legal policy 5, 25, 31, 35, 40, 45, 46, 47, 48,
    49–51, 60, 62, 65, 103, 107, 108, 110,
    134, 140, 141
Liberals (FDP) 27, 33, 39, 66, 70, 75, 84,
    86, 91, 92, 94, 127
Lowi, Theodore 5, 57, 140

media 5, 12, 31
military policy 123, 128
ministers 41, 43 f., 45 f., 59, 70, 71–75, 99,
    111

NATO 60, 74
network 7–10, 33, 39 f., 42, 52–59, 137
new social movements 7, 16–18, 44, 49
non-decision 4, 131

ombudsman 115, 123
opposition 15, 20, 29, 30–32, 33, 39 f.,
    41–44, 45, 63, 66, 68 f., 75, 76–81, 85,
    110, 111, 125, 127, 129, 141, 146
organized crime 30, 56, 131
'Ostpolitik' 93 f., 107

parliamentary groups 20–22, 29–37, 42–44,
    48, 64, 69, 70, 72–75, 78, 79, 81–95,
    141
parliamentary secretaries of state 11, 41,
    43 f.
parties 9 f., 15–22, 42–45, 48, 58 f., 72–74,
    79, 84–95, 145–147
party discipline 74, 81–95
party finance 73
party law 32, 73, 110
PDS (Postcommunists) 78, 79, 80 f., 83, 98,
    142
penal law reform 26, 37, 40, 44, 48, 74,
    121, 123, 132
pluralism 7–9, 45–62, 140
policy advice 23–25, 26–27
policy analysis 1–3, 147
professionalization of deputies 88, 145
promotional groups 49–57, 140
public interest groups 50

questions (in parliament) 75, 80, 81

Rational Choice 43, 82, 88
refugees 5 f., 56, 101, 123, 129, 130 f., 135, 140
regional development plan 126
regulation 4–7, 13, 45, 46, 66, 67, 76, 88, 89, 90, 109, 110, 116, 120, 123, 130
retirement allowances 91
reunification of Germany 10, 29, 36, 49, 54, 72, 74, 91, 94 f., 96, 101, 117–119, 124, 129 f., 133, 140
roll call 5, 81–95

Schmidt, Helmut 21, 70, 73, 84, 100
social policy 5, 22, 32, 34, 39 f., 46, 47, 48, 49–57, 66, 67, 70, 72, 78, 89, 90, 103, 107, 108, 110, 123, 126, 129, 132, 134, 136
SPD (Social Democratic Party) 15 f., 19, 30–32, 39, 66, 74, 76, 78, 82, 85, 86, 91, 92, 97, 101, 111, 127, 129
speaker 42, 73, 80, 82, 83, 84
status groups 34, 45, 49–62, 66, 140–141
steering/control 37, 42–44, 78, 87, 137–147

Strauss, Franz-Josef 71, 79
sunset legislation 23
symbolic policy 115, 119, 122–127, 131, 137, 141

tax policy 107
technology 13, 23–25, 125–127
terrorism see: antiterrorist laws
trade unions 19 f., 34, 49–51, 59, 60, 68, 136, 140
trusteeship organization (Treuhand) 117, 118

United Kingdom 10, 38, 58, 76, 81
United Nations 92
university reform 77, 118, 128, 131
USA 2, 9, 10, 38, 43, 58, 65, 86, 88, 95, 133, 135, 143, 144 f.

vocational training 33, 60, 111, 131
voting (on bills) 69, 81–95

wage policy 92, 118
women 56, 71 f., 80, 82, 83, 125